Asia and the Drafting of the Universal Declaration of Human Rights

Robin Ramcharan • Bertrand Ramcharan

Asia and the Drafting of the Universal Declaration of Human Rights

palgrave
macmillan

Robin Ramcharan
Webster University
Bangkok, Thailand

Asia Centre
Bangkok, Thailand

Bertrand Ramcharan
Emeritus President, UPR Info
Alyth, Perthshire, UK

ISBN 978-981-13-2103-0 ISBN 978-981-13-2104-7 (eBook)
https://doi.org/10.1007/978-981-13-2104-7

Library of Congress Control Number: 2018955440

Cover Design by Tom Howey

This Palgrave Macmillan imprint is published by the registered company Springer Nature Singapore Pte Ltd.
The registered company address is: 152 Beach Road, #21-01/04 Gateway East, Singapore 189721, Singapore

Dedicated to Dr. Lily Ramcharan, BA, MA, DES, Ph.D. (Kent)
Our inspiration

Foreword

This is a highly original and much needed book. Based on the actual records of the drafting of the Universal Declaration of Human Rights (UDHR), it shows convincingly that Asian States and experts played a leading role in shaping the Declaration, which very much represents Asian values: the values of freedom, tolerance, equality, equity, respect, and diversity.

At the same time, it brings out with clarity that Asia has many human rights problems that need to be tackled urgently. The authors write, "Implementation, prevention, protection, equality, and equity are the challenges of the present and the future in Asia." This is the call of civil society in Asia.

The protection of human rights must first be done at home, inside each country. Strengthening national protection systems is vital. An essential part of this is human rights education for the young. The historic Asian heritage of humanism is given concrete content by instruments such as the Universal Declaration of Human Rights.

Regional institutions for the promotion and protection of human rights are largely lacking in Asia. The ASEAN Intergovernmental Commission on Human Rights (AICHR) is just beginning its efforts, and it faces many challenges stemming from the defensiveness of the members of the Association of Southeast Asian Nations (ASEAN) in giving the ASEAN Commission the requisite teeth to tackle numerous pressing problems.

With the paucity of national and regional or sub-regional bodies for promoting and protecting human rights, civil society organizations are demonstrating great courage and dynamism in advocating for the protection of human rights. It is vital that the role of civil society nationally and regionally be supported and reinforced.

This book will give heart to civil society in Asia. The proof it brings forth that the Universal Declaration of Human Rights rests on Asian values and drew upon Asian inspiration and expertise will reinforce the efforts of civil society.

The authors are in a unique position to make this contribution. One has been a specialist in the conflict prevention of ASEAN, was Professor of International Relations and Law at Alliance University, Bangalore, and teaches on human rights at Webster University Thailand. The other has been Professor of Human Rights at the Geneva Graduate Institute of International and Development Studies and, before that, served in the position of UN High Commissioner for Human Rights.

Originating from Asia, they are giving back to the continent of their origins in pleading for a world of human dignity, human rights, and justice for all.

Asia Centre
Bangkok, Thailand

James Gomez

The Asian Quest

Mr. Malik (Lebanon) "...suggested that such a bill [the proposed international bill of human rights] must provide not only for freedom of thought and conscience, but for *the freedom of being and of becoming what one's conscience required one to become*, that is to say, freedom to change...."[1]

"...Provisions for implementation would have to be found, as without them all discussions of human rights would be futile. He favoured individuals as members of the Commission on Human Rights."[2]

Mr. Chang (China) "recalled the development of human rights during the last one hundred and fifty years and felt that *there existed now a new humanism*, as otherwise there would be no incentive for the efforts that were made. Those incentives must be the ideals of human freedom and human dignity."[3]

Mrs. Mehta (India) "considered...that this bill [the international bill of rights] should eventually become *an integral part of the Charter and a fundamental law of the United Nations.*"[4]

General Romulo (Philippine Republic) "pointed out that *the power of might to rule over weaker nations had succeeded the divine right of kings to rule over individuals*; he called upon the Commission [on Human Rights] to take that factor into consideration during the discussion of the universal standards to be written into the Preamble."[5]

Mr. Ghani (Iran) "felt that freedom of expression and of opinion were possible only in countries where the standard of education was high enough to allow the masses to form a sound opinion, and so he wished the United Nations to take steps first of all to eliminate illiteracy and promote education, by such means as granting financial assistance to backward countries."[6]

Mr. Yazici (Turkey) "expressed full agreement with all recommendations of the Human Rights Commission Report, and stated that a Human Rights group has been established in Turkey."[7]

Mr. Ebeid (Egypt) "recalled the disillusionment and conflicts which had followed the proclamation of President Wilson's fourteen points after the First World War. *The principles of human rights should be set forth in clear terms.* The peoples of the world would greet with enthusiasm the first action taken by the United Nations to enforce redressment of wrongs."[8]

Notes

1. E/SR.19, 31 May, 1946, in William Schabas, *The Universal Declaration of Human Rights, The travaux préparatoires*, VOLUME I. October 1946 to November 1947 (Cambridge: Cambridge University Press, 2013), p.64. This work also uses Volume II of Schabas, which covers, December 1947 to December 1948.
2. Ibid.
3. E/SR.20, 31 May 1946 (Schabas, p. 65–66).
4. E/CN.4/SR 7, 31 January 1947. (Schabas 169).
5. E/CN.4/SR 8, 31 January 1947, (Schabas 171).
6. E/CN.0.4/SR 14, 4 February 1947, (Schabas, 200).
7. E/439, 14 March 1947; Summary record of the Six to eight meeting of the Economic and Social Council. (Schabas, 241).
8. E.CN.4/SR 8, 31 January 1947. (Schabas, 173) (Mr. Ebeid represented Egypt, an African country, whose aspirations were similar to those of Asian States.

Preface: The Asian Case for a New Humanism

The Universal Declaration of Human Rights bears strong Asian imprints, and it is the aim of this book to bring this out, a story that has hitherto not been told. Shortly after the establishment of the United Nations, an advance, preparatory, "Nuclear Commission" was established to pave the way for the future Commission on Human Rights envisaged in Article 68 of the Charter and for its work in drafting an International Bill of Rights as decided upon at the UN founding conference in San Francisco. Serving on this "Nuclear Commission" of seven persons were Mr. K.C. Neogi of India, Dr. C.H. John Wu of China, and Dr. Chin-Lin Hsia of China. They were both active participants in the discussions and helped shaped the outcome of the work of the "Nuclear Commission."

K.C. Neogi was a member of the Indian Central Assembly from 1921 to 1924 and again from 1942 to 1945. He had been Chairman of the Railway Enquiry Committee in 1947 and later served as the first Chairman of the Indian Finance Committee in 1952.[9] Mr. Neogi was the Rapporteur of the first session of the Nuclear Commission.[10] John Ching Hsiung Wu was a lawyer and translator who played a leading role in drafting the Constitution of the Republic of China.[11] Chin-Lin Hsia, a Chinese scholar and diplomat, was the author of *Studies in Chinese Diplomatic History*.[12] He chaired the committee on war criminals of the Far Eastern Commission, the inter-allied body responsible for oversight of the occupation of Japan.[13]

As the "Nuclear Commission" began its work, Mr. Neogi counselled at a meeting on 30 April 1946 that since not all members of the "Nuclear Commission" probably had a chance to acquaint themselves with the contents of the literature concerning human rights, the following sources might be of interest to them:

1. A document prepared by a committee of the London *Daily Herald* under the chairmanship of Lord Sankey, a judge in the House of Lords.
2. The issue on essential human rights of the *Annals of the American Academy of Political and Social Science* (January 1946).[14]

At the sixth meeting of the "Nuclear Commission" held on 6 May 1946, Mr. Neogi, attentive to sovereignty, "suggested that it might be wise to study existing constitutions many of whom have human rights provisions and to find out whether these provisions have been adhered to. He felt strongly that that it would be important to write a Declaration of Human Rights which any nation who might want to join the United Nations would have to accept."[15]

Dr. Hsia, for his part, supported the idea that the necessary means be provided for supervision and control. He noted that "all authorities who had discussed the work of the Commission on Human Rights had expressed themselves strongly in favour of some kind of enforcement agency, that one group of experts had suggested that the Commission should have the right to: 'Inquiry, investigation and advice.'"[16]

When, the next year, the Economic and Social Council discussed the report of the Commission on Human Rights, the Lebanese delegate, Charles Malik, said that the forthcoming Declaration offered the United Nations the opportunity to answer the question, "What is man." The Declaration would provide meaning to the phrase, "dignity and worth of the human person," in the preamble of the Charter of the United Nations.[17]

The Chinese delegate, Peng Chun Chang, commented that "after the myopia of the last hundred and fifty years, nations were at least on the threshold of a new humanistic period." The International Bill of Human Rights envisaged should be based on the aspiration for a new humanism.[18]

During his participation in the deliberations of various bodies considering the proposed Universal Declaration of Human Rights and the more extensive International Bill of Rights, Mr. Chang would repeatedly refer to the atrocities that had been perpetrated on the people of China and on other peoples, and would eloquently make the case for a new humanism, as we shall see in the pages below.

Bangkok, Thailand Robin Ramcharan
Alyth, UK Bertrand Ramcharan

Notes

9. Schabas, p. 20.
10. See E/HR/19, 15 May 1946: *Draft Report of the Commission on Human Rights to the Second Session of the Economic and Social Council.* Rapporteur Mr. K.C. Neogi (India), in Schabas p. 49.
11. Ibid.
12. Ching-Lin Hsia, *Studies in Chinese Diplomacy* (Harrisonburg, V.A.: The Commercial Press, 1925).
13. See Schabas, p. 35.
14. Issue 243(1) of the *Annals of the American Academy of Political and Social Science*, edited by William Draper Lewis and John R. Ellington, devoted to "Essential Human Rights." It contained articles on various aspects of human rights, including contributions by Carlos P. Romulo of the Philippines. See Schabas, p. 39.
15. Schabas, p. 42.
16. Eighth meeting of the "Nuclear Commission", 8 May 1946, reproduced in Schabas, p. 48.
17. E/SR.69, in Schabas, p. 5.
18. Ibid, pp. 7–8.

References

Primary Documents: United Nations Documents from Drafting Process in William Schabas:
E/SR.69.
E/HR/19, 15 May, 1946.

Hsia, Ching-Lin. *Studies in Chinese Diplomacy* (Harrisonburg, V.A.: The Commercial Press, 1925).

Lewis, William Draper and John R. Ellington, Eds., *Annals of the American Academy of Political and Social Science*, Issue 243(1)

Schabas, William T*he Universal Declaration of Human Rights, The travaux préparatoires*, Volumes 1 and 2. October 1946 to November 1947 (Cambridge: Cambridge University Press, 2013), p. 64.

Contents

Abbreviations

AHRD	ASEAN Human Rights Declaration
AICHR	ASEAN Intergovernmental Commission on Human Rights
ASEAN	Association of Southeast Asian Nations
CEDAW	Convention on the Elimination of All Forms of Discrimination Against Women
CIL	Customary international law
ECOSOC	Economic and Social Council (United Nations)
GA	General Assembly (United Nations)
GANRHI	Global Alliance of National Human Rights Institutions
HRC	Human Rights Council
ICCPR	International Covenant on Civil and Political Rights
ICESCR	International Covenant on Economic, Social and Cultural Rights
ILO	International Labour Organization
KMT	Kuomintang
MDG	Millennium Development Goals
NAM	Non-Aligned Movement
NGO	Non-governmental organization
NHRI	National Human Rights Institution
OHCHR	Office of the High Commissioner for Human Rights
SDG	Sustainable Development Goals
UDHR	Universal Declaration of Human Rights
UN	United Nations
UNDP	UN Development Programme
UNESCO	UN Educational, Scientific and Cultural Organization
UPR	Universal Periodic Review
USA	United States of America
USSR	Union of Soviet Socialist Republics

List of Tables

CHAPTER 1

Introduction

Philosophy, A.J. Ayer wrote in his review of the twentieth century, is the study of evidence.[1] This book is a study of the evidence on Asia's contribution to the drafting of the Universal Declaration of Human Rights, keeping in mind Asia's contemporary policies on human rights, and Asian consensual approaches to the promotion and protection of human rights worldwide. Yes, there are numerous human rights problems in Asia. Yes, there are numerous analyses of these problems. And, yes, this is a period in which China is asserting its power and seeking recognition of its perspectives on various issues of international affairs. It is important to realize that the Universal Declaration of Human Rights remains the central document, the reference point from which future Asian policies and strategies on human rights must continue to be guided.

This book presents convincing historical evidence that Asia played a central part in the drafting of the Universal Declaration of Human Rights. That evidence is marshalled in the chapters that follow. It is important to link this with evidence of contemporary Asian international policies on human rights. This is because, whatever problems are being experienced on the ground, the evidence sustains the conclusion that Asian governments are professing continuing faith in the Universal Declaration and in universal human rights standards. Formally, at least, the principal Asian powers, 70 years after the adoption of the Universal Declaration, continue to profess their faith in the Declaration, in universal human rights, and in rights-based strategies of governance and development. This may be seen

R. Ramcharan, B. Ramcharan, *Asia and the Drafting of the Universal Declaration of Human Rights*,
https://doi.org/10.1007/978-981-13-2104-7_1

in the national reports of the principal Asian powers submitted to the UN Human Rights Council within the framework of its Universal Periodic Review (UPR) system.

Under the UPR system, each member state of the United Nations now submits once every four and a half years a national report on its efforts to promote and protect human rights. The principal Asian powers have all reaffirmed their faith in the Universal Declaration in their latest reports.

China, for example, stated in its last report of 2013 that it respects the principle of universality of human rights and is of the view that all countries have a duty to take measures, commensurate with their national conditions, continuously to promote and protect human rights in accordance with the purposes and principles of the Charter of the United Nations and the basic spirit of the Universal Declaration of Human Rights and the relevant international human rights. The international community should accord equal attention to the achievement of civil and political rights; economic, social, and cultural rights; and the right to development; it should also promote the coordinated development of individual and collective human rights. China, it added, "is committed to carrying out exchanges and cooperation on human rights with all countries, and to promoting the resolution of human rights issues in a fair, objective and non-selective manner by the international community."[2]

India, in its report of 2017, stated that with one-sixth of the global population, India is the world's largest democracy that is home to a multi-ethnic, multi-religious, multi-lingual population that has lived together for millennia with an ethos of respect for diversity and plurality. Supported by a rights oriented constitutional framework, a secular polity, and independent judiciary, a range of national and state level commissions that monitor compliance with human rights, a free press, and a vibrant and vocal society, India continues its endeavours towards fulfilling its human rights obligations. Recognizing the universality, indivisibility, and inter-relatedness of all human rights, India places equal emphasis on the civil and political rights and freedoms of its citizens as well as their socio-economic development. It is aware that historical factors and extant social structures "can render certain communities more vulnerable to exclusion, marginalization and human rights violations," and it "prioritises, through a range of protective and affirmative measures, the attainment of liberty and development for all. In the spirit of leaving no one behind, India follows the motto of 'Sabka Saath, Sabka Vikas' (all together and development for all)."[3]

Indonesia, in its report of 2017, stated that as a country it has been resolute in upholding its constitutional mandate and commitment to the global norms on human rights. It underscored the importance of the UN Human Rights Council's mechanism on the UPR. "Taking action on the UPR recommendations is crucial to support the efforts to realize the full enjoyment of human rights for all in Indonesia."[4]

Malaysia, in its 2013 report, stated that the government continued to be characterized by, among others, "a strong commitment to the rule of law, to upholding respect for human rights, and a commitment to continue widening the democratic space…."[5]

Pakistan, in its 2017 report, stated that "Pakistan's commitment to human rights emanates in the first place from its Constitution and duty towards its people. We are determined to ensure that every Pakistani citizen lives in equality, dignity, and freedom. The words of the Founding Father, Quaid-e-Azam Muhammad Ali Jinnah, are the guiding principle of our policy: 'We are equal citizens of one State'. Therefore, the Government attaches high priority to advancing the mutually reinforcing objectives of development, human rights and democracy and there is a strong and unequivocal political commitment in this regard."[6] A Ministry of Human Rights had been established in 2015.[7]

The Philippines, in its 2017 report, stated: "In his 2016 State of the Nation Address, the President committed that his administration shall be sensitive to the State's obligation to promote, protect, fulfil the rights of our citizens, especially the poor, the marginalized and the vulnerable, and social justice shall be pursued, even as the rule of law shall prevail at all times. This administration shall implement a rights-based approach to development and governance, as we improve our people's welfare in the areas of health, education, adequate food and water, housing, environmental preservation and respect for culture. 'Human rights must work to uplift human dignity.'"[8]

Singapore, in its 2015 report, stated: "We are fully committed to the protection and promotion of the human rights of our citizens. We take a practical, not an ideological approach to the realisation of human rights. Human rights exist in specific cultural, social, economic and historical contexts. In every country, accommodation must be reached among the competing rights of the individuals who make up the nation and the interests of society as a whole. We therefore firmly apply the rule of law to ensure stability, equality and social justice, which are the necessary conditions for respecting the fundamental human rights enshrined in our

Constitution and the Universal Declaration of Human Rights. We also focus on delivering good socio-economic outcomes through pragmatic public policies."[9]

Thailand, in its 2016 report, stated that "The Government attaches utmost importance to the promotion and protection of human rights of all groups of people. In its Policy Statement to the National Legislative Assembly (NLA) on 122 September 2014, the Government identified addressing social and economic inequalities as well as the adherence of the rule of law and protection of human rights as 2 of 11 main policies."[10]

Vietnam, in its report of 2013, stated that "The State of Vietnam always sees the promotion and protection of human rights and fundamental freedoms of the people as the essential elements of all Viet Nam's socio-economic development strategies. In doing so, Vietnam also delivers upon its commitments as a party to international instruments on human rights, including the UPR recommendations that Viet Nam already accepted." The report added: "Building a State of the people, by the people, for the people and the promotion and protection of human rights are both enshrined in the 1992 Constitution (amended in 2001). The legal system has been developed harmoniously and consistently throughout the legal building programs and ordinance issuance of the National Assembly and also the policies and mechanisms to implement these legal documents."[11]

The foregoing statements contained many shades and nuances and disclosed many problems to be tackled. Yet, they all professed adherence to universal human rights, which was the vision of the Asian drafters of the Universal Declaration: human rights strategies of governance and development.

Having made the points that Asia played a central part in the drafting of the Universal Declaration and that Asian countries continue to profess faith in universal human rights, it is appropriate that we refer, next, to some of contemporary academic debates on human rights in the "Asian Century."

Human Rights in the Asian Century

The twenty-first century, with familiar as well as unprecedented challenges, needs to search for solutions firmly grounded in universal human rights. However, the first two decades of the twenty-first century have featured a continuing dialogue on the universality of human rights in the "Asia-Pacific Century." While the Asian values debate of the 1990s may have subsided and even though the international community upheld the universality of human rights at the World Conference on Human Rights in Vienna in 1993, the rise of new powers in Asia and the regression in democracy, the rule of law, and liberal rights across the region have given rise to concern about the future of human rights.

Powerful regimes across the region openly flout long-established human rights norms and international law. With Europe and the United States seemingly prevaricating on the international human rights protection front, a speculative case for the end of human rights has been advanced. Rieff has argued that "Brexit, Donald Trump's presidency, and the steady rise of China have shattered the human rights movement's narrative that progress is inevitable."[12] Rieff references a 2001 work by Michael Ignatieff, *Human Rights as Politics and Idolatry*, in which he argued that over the next half century, "we can expect to see the moral consensus that sustained the Universal Declaration [of Human Rights] in 1948 splintering still further.... There is no reason to believe that economic globalization entails moral globalization." Similarly, Stephen Hopgood has issued a stinging attack on the "hijacking" of human rights by great powers for their self-interests.[13] Forsythe,[14] in a book review, surveys similar arguments about the alleged demise of human rights, namely, that the "hard times for human rights" are due to the decline of Western-dominated international relations that parallels the decline of the United States (Moyne[15]) and the misguided endorsement of a one-size-fits-all legal recipe that does not suit a diverse world (Posner[16]). The relevance and effectiveness of the entire system has been called into question. We do not subscribe to these doomsday pronouncements.

Asian economic and political dynamism are changing the world and are expected to contribute in a major way to shaping the world in this century. Gideon Rachman, a leading strategic thinker of the *Financial Times* of London, argues that the West's domination of world politics is coming to a close. The flow of wealth and power is turning from West to East in a process of what he calls "Easternization," and he thinks that a new era of global instability has begun.[17] Easternization, argues Rachman, is the defining trend of our age—the growing wealth of Asian nations is transforming the international balance of power. This shift to the East is shaping the lives of people all over the world, the fate of nations, and the great questions of war and peace.

A rising China, it is asserted, may now challenge America's supremacy, and the ambitions of other Asian powers—including India, Indonesia,

Japan, Pakistan, and North Korea—have the potential to shake the whole world. Meanwhile, the West is caught up with economic malaise and political populism, the Arab world is in turmoil, and Russia strives to reclaim its status as a great power.

Geoff Dyer, previously the correspondent of the *Financial Times* in Beijing, wrote in *Contest of the Century* that the contest will be very much about the rules of international order and about the values of human rights elaborated by the United Nations.[18] The struggle over values is also told in Daniel Bell's *The China Model*,[19] and Jiang Quing has made the case for *A Confucian Constitutional Order*.[20] While China is engaging more in multilateralism, some charge that it is at the same time chipping away at the international human rights architecture. Warden has noted that while China has embraced multilateralism and its emerging leadership role in the United Nations system, it is also deftly pursuing a "human rights with Chinese characteristics" agenda. Its vision of "building a community of shared future" made its way into UN Human Rights Council Resolutions in 2017 at its 34th session.[21] The Chinese Permanent Mission in Geneva stated that this "demonstrates China's growing influence and ability to set the agenda in international human rights governance."[22] At the 35th session in 2017, a side event saw Chinese Ambassador to the UN in Geneva, Ma Zhaoxu, deliver a joint statement on behalf of some 140 countries, "Joining Hands to Reduce Poverty, Promote and Protect Human Rights," that peace and development were the prerequisites for human rights, and "development provides the basic conditions for realizing various human rights."

In evaluating this statement, one needs to take account of the consensus language of UN resolutions and declarations China has agreed to, such as the Vienna Declaration and Programme of Action (VDPA) (1993) that provides:

> Paragraph 5. All human rights are universal, indivisible and interdependent and interrelated. The international community must treat human rights globally in a fair and equal manner, on the same footing, and with the same emphasis. While the significance of national and regional particularities and various historical, cultural and religious backgrounds must be borne in mind, it is the duty of States, regardless of their political, economic and cultural systems, to promote and protect all human rights and fundamental freedoms.

Paragraph 8. Democracy, development and respect for human rights and fundamental freedoms are interdependent and mutually reinforcing. Democracy is based on the freely expressed will of the people to determine their own political, economic, social and cultural systems and their full participation in all aspects of their lives. In the context of the above, the promotion and protection of human rights and fundamental freedoms at the national and international levels should be universal and conducted without conditions attached.

Paragraph 10. The World Conference on Human Rights reaffirms the right to development, as established in the Declaration on the Right to Development, as a universal and inalienable right and an integral part of fundamental human rights. As stated in the Declaration on the Right to Development, the human person is the central subject of development. While development facilitates the enjoyment of all human rights, the lack of development may not be invoked to justify the abridgement of internationally recognized human rights.

China sponsored a resolution at the Human Rights Council in 2017, "The Contribution of Development to the Enjoyment of all Human Rights," ultimately adopted, which aimed at advancing the view that development preceded human rights. This view, which prioritized economic development over civil and political rights, has been contested, notably by the United States. The latter has rejected the "development first" approach, which, it asserts, runs counter to China's own commitments to universality and indivisibility. The EU, through Germany, also rejected attempts to artificially separate development and human rights.[23]

Human rights, a key pillar of the UN's engagement with the world (along with development and peace and security), was not mentioned in a Chinese position paper on a UN reform agenda. UN Secretary-General Antonio Guterres was also vague on human rights in his statements on UN reform. Candela has argued that China seeks to fill an increasingly large void as the US's influence recedes in order to expand its influence through multilateral frameworks and in order to diminish the human rights architecture. She notes that China is "renowned in the UN for blocking the promotion of human rights," notably through the UN budget committee, where it has objected to requests from the Office of the High Commissioner for Human Rights for increased financing and proposed reorganization in the field.[24] Sceats and Breslin have argued that despite its subscription to various human rights instruments, China sees human rights in aspirational terms and not in legal terms. As it assumes its role as a responsible global player, it faces tensions between its traditional adherence to non-interference and the need for intervention, such as in the Libyan case in 2011. Amidst the Arab Spring revolts, it has emphasized the need for strong government. The concern with domestic stability and avoidance of criticism at the UN on human rights continue to guide its approach to human rights in the world.[25]

It has been asserted that there is a clear turning point in history, which Rieff described as follows: "the global balance of power has tilted away from governments committed to human rights norms and toward those indifferent or actively hostile to them. Into the latter camp fall, most obviously, China, Russia, Turkey, the Philippines, and Venezuela."[26]

Human rights values will play a critical role in debates concerning the foundations of the future Asian and world orders, and it is crucial that everyone in Asia realizes that the values of the UDHR (1948) are very much Asian values. Easternization may be under way but it has a while to run and a road map is needed to guide the turbulent process that will define the international politics of the twenty-first century. The Universal Declaration of Human Rights remains that road map.

The Asian Versus Universal Rights Debate

The assertion that human rights are Asian values has been reinforced after a hard-fought battle against states in the region that had sought to argue that Asian values are somehow different from those proclaimed in the UDHR. While the "Asian values" debate has subsided, one still hears some voices arguing for this position in the twenty-first century. The global dialogue on universality continues, but all member states of the UN participating in the UPR process affirm their commitment to universality. The UDHR proclaimed a universal value in 1948 for the first time, and while it has become part of international human rights law, both treaty and customary, one still hears contrarian voices on occasions.

This work is located in a constructivist framework to the elaboration and diffusion of universal norms, namely that there is a global dialogue between states and societies in the development of such norms. The irrefutable elucidation of the Asian contribution in this work, using primary evidence, is part of this dialogue and supports the claims of universality in the UDHR.

The Asian values debate of the 1990s, led by leaders of economically successful states with powerful leaders like in Malaysia and Singapore, had argued for a cultural "relativist" position that sought to challenge the universal rights approach.[27] The challenge was not unique to East Asia as other parts of the Asian continent had also critiqued the "Western" values in the UDHR.[28] Together, they argued that human rights had to be adapted to local traditional customs, culture, and religious practices. They could draw upon the warning issued by the American Anthropological Association to the UN Commission on Human Rights in 1947, during the drafting of the UDHR, about the danger of erasing cultural diversity. The Society pointed to the West's history of "ascribing cultural inferiority" to non-European peoples.[29]

Countries expounding the relativist argument in the early 1990s, according to Cerna, included China, Indonesia, Iran, Iraq, Malaysia, Myanmar, Pakistan, Singapore, Syria, Vietnam, and Yemen.[30] In the lead-up to the 1993 Vienna Conference, the Asian States, which were the loudest proponents of cultural relativism and "Asian values," issued the Bangkok Declaration which stated that "while human rights are universal in nature, they must be considered in the context of a dynamic and evolving process of international norm-setting, bearing in mind the significance of national and regional particularities and various historical, cultural and religious backgrounds."[31] Later on, an analysis of the relativist positions in the UPR of the Human Rights Council noted several forms of cultural relativism by 2011: one based on political factors and/or revolutionary discourse, notably in the UPRs of China, Vietnam, and Myanmar; another based on Islamic cultural relativism Yemen, Iran, and Pakistan; a mixture of both in Iran; and one based on diversity and respect for the self-determination of local communities, such as Indonesia.[32] The revolutionary form was related "to regimes with a revolutionary origin and to have its main friction with international human rights standards in the denial of political plurality and frequent association with 'colonizing lobbies.'"[33]

The preservation of regional diversity was argued for by revolutionary China at the 1993 Bangkok meeting. At that time, a complementary and different line of justification for relativism was offered by Singapore's late Prime Minister Lee Kuan Yew who defended **strong leadership** "on the ground of their alleged effectiveness in promoting economic success," an assertion that was critically examined and refuted by Nobel laureate Amartya Sen.[34] The latter usefully warned against the "orientalist" temptation to view "Asia" as a homogenous term at the expense of its great diversity.

The Asian values challenge persists in places, especially the revolutionary form and the complementary arguments once defended by the late Lee Kuan Yew. It has gained traction with the rise of a powerful and influential China. It has led to fears among the international human rights advocates over the possible "implicit, meta-level challenge [China's] rise poses to the argument that increased observance of human rights is a sine qua non for development and enhanced global influence."[35] The appeal of such a "Chinese Model" may not come from any active Chinese exporting of norms, which it claims it is not engaged in, but rather in the powerful suggestion that each state must define its own human rights priorities. As Xue Hanqin, a Chinese judge on the International Court of Justice, has argued: "China's position on cultural relativism is not intended to challenge Western values and its liberal rights models, but to argue that these models and values are not the only way to promote and protect human rights."[36]

This international dialogue on international human rights standards, as demonstrated by scholars such as Kathryn Sikkink and others,[37] began with the drafting of the UDHR and the promulgation of the universal values in this Declaration. These were in turn transformed—through power tactics, through agreements, through institutionalized socialization and inter-societal engagement—into the core binding international human rights instruments, many of which China has signed up for, and into customary international law as the UDHR was incorporated into many state's policies and legislation. This "international norms cascade" arguably continues today and needs reinvigoration as China and "illiberal democracies" rise, and as liberal democracies succumb to populism and identity-based politics.[38]

This work takes into account the following elements in Donnelly's framework to explaining human rights in his work, *Universal Human Rights in Theory and Practice* (2013).[39] First, in explaining modern international human rights, historical accuracy is required. The promulgation of "universal" "human" rights is a post-Second World War movement. It came after two world wars in the space of 30 years and the Holocaust. Whereas traces of human rights values and norms can be found in different cultures, religions, political traditions in other times across the world, it may be historically inaccurate to frame these in a modern "human rights" term. The attempts to do so, however difficult, do nevertheless point to the powerful new global normative rights framework, which serves as a reference point for all governments and societies.

Second, human rights is a moral project rather than a pre-existing fact of nature and a social project grounded in the implementation of international human rights law. There is a dialectic between overlapping transcendental or "comprehensive doctrines"/philosophical traditions (such as natural law, Kantianism, utilitarianism) and religious traditions (such as Christianity, Buddhism, Islam, Judaism).

Third, flowing from this, the UDHR provided a list of the minimum number of things needed for a life of dignity, not only for health and physical sustenance but also for mental and social well-being. It is a historical fact that the "new" humanism of the late seventeenth century[40]—the European enlightenment, the American revolution, and the French revolutions—powerfully influenced the framing of "human" rights in the twentieth century, as those things that are required for a life of "dignity." Donnelly argues for an "overlapping consensus on internationally recognised human rights norms," which means that "there is a striking convergence on a vision of the limits of political legitimacy in the contemporary world."[41] China, for example, recognized universal rights at Vienna in 1993 and amended its Constitution in 2004, which stated that it recognized and protected human rights.[42]

Fourth, the UDHR Model has been the basis for dialogue. The model comprises: (a) a short list of substantive rights recognized in the document and subsequent conventions; (b) rights rooted in a conception of those rights being inherent to human dignity; (c) universal rights needed to implement values; (d) individuals, not corporate entities, hold these rights as they are at the same time deeply entrenched in natural and voluntary groups; (e) internationally recognized human rights are interdependent and indivisible; and (f) although they are universal rights, states have the responsibility to implement these rights for their own nationals.[43]

The idea of "overlapping consensus" implies contestation and ongoing dialogue. It is vitally important that the case for universality be buttressed further. The ASEAN Human Rights Declaration of 2012 contained a commitment to the Universal Declaration of Human Rights, the Charter of the United Nations, the Vienna Declaration and Programme of Action. At the same time, it stipulated in Article 7 that while "all human rights are universal, indivisible, interdependent and interrelated," "the realisation of human rights must be considered in the regional and national context bearing in mind different political, economic, legal, social, cultural, historical and religious backgrounds." The 2009 Terms of Reference of the ASEAN Intergovernmental Commission on Human Rights (AICHR) also proclaimed adherence to universal values (Article 2.2) while, at the same time, promoting "human rights within the regional context, bearing in mind national and regional particularities and mutual respect for different historical, cultural and religious backgrounds, and taking into account the balance between rights and responsibilities" (Article 1.4).[44]

In order to steer the members of ASEAN and other governments in Asia, to buttress their civil societies and rights advocacy, and to shape the "arc of history towards justice," the case for universal values must be reinforced. One important way of doing so is to clearly show that Asian values ***are consistent with*** universal values. An NGO Bangkok Declaration in 1993, reflecting CSOs commitment to universalism, hailed universality as "encompassing the richness and wisdom of Asia-Pacific cultures." A large number of NGOs (240) advanced the argument that "[t]here is emerging a new understanding of universalism encompassing the richness and wisdom of Asia-Pacific cultures. The human rights are of universal concern and are universal in value, the advocacy of human rights cannot be considered to be an encroachment upon national sovereignty."[45]

Asian Values Are Universal Values

Buttressing this argument, this work will demonstrate, from the records of the drafting of the Declaration, that it drew upon detailed Asian blueprints from China, India, Lebanon, Vietnam, and Indonesia. Such an exploration has hitherto not been made in so explicit a manner, though some authors have examined the drafting of the UDHR and others have examined the progress of universal human rights values in Asia generally. An edited work by Bunte and Dressel has examined the uptake and compliance with international human rights across constitutions in Southeast Asia. Its focus is on the diversity of constitutional frameworks and constitutional safeguards for human rights in the contemporary economic, political, and social context of the region.[46] An earlier work by Philip Eldridge noted the political contestation in Southeast Asia over universal rights up to the early 1990s. He surveyed the varying degrees of uptake among authoritarian states at the time (Cambodia, Indonesia, and Malaysia) and contrasted them to more progressive, democratic states of the time (Philippines and Thailand). Differences over understandings about universality in the political economy at the time, he noted, might be overcome by ASEAN's inclusion in international human rights treaties.[47] In another edited work by Nasu and Saul, authors consider the challenges facing regional institutional frameworks in the Asia Pacific. The work challenges assumptions that Asia is not ready for greater institutionalization.[48]

The present work focuses squarely on Asian contributions to the UDHR and its subsequent uptake in the region. The drafting of the UDHR and the role of the Commission on Human Rights have been explored in a number of works. A brief survey is warranted here, to make the point that they do not specifically discuss Asian contributions.

Ashild Samnoy, in 1993, examined the historical origins of the 1948 international consensus over the UDHR, which would become a "fundamental frame of reference to international legal and political discourse."[49] Samnoy notes a critical factor in the adoption of the Declaration, *timing* (notably the impact of the war and the Holocaust), which allowed for consensus among the UN's 58 states that represented most, if not all, parts of the world. While tracing the origins of the Declaration, the setting up of the drafting process and the Commission on Human Rights, Samnoy notes the significant contribution of a united Latin America, of Charles Malik (Lebanon) and of P.C. Chang (China), though his account depicts largely the dominant roles of great powers in setting up the mechanism. He notes debates of the form of an international instrument, whether to adopt a declaration or a convention, with smaller states (including India, Lebanon, and the Philippines) preferring a binding instrument.[50] The Chinese delegate in the General Assembly debates over the drafting of universal values in 1948, T.Y. Wu, would argue that the Declaration would "serve as a moral standard to which mankind could aspire" and Malik of Lebanon would stress the authoritative character of the document.[51] He notes a number of factors that facilitated the drafting, including: (1) avoidance of great controversies (such as the problem of minorities), (2) general or vague formulations of controversial issues, (3) the use of limitation clauses, and (4) not grounding the document in any religious or philosophical tradition, resulting in the text of Article 1.

Johnson and Symonides' 1998 survey of the UDHR, marking its 40th anniversary, provide a general overview of the drafting and impact of the Declaration. Johnson usefully outlines the key rights issues included as well as some of the contentious issues that were omitted: petitions, rights of minorities, dependent territories, rights to resist oppression, and women's rights.[52]

Johannes Morsink's meticulous examination in 1999 of the crafting of the UDHR through a thematic approach discusses the contemporary influences on the drafters—including war, the Holocaust, ideology, East vs. West geopolitical competition at the start of the Cold War, the women's lobby, civil society, and Latin American socialism. He set out to rebut charges that the Declaration was in any way ethnocentric, though he concedes that parts of Asia and Africa were not represented.[53]

Mary Glendon, in the same year, argued that despite the non-representation of many peoples from Africa and Asia, the UDHR was very much a "multicultural" document and that the framers "never claimed to have produced the last word on human rights.[54] She noted an ongoing "contest for the meaning of the declaration" and argued that the contribution of developing countries was by no means negligible. She called attention to the role of Chinese, Indian, and Lebanese delegates in shaping the discussions of the Commission on Human Rights. She noted that it is unlikely that any other political document in history has ever drawn from such diverse sources, or received the same worldwide consideration and scrutiny, as the Declaration underwent over its two years of preparation."[55]

Alfredsson and Eide's 1999 comprehensive and systematic treatment of the UDHR did not specifically discuss the contribution of Asian drafters, but rather very usefully analysed the substantive rights and duties in each article in the Declaration.[56]

More recently, the contribution of the Global South was examined by Kathryn Sikkink, who demonstrates that the drafting of the UDHR was shaped by significant figures from Asia and Latin America. In her recent work she refutes the notion that "powerful states of the Global North proposed the idea of international protection of human rights, wrote human rights laws, and imposed them on the weak states of the Global South against their will."[57] She outlined in detail the role of Latin Americans in particular, who presented a very unified front in the process and on the content. She stresses the contentious nature of human rights dialogue since 1948, both in the Global South and in the Global North. She notes that human rights are a process and not an end point and argues for their increased effectiveness over time in offering protection.[58]

Thus far, however, none has systematically analysed the contribution of Asian drafters of the UDHR and their contribution to framing universal values. This book draws on the documentary evidence from the Commission on Human Rights, many of which were included in a collection of documents by William Schabas.[59] Other documents were available through personal collections of Bertrand Ramcharan from decades in the UN Human Rights Programme, through the United Nations online documents and through the UN library archives. ***A brief word*** on the coding of UN documents is in order. Simply put, documents from the various United Nations entities carry the following types of codes (sample numbers provided): A/ (General Assembly document) -; E/ (Economic and Social Council or ECOSOC); E/CN.4 (Commission on Human Rights of the ECOSOC); and A/HRC (Human Rights Council).[60]

The book begins, in Chap. 2, by briefly outlining the universal values contained in the UDHR, the context in which they were drafted, their reinforcement and codification in international human rights law, and the mechanism through which Asian drafters began their engagement with universal values. It describes their engagement with the early stages of setting up the Commission on Human Rights and the contributions of Asians at this stage. Chapter 3 provides sketches of the Asian drafters and their inputs on universal values. Chapter 4 elaborates the visions of human rights that they proposed throughout the various phases of the drafting process. Subsequent chapters proceed to examine Asian contributions to the substantive foundation provisions of the UDHR (Chap. 5), to the principle of humanity (Chap. 6), to discussions on dignity, equality and equitable life chances (Chap. 7), and to implementation challenges (Chap. 8). Chapter 9 traces the "future" of the UDHR since 1948. The book concludes by validating universal rights as Asian values based on the historical evidence presented.

This book has a simple message: that the values of the Universal Declaration are very much Asian values and that the future of the world must continue to be inspired by those values.

Notes

1. A.J. Ayer (1984), *Philosophy in the Twentieth Century* (New York, Vintage books), p. 18.
2. Human Rights Council, A/HRC/WG.6/17/CHN/1, para.4.
3. Human Rights Council, A/HRC/WG.6/27/IND/1, para. 1.
4. Human Rights Council, A/HRC/WG.6/27/IDN, para. 1.
5. Human Rights Council, A/HRC/WG.6/17/MYS/1, para. 9.
6. Human Rights Council, A/HEC/WG.6/28/PAK/1, para. 2.
7. Ibid, para. 19.

8. Human Rights Council, A/HRC/WG.6/27/PHL/1, para. 3.
9. Human Rights Council, A/HRC/WG.6/24/SGP/1, para. 4.
10. Human Rights Council, A/HRC/WG.6/25/THA/1, para. 14.
11. Human Rights Council, A/HRC/WG.6/18/VNM/1, paras. 6–7.
12. David Rieff, "The End of Human Rights? Learning from the failure of the Responsibility to Protect and the International Criminal Court." *Foreign Policy.* April 9 2018. http://foreignpolicy.com/2018/04/09/the-end-of-human-rights-genocide-united-nations-r2p-terrorism/
13. Stephen Hopgood. *The Endtimes for Human Rights.* (Ithaca: Cornell University Press, 2014).
14. D. Forsythe, "Hard times for human rights." *Journal of Human Rights,* Vol. 16, No. 2, 2017, pp. 242–253.
15. S. Moyn, *The Last Utopia: Human Rights in History* (Cambridge MA: Harvard University Press, 2012).
16. E. Posner, *The Twilight of Human Rights Law* (Oxford: Oxford University Press, 2014).
17. See Gideon Rachman, Easternization. *War and Peace in the Asian Century.* (London: The Bodley Head, 2016).
18. Geoff Dyer (2014), *Contest of the Century*, New York: Vintage Books.
19. Daniel Bell, *The China Model* (Princeton and Oxford, Princeton University Press, 2015).
20. Jiang Quing, *A Confucian Constitutional Order.* (Princeton and Oxford: Princeton University Press, 2013).
21. Human Rights Council, 34th session (HCR34) in March 2017: a resolution on the "Question of the realization in all countries of economic social and cultural rights" (A/HRC/34/L.4/Rev.1) and a resolution on "The right to food" (A/HRC/34/L.21).
22. Andrea Worden, China Pushes 'Human Rights With Chinese Characteristics' at the UN, *China Change*, October 9, 2017. https://chinachange.org/2017/10/09/china-pushes-human-rights-with-chinese-characteristics-at-the-un/ 4/12
23. Worden (2017), p. 8.
24. Kacie Candela, China's Notions of UN Reform: Filling the Growing Vacuum Left by the US," *Pass Blue*, January 3, 2018, p. 11. Accessed at http://www.passblue.com/2018/01/03/chinas-notions-of-un-reform-filling-the-growing-vacuum-left-by-the-us/ 1/7.
25. Sonja Sceats and Shaun Breslin, *China and the International Human Rights System.* (London: Chatham House, 2012).
26. Rieff, op.cit., (2018).
27. See Diane K. Mauzy (1997), "The human rights and 'Asian values' debate in Southeast Asia: Trying to clarify the key issues," *The Pacific Review*, Vol. 10 No. 2, p. 210 (pp. 210–236). Ole Bruun and Michael Jacobsen, Human

Rights and Asian Values: Contesting National Identities and Cultural Representations in Asia (London: Routledge, 2003); Kingsbury, D. Leena Avonius, Eds., *Human Rights in Asia: A Reassessment of the Asian Values Debate* (Springer, Palgrave Macmillan, 2008).

See also Michael Freeman (2007), "Human Rights, Democracy and Asian Values," Michael Freeman (2007) Human rights, democracy and 'Asian values', *The Pacific Review*, 9:3, 352–366. On cultural relativism generally see, Jack Donnelly (1984), *Human Rights Quarterly*, Vol. 6, No. 4 (Nov., 1984), pp. 400–419.

28. See An-na'im, Abdullahi Ahmed (ed.). Human Rights in Cross-cultural Perspectives: A Quest for Consensus. Philadelphia: University of Pennsylvania Press, 1992..
29. Roger Blackburn, *Cultural Relativism in the Universal Periodic Review of the UN Human Rights Council.* Institut CAtala International, Working Paper No. 3, 2011. Available at https://www.upr-info.org/sites/default/files/general-document/pdf/-blackburn_upr_cultural_relativism.09.2011.pdf
30. C. Cerna (1994), "Universality of Human Rights and Cultural Diversity: Implementation of Human Rights in Different Socio-Cultural Contexts," *Human Rights Quarterly*, Vol. 16, No. 4, pp. 740–752.
31. *NGO Bangkok Declaration on Human Rights*, World Conference on Human Rights, 19 April 1993, UN Doc. A Conf.157/PC/83.
32. Blackburn (2011), p. 33.
33. Blackburn (2011), p. 34.
34. Amartya Sen, "Human Rights and Asian Values," 16th Annual Morgenthau Memorial Lecture on Ethics and Foreign Policy, 1997.

    May 25, 1997, https://www.carnegiecouncil.org/publications/archive/morgenthau/254
35. Sceats and Breslin (2012), p. 41.
36. Quoted in Sceats and Breslin (2018), p. 42.
37. Martha Finnemore and Kathryn Sikkink (1998), "International Norm Dynamics and Political Change," International Organization, Vol. 52, No. 4, (Autumn, 1998), pp. 887–917.
38. Fareed Zakaria, *The Future of Freedom: Illiberal Democracy at Home and Abroad.* London and NY: WW Norton and Co. 2007. First published in 2003; Zakaria, "The rise of illiberal democracy," *Foreign Affairs,* Nov/Dec, 1997, pp. 22–43.
39. Donnelly (2013), *Universal Human Rights In Theory and Practice,* Ithaca: Cornell University Press, 2013. p. 53.
40. See, for example, Valentine Zuber, *Le Culte des Droits de l'Homme.* (Paris: Galimard, 2014). Zuber traces the passage from a religious based order to a new secular, humanist order at the time of the French Revolution.

41. Donnelly (2013), p. 58.
42. See M. Ulric Killion, "China's Amended Constitution: Quest for Liberty and Independent Judicial Review, *Washington. University Global Studies. Law Review.* Vol. 43, No. 4, 2005., pp. 43–80, Available at http://open-scholarship.wustl.edu/law_globalstudies/vol4/iss1/3
43. Donnelly (2013), p. 28.
44. AICHR (2009), Terms of Reference. Accessible at: http://www.asean.org/storage/images/archive/publications/TOR-of-AICHR.pdf
45. *NGO Bangkok Declaration on Human Rights*, World Conference on Human Rights, 19 April 1993, UN Doc. A/CONF.157/PC/83.
46. Bünte, M. and B. Dressel. *'Politics and Constitutions in Southeast Asia.'* (London, New York: Routledge 2017). See especially first chapter of Part 3.
47. Philip J. Eldridge, *The Politics of Human Rights in Southeast Asia*, (Routledge, London and New York, 2002)
48. Hitoshi, Nasu, Ben Saul, *Human Rights in the Asia-Pacific Region: Towards Institution Building*, Routledge, 2011.
49. Ashild Samnoy, *Human rights as international consensus: The Making of the Universal Declaration of Human Rights, 1945–1948*, Chr. Michelsen Institute Bergen, Norway, 1993, p. 1.
50. Ibid, p. 61.
51. Ibid, pp. 72–73.
52. M. Glen Johnson and Janusz Symonides, *The Universal Declaration of Human Rights: A History of its Creation and Implementation*, 1948–1998, UNESCO Publications, 1998. http://unesdoc.unesco.org/images/0011/001144/114488E.pdf
53. Johannes Morsink, *The Universal Declaration of Human Rights: Origins, Drafting, and Intent* (Philadelphia: University of Philadelphia 1999/2010).
54. Mary Glendon (1999), "Foundations of Human Rights: The unfinished Business," *American Journal of Jurisprudence*, Vol. 44, No. 1, 1999, p. 7.
55. Glendon (1999), p. 8.
56. Gudmundur Alfredsson and Asbjorn Eide (Ed.s), the Universal Declaration of Human Rights: A common Standard of Achievement (the Hague: Martinus Nijhoff, 1999).
57. Kathryn Sikkink, Evidence for Hope: Making Human Rights Work in the 21st Century. Princeton: Princeton University Press, 2017, p. 56.
58. See also Fariss, C. "Respect for human rights has improved over time: Modeling the changing standard of accountability." *American Political Science Review*, Vol. 108, No. 2., May 2014, pp. 297–318.
59. William Schabas (2014), op.cit.
60. The lengthy titles of UN documents are mostly excluded. The specific UN codes are used in this work. A useful explanation is provided on Wikipedia,

"UN Document Codes," at https://en.wikipedia.org/wiki/United_Nations_Document_Codes.Middle codes, mean as follows:

> __/RES/ (A resolution of the body); __/PV.67/ (A full, first-person account of the proceedings of the 67th meeting (of the year, or since the start of the UN) known as a "proces verbal" or "Verbatim record"); __/SR.67/ (A third-person condensed version of the above meeting, known as the "Summary record"); ___/L.45/ (is a enjoys limited distribution, for example a draft resolution before a voted on the same); __/ES-10/ (A "meeting" of the Tenth "emergency special session"). Finally, the trailing codes mean: _/__/Add.3 – (Addendum to a document); __/__/Rev.1 (First revision of a document) and __/__/Corr.1 (Corrigendum to a document).

References

Primary Documents: Human Rights Council:

Human Rights Council, A/HRC/WG.6/17/CHN/1, para.4.

Human Rights Council, A/HRC/WG.6/27/IND/1, para. 1.

Human Rights Council, A/HRC/WG.6/27/IDN, para. 1.

Human Rights Council, A/HRC/WG.6/17/MYS/1, para. 9.

Human Rights Council, A/HEC/WG.6/28/PAK/1, para. 2.

Human Rights Council, A/HRC/WG.6/27/PHL/1, para. 3.

Human Rights Council, A/HRC/WG.6/24/SGP/1, para. 4.

Human Rights Council, A/HRC/WG.6/25/THA/1, para. 14.

Human Rights Council, A/HRC/WG.6/18/VNM/1, paras. 6–7.

AICHR. (2009), Terms of Reference. Accessible at: http://www.asean.org/storage/images/archive/publications/TOR-of-AICHR.pdf

Alfredsson, Gudmundur and Asbjorn Eide (Eds.), *The Universal Declaration of Human Rights: A common Standard of Achievement* (the Hague: Martinus Nijhoff, 1999)

An-na'im, Abdullahi Ahmed (ed.). *Human Rights in Cross-cultural Perspectives: A Quest for Consensus.* (Philadelphia: University of Pennsylvania Press, 1992).

Bell, Daniel. *The China Model* (Princeton and Oxford, Princeton University Press, 2015).

Blackburn, Roger. *Cultural Relativism in the Universal Periodic Review of the UN Human Rights Council.* Institut CAtala International, Working Paper No. 3, 2011. Available at https://www.upr-info.org/sites/default/files/general-document/pdf/-blackburn_upr_cultural_relativism.09.2011.pdf

Bünte, Marco and B. Dressel. *Politics and Constitutions in Southeast Asia.* (London, New York: Routledge, 2017).

Candela, Kacie China's Notions of UN Reform: Filling the Growing Vacuum Left by the US, *Pass Blue*, January 3, 2018, p. 11. Accessed at http://www.passblue.com/2018/01/03/chinas-notions-of-un-reform-filling-the-growing-vacuum-left-by-the-us/ 1/7

Cerna, Christina, "Universality of Human Rights and Cultural Diversity: Implementation of Human Rights in Different Socio-Cultural Contexts," *Human Rights Quarterly*, Vol. 16, No.4, (1994), pp.740–752.

Donnelly, Jack, *Human Rights Quarterly*, Vol. 6, No. 4 (Nov., 1984), pp. 400–419

Donnelly, Jack, *Universal Human Rights In Theory and Practice* (Ithaca: Cornell University Press, 2013), p. 53

Dyer, Geoff, *Contest of the Century*, New York: Vintage Books.

Eldridge, Philip J. *The Politics of Human Rights in Southeast Asia*, (Routledge, London and New York, 2002)

Fariss, C. "Respect for human rights has improved over time: Modeling the changing standard of accountability." *American Political Science Review*, Vol. 108, No. 2., May 2014, pp. 297–318.

Finnemore, Martha and Kathryn Sikkink (1998), "International Norm Dynamics and Political Change," International Organization, Vol. 52, No. 4, (Autumn, 1998), pp. 887–917.

Forsythe, David, "Hard times for human rights." *Journal of Human Rights,* Vol. 16, No. 2, 2017, pp. 242–253.

Freeman, Michael, "Human Rights, Democracy and Asian Values," *The Pacific Review*, Vol. 9, No.3, 1997, 352–366.

Glendon, Mary, "Foundations of Human Rights: The unfinished Business," *American Journal of Jurisprudence*, Vol. 44, No. 1, 1999, p. 7.

Hopgood Stephen, *The Endtimes for Human Rights.* (Ithaca: Cornell University Press, 2014).

Human Rights Council, 34th session (HCR34) in March 2017: a resolution on the "Question of the realization in all countries of economic social and cultural rights" (A/HRC/34/L.4/Rev.1) and a resolution on "The right to food" (A/HRC/34/L.21).

Johnson, M. Glen and Janusz Symonides, *The Universal Declaration of Human Rights: A History of its Creation and Implementation*, 1948–1998, UNESCO Publications, 1998. http://unesdoc.unesco.org/images/0011/001144/114488E.pdf

Killion, M., Ulric "China's Amended Constitution: Quest for Liberty and Independent Judicial Review," *Washington. University Global Studies. Law Review.* Vol. 43, No.4,, 2005., pp. 43–80, Available at http://openscholarship.wustl.edu/law_globalstudies/vol4/iss1/3

Kingsbury, Damien, Leena Avonius, Eds., *Human Rights in Asia: A Reassessment of the Asian Values Debate* (Springer, Palgrave Macmillan, 2008).

Mauzy, Diane, "The human rights and 'Asian values' debate in Southeast Asia: Trying to clarify the key issues," *The Pacific Review*, Vol.10 No.2, 1997, pp. 210–236.

Morsink, Johannes, *The Universal Declaration of Human Rights: Origins, Drafting, and Intent* (Philadelphia: University of Philadelphia 1999/2010)

Moyn, S., *The Last Utopia: Human Rights in History* (Cambridge MA: Harvard University Press, 2012).

Nasu, Hitoshi and Ben Saul, *Human Rights in the Asia-Pacific Region: Towards Institution Building*, Routledge, 2011.

NGO Bangkok Declaration on Human Rights, World Conference on Human Rights, 19 April 1993, UN Doc. A Conf.157/PC/83,

Ole Bruun and Michael Jacobsen, Human Rights and Asian Values: Contesting National Identities and Cultural Representations in Asia (London: Routledge, 2003)

Posner, E. *The Twilight of Human Rights Law* (Oxford: Oxford University Press, 2014)

Quing, Jiang, *A Confucian Constitutional Order.* (Princeton and Oxford: Princeton University Press, 2013).

Rachman, Gideon, *Easternization: War and Peace in the Asian Century.* (London: The Bodley Head, 2016).

Rieff, David, "The End of Human Rights? Learning from the failure of the Responsibility to Protect and the International Criminal Court." *Foreign Policy. April 9 2018.* http://foreignpolicy.com/2018/04/09/the-end-of-human-rights-genocide-united-nations-r2p-terrorism/

Samnoy, Ashild, *Human rights as international consensus: The Making of the Universal Declaration of Human Rights, 1945–1948* (Chr. Michelsen Institute Bergen, Norway, 1993).

Sceats, Sonja and Shaun Breslin, *China and the International Human Rights System.* (London: Chatham House, 2012).

Sen, Amartya, "Human Rights and Asian Values," Sixteenth Annual Morgenthau Memorial Lecture on Ethics and Foreign Policy, May 25, 1997, https://www.carnegiecouncil.org/publications/archive/morgenthau/254

Sikkink, Kathryn, Evidence for Hope: Making Human Rights Work in the 21st Century. Princeton: Princeton University Press, 2017, p.56

Worden, Andrea, "China Pushes 'Human Rights With Chinese Characteristics' at the UN," *China Change*, October 9, 2017. https://chinachange.org/2017/10/09/china-pushes-human-rights-with-chinese-characteristics-at-the-un/4/12

Zakaria, Fareed, *The Future of Freedom: Illiberal Democracy at Home and Abroad.* London and NY: WW Norton and Co. 2007. First published in 2003

Zakaria, "The rise of illiberal democracy," *Foreign Affairs,* Nov/Dec, 1997, pp. 22–43.

Zuber, Valentine, *Le Culte des Droits de l'Homme.* (Paris: Galimard, 2014).

CHAPTER 2

Crafting Universal Values: The UDHR Model, Context, and Process

The UDHR proclaimed universal values in 1948. Asians contributed to elaborating the 30 articles in the document, process undertaken at a time of great upheaval following unprecedented devastation following the Second World War. This chapter outlines the values, the context in which they were elaborated, their reinforcement and codification in international human rights law, and the drafting mechanism adopted to come up with universal human rights.

The UDHR Model and International Human Rights Law

The Universal Declaration adopted by General Assembly Resolution 217/A on 10 December 1948 contained 30 articles. Subsequent conventions adopted in 1966, the ICCPR and the ICESCR, transformed these into binding obligations for State Parties. Twenty years after their adoption, the Proclamation of Teheran, issued at the International Conference on Human Rights in Teheran from 22 April to 13 May 1968, hailed the "common understanding, of the peoples of the world concerning the inalienable and inviolable rights of all members of the human family" in the UDHR, "which constitutes an obligation for the members of the international community."[1] At the 1993 Vienna Conference, as noted in the Introduction, an even greater number of member states of the UN

R. Ramcharan, B. Ramcharan, *Asia and the Drafting of the Universal Declaration of Human Rights*,
https://doi.org/10.1007/978-981-13-2104-7_2

upheld the universality of human rights. In addition, today there are ten international human rights treaties that have built on the International Bill.[2] The list of internationally recognized rights across these three instruments, known as the International Bill of Human Rights, are found in Table 2.1, which was adapted from Donnelly.[3]

International human rights law, which now encompasses 18 core international instruments[4] and customary international law based on practice by states, has upheld universal values and rights. The Universal Declaration, it has been argued, has achieved the status of customary law through its invocation and adoption into many constitutions around the world as well as its invocation by the peoples of all states. Rights beyond the list in the UDHR have also been advanced as binding obligations.[5] Hilary Chadwell has noted that broad international acceptance of the UDHR over the last

Table 2.1 Internationally recognized human rights under the International Bill of Human Rights

Equality of rights without discrimination
Equality of rights without discrimination
Life
Liberty and security of person
Protection against slavery
Protection against torture and cruel and inhumane treatment
Recognition as a person before the law
Equal protection of the law
Access to legal remedies for rights violations
Protection against arbitrary arrest or detention
Hearing before an impartial and independent judiciary
Presumption of innocence
Protection against ex post facto law
Protection of privacy, family, and home
Freedom of movement and residence
Seek asylum from persecution. Nationality
Marry and found family
Own property
Freedom of thought conscience and religion
Freedom of opinion, expression, and the press
Freedom of assembly and association
Political participation
Social security
Work, under favourable conditions

(*continued*)

Table 2.1 (continued)

Free trade unions
Rest and leisure
Food, clothing, and housing
Health care and social services
Special protections for children
Education
Participation in cultural life
A social and international order needed to realize rights
Self-determination
Humane treatment when detained or imprisoned
Protection against debtor's prison
Protection against arbitrary expulsion of aliens
Protection against advocacy of racial or religious hatred
Protection of minority culture

Source: Adapted from Donnelly (2013), p. 27

60 years has given its principles some legal status. The UDHR is referred to in the preambles of almost all international and regional human rights treaties, such as the ICESCR, the ICCPR, the European Convention for the Protection of Human Rights and Fundamental Freedoms (1950), the American Convention on Human Rights (1969), and the African Charter on Human and Peoples' Rights (1981). Many of the provisions of the UDHR were given treaty status in the ICESCR and ICCPR.

The Context

The historical juncture at which the Declaration was drafted, according to Samnoy, may have been a critical factor to adoption of "universal" values. The UDHR was drafted at a time of great upheavals, at the end of two world wars in the space of 30 years, unprecedented deaths and destruction, the Holocaust, and the ravages of Japanese imperialism across East Asia.[6] The search for universal values, begun during the League of Nations that would underpin the "society of nations," would move beyond European notions of "civilization" to encompass much broader visions from around the world.[7] While many of the Southeast Asian States had not yet achieved independence, representatives of the region would make significant contributions to framing universal values.

At the time of the drafting of the Universal Declaration of Human Rights, the two great Asian countries with the weight to impact on world affairs and thought were China and India. China was the heir to a great civilization but it was then in political crisis internally and internationally, with imposed treaties and external invasions. President Roosevelt saw China as a counterweight to Japan and the Soviet Union and arranged to bring it into the Big Four.[8]

One needs to keep in mind the nature of Chinese governance at the time. Following the 1911 Revolution, the Guomindang Party created by Sun Yat-sen had been both Leninist and authoritarian. After the party's break with the Communists in 1927, the party, under the leadership of Chiang Kai-shek, promoted an organic law that still "entrenched single-party rule by the KMT government."[9]

Francis Fukuyama observes that while the constitutions of the early twentieth century were largely meaningless, the same could not be said of the revisions to the civil code published by the KMT in 1929–1930. There were three major areas of reform: The first was the shift from the old Qing Code's schedules of proscriptions and punishments to a system recognizing the rights and responsibilities of citizens. "For the first time, Chinese citizens were seen not simply as the subjects of state power but as individuals with positive legal entitlements."[10] The second shift was economic. The old Qing Code had embedded property rights in the lineage or patrilineal kin group, and the right to alienate property was severely entailed by the obligations of one family member to another. The KMT code, by contrast, recognized property rights that were individual and freely alienable. It put into effect a whole domain of private law involving contract and torts, which had been regarded as "minor matters" in Qing law. And finally, it attacked the legal basis of the patrilineal family by giving women full rights to inherit property and the ability to contest those rights before the courts. This was one area in which Chinese legal reform outpaced reform that had taken place in Japan up to that date.

The KMT government represented in the war-time discussions about the establishment of a new international organization was riddled with corruption and oppression, and was hardly a paragon of human rights. Individual Chinese representatives, however, were highly competent and cultured, and these included Mr. Wellington Koo, who led China's delegation to international meetings such as at Dumbarton Oaks, and Mr. P.C. Chang, China's representative on the UN Commission on Human Rights, who made a distinguished contribution to the drafting of the Universal Declaration of Human Rights.

India, though engaged in a struggle for freedom from British rule, which it finally achieved in 1948, had large numbers of troops fighting on the Allied side and, again at the urging of President Roosevelt, was invited to participate in international conferences planning for the post-war world. Specific human rights proposals advanced by Indian representatives—as indeed by Chinese representatives—will be outlined later in this book. But India's influence on the human rights policy content of the post-war world stemmed from two sources: its struggle for independence that would inspire the subsequent movement for decolonization and the political thought of Mahatma Gandhi.

Gandhi absolutely rejected the use of violent means to achieve political ends. He considered that violence dehumanized the practitioner as well as the victim and urged Indians to fight British imperialism through non-violent civil disobedience. Gandhi took over the leadership of the movement for independence in 1919. Dennis Dalton, Emeritus Professor of Political Science at Columbia University, studied the political thought of Gandhi extensively and wrote a 1982 book, *The Indian Idea of Freedom*, that greatly helps to locate the place of Gandhian political thought among the human rights ideas of the twentieth century. Gandhi, according to Dalton, believed greatly in inclusivity, rather than the exclusivity of people like Hitler. Gandhi's first concept of inclusivity was *swaraj*, meaning rule over oneself (self-discipline), which produces true liberation. His second concept of inclusivity was *satya*, meaning the pursuit of truth. His third concept of inclusivity was *ahimsa*, meaning the practice of non-violence. *Ahimsa* and *satya* were intertwined. Gandhi's fourth concept of inclusivity was *satyagraha*, which was the power generated by truth and non-violence. Gandhi's fifth concept of inclusivity was *sarvodaya*, meaning equality. As Dalton put it, Gandhi believed "that in perceiving the essential unity of humanity, we will desire to uplift others."[11] Through non-violent action, economic and social equality can be reconciled with individual freedom.

Ideas such as these may not have found direct expression in war-time or immediate post-war conferences, but they infiltrated the global intellectual environment and ideas such as self-determination, equality, dignity, and justice for all would pervade the Charter and the Universal Declaration of Human Rights, which was drafted between 1946 and 1948.

The Drafting Process and Mechanism

Universal values were crafted over several phases. The UDHR was the outcome of a process set up within the Economic and Social Council (ECOSOC) of the United Nations.[12] ECOSOC set up a Preparatory Committee ("The Nuclear Commission"), which elaborated the terms of reference, membership, size, and so on, of the new Commission on Human Rights. The Nuclear Commission, which included Dr. C. L. Hsia (China) and Mr. K. C. Neogi (India), determined in April to May 1946 that the Commission should focus on submitting proposals, recommendations, and reports for an International Bill of Human Rights. At the first meeting of the Nuclear Commission on 29 April 1946, it was Dr. Hsia who nominated Mrs. Eleanor Roosevelt to be the Chair of the Commission. Mr. Neogi was nominated for the position of rapporteur.[13] The Commission, via ECOSOC Resolution 9(II), requested the secretary-general to collect all information about human rights from all governments and stakeholders. The Division of Human Rights of the UN Secretariat subsequently undertook a comprehensive study of human rights documents submitted. The Nuclear Commission's report,[14] which was submitted to the second session of the Economic and Social Council, stated that an International Bill of Human Rights should be elaborated as soon as possible and that "It fully realized the importance of ..achieving and promoting the recognition- and observance of human rights and fundamental freedoms for all, in the hope of drawing from the last world war which demanded the sacrifice of so many lives, the lessons which will aid us to achieve the highest aspirations of mankind."[15]

The task of drafting of a declaration was started by Mrs. Eleanor Roosevelt (United States), Dr. Peng Chun Chang (China), and Charles Malik (Lebanon), with assistance from the UN Secretariat, notably Mr. John Humphrey, Director of the UN Secretariat's Division for Human Rights. A formal Drafting Committee was created and enlarged to eight members following a letter from Mrs. Roosevelt to the President of ECOSOC requesting the same.[16] The institutions involved, phases, and chronology of the drafting process are summarized in Fig. 2.1 and Table 2.2. The UDHR was drafted over two years over some 12 sessions across the Drafting Committee, the Commission on Human Rights, the ECOSOC, and the General Assembly. Key questions were treated in the different phases.

Short History of the UDHR Project
Phase 1: Germination
1945: The UN is created in San Francisco. Human rights is included in the UN Charter and the ECOSOC is requested to appoint a Human Rights Commission charted to produce an appropriate international framework
Phase 2: Drafting
1946-1948: The Human Rights Commission in various committees, worked on drafting the UDHR fortwo years. Key questions addressed in this phase included: would there be a single document? What form should it take? - Should it be only a statement of principles or a binding instrument? A non-binding Declaration was chosen, followed by legally binding conventions.
Phase 3. Formal Debate in the General Assembly on the Draft
Fall 1948. The adopted draft is formally submitted to the UNGA's Third Committee for formal debate by UN delegates. December 1948. Modified draft of UDHR debated in full plenary of GA and adopted without a dissenting vote. (8 abstentions)
Phase 4. Drafting of Conventions.
1966. Two legally binding covenants are adopted and opened for ratification. The International Covenant on Civil and Political Rights and the International Covenant on Economic Social and Cultural Rights entered into force in 1976. Together with the UDHR, they comprise the international bill of human rights and form the bedrock of international human rights law today.
Adapted from Donnelly, Morsink, Samnoy, UN website and other sources

Fig. 2.1 Short history of the UDHR project. (Adapted from Donnelly, Morsink, Samnoy, UN website, and other sources)

Asian Input in Early Drafting Stages

Schabas, in introducing documents on the drafting of the UDHR, recalled John Humphrey's words, that there was no Jefferson. Indeed, "the Declaration's great strength was the collective dimension of its authorship."[17]

The Secretariat draft drew on the detailed constitutional provisions of ten key Asian countries in distilling the norms in the Universal

Table 2.2 Drafting process for the UDHR

General Assembly	*ECOSOC (Sessions relevant to human rights drafting process)*	*Commission on HR sessions on drafting of the UDHR*	*Drafting Committee sessions on UDHR*
1946			
		Nuclear Commission on Human Rights 29 April to 21 May 1946 Report to ECOSOC E/38/REV.1	
	Second session 25 May to 21 June 1946 Resolution adopted on Commission on HR E/RES/9(II)		
1947			
		First session 27 January to 10 February 1947 New York Report to ECOSOCE/259(SUPP)	
	Fourth session 28 February to 29 March 1947 Resolutions adopted on Human rights E/RES/46(IV) Women E/RES/48(IV) Trade unions E/RES/52(IV)		
			First session, 9 to 25 June 1947 New York Report to Commission on Human Rights E/CN.4/21

(*continued*)

Table 2.2 (continued)

General Assembly	*ECOSOC (Sessions relevant to human rights drafting process)*	*Commission on HR sessions on drafting of the UDHR*	*Drafting Committee sessions on UDHR*
		Second session 2 December – 10 December 1947 Report to ECOSOC E/600(SUPP)	
1948			
	Sixth session 2 February to 11 March 1948 New York Report of the CHR E/RES/116(VI)		
			Second session from 3 to 22 May 1948, New York Report to Commission on Human Rights E/CN.4/95
		Third session 24 May to 18 June 1948 Report to ECOSOC E/800 and addendum E/800/ADD.1	
	Seventh session 19 July to 29 August 1948 Geneva Resolution 151(VII) of 26 August 1948, transmitting the draft International Declaration of Human Rights to the General Assembly		

(*continued*)

Table 2.2 (continued)

General Assembly	*ECOSOC (Sessions relevant to human rights drafting process)*	*Commission on HR sessions on drafting of the UDHR*	*Drafting Committee sessions on UDHR*
3rd session, Third Committee 30 September to 7 December 1948 Paris Draft UDHR adopted (A/PV.178) A/777 3rd session, Plenary 21 September to 2 December 1948 Paris Adoption of the UDHR A/RES/217(III)			

Sources: From United Nations website: www.un.org

Declaration. Asian experts made brilliant distillations of philosophical ideas and values coming from different parts of the world, especially Asia.

While preparing to draft the UDHR, the UNESCO asked leading thinkers and statesmen to share their insights on rights and what might be included in the Declaration. In his response, Mahatma Gandhi pointed out that, in India, emphasis had been placed, historically, on the individual's duties to the community. [27]

Besides China and India, *the Philippines* also made a significant contribution to the shaping of the Universal Declaration of Human Rights. During the second session of the Drafting Committee of the Commission on Human Rights, on 5 December 1947, Carlos Romulo of the Philippines proposed to redraft Article 1 as discussed in the first session in June 1947 on the basis of Rene Cassin's draft proposal. In response, the chairman invited the French and Philippine representatives to submit a new text of the article. At the ninth meeting of the Drafting Committee, on 10

December 1947, Romulo proposed the following text: "All men are brothers. Being endowed by nature with reason and conscience, they are born free and possess equal dignity and rights."[7]

Following further discussion, the following text proposed by the Philippines and France was adopted: "All men are born free and equal in dignity and rights. They are endowed with reason and conscience and should act towards one another like brothers."[8] With some subsequent polishing, the following is what was adopted as the UDHR's opening article: "All human beings are born free and equal in dignity and rights. They are endowed with reason and conscience and should act towards one another in a spirit of brotherhood."

The Philippines also proposed an article stating that everyone had the right to participate in their government, both directly or indirectly, through elections that are periodic, free, and conducted by secret ballot.[11]

In China, India, Vietnam, Indonesia, and throughout Asia, the quest for self-determination was a battle cry throughout Asia at the time of the drafting of the Universal Declaration. The principle of self-determination had come into prominence from the second decade of the twentieth century through the lofty pronouncements of US President Woodrow Wilson, but though characterized as a foundation principle, it did not itself receive principled application even from its sponsor, President Wilson, and only saw application in Central and Eastern Europe. Colonial territories, countries of deep racial discrimination, and colonial territories providing raw materials to imperialist powers were left to their fates by the imperial powers.

But the quest for freedom from foreign rule in places like India predated President Wilson's advocacy of the principle of self-determination and while segregation was rife in the south of the United States, governments in that country were keen to gain access to markets in places like the British Empire and therefore favoured anti-colonial policies. On top of this, leaders in British, French, and Dutch colonies sought to capitalize on the predicaments of these countries during the Second World War to advance the cause of independence. While the imperial powers feigned lip service to the doctrine of internal self-government, they had no intention of granting independence to their colonial possessions.[18] The political and economic weaknesses of imperial powers at the end of the Second World War, and struggle within colonial territories in Asia and Africa, would lead to the great decolonizations that took place after the Second World War.

It was through a combination of these circumstances that self-determination featured in the minds of American and British post-war planners in the Atlantic Charter (although Prime Minister Churchill never saw the principle of self-determination applying to the British Empire) and also in the thinking of post-war planners from in the USSR.[19] Nevertheless, as noted by Goodrich, Hambro, and Simons, "the principle of equal rights and self-determination received no mention in the Dumbarton Oaks Proposals" and was only added at the San Francisco conference.[20] The right of self-determination was later added as the opening right in the two international covenants on human rights.

In the historical march of the human rights movement, one of the seminal moments had been the development of arrangements within the League of Nations for monitoring the rights of minorities as a group in selected countries.[21] The idea of protecting minorities as groups was abandoned in the war-time and immediate post-war discussions in favour of the protection of individual human rights worldwide. As Professor Mark Mazower has written, "Mention of minorities was excluded from the Charter and later even from the Universal Declaration too. Minority rights were shunted off into an obscure sub-commission which led a twilight and futile existence for the next few decades."[22]

Professor Mazower is not quite right in his assessment of the Sub-Commission on the Prevention and Protection of Minorities. It was the Sub-Commission that initiated a study on the rights of minorities, which contained normative suggestions that would eventually make their way into the UN's 1992 declaration on the protection of minorities. But that is not the issue of primary interest here. What is of interest for our purposes was the abandonment of the idea of the protection of minority rights as group rights. Writing in *Foreign Affairs* in January, 1942, Czech President Eduard Benes wrote: "The protection of minorities in the future should consist in the defense of human democratic rights and not of national rights. Minorities in individual states must never again be given the character of internationally recognized political and legal units, with the possibility of again becoming sources of disturbance."[23] President Benes called instead for a charter of human rights throughout the whole world after the war.[24]

Professor Mazower commented: "Collapsing minority rights into individual human rights appealed to the Great Powers too. It had, after all, been British and French reluctance to give the interwar system teeth that had doomed to frustration Weimar attempts to take it seriously."[25] He recalled that to the British delegation at San Francisco, the Foreign Office had laid down the following guidelines: We should abandon the idea of a special international system on League of Nations lines for the protection of minorities and should rely for what it is worth upon action by the UNO and its members under the provisions of the UN Charter [the universal 'Bill of Rights].[26]

At the time of the drafting of the Universal Declaration of Human Rights, there would be great debates over issues such as self-determination and the protection of minorities. In the end, the Universal Declaration made responsible choices, and the issues of self-determination and the rights of persons belonging to minorities would be taken up in the later International Covenant on Civil and Political Rights (1966), which drew its inspiration from the Universal Declaration. The Universal Declaration was the mother instrument.

It deserves to be noted, however, that Asia had sought to include an article on the protection of minorities in the Universal Declaration. Participating in the 11th meeting of the First Session of the Sub-Commission on Prevention of Discrimination and Protection of Minorities, on 1 December 1947, the Iranian expert on the Sub-Commission, Mr. Shafaq, reported that three members of a Committee of Four that had been designated to consider the matter, including himself, had agreed on the following text:

> In States inhabited by well-defined ethnic, linguistic or religious groups which are clearly distinguished from the rest of the population and which want to be accorded differential treatment, citizens belonging to such groups shall have the right as far as is compatible with public order and security to establish and maintain their schools and cultural or religious institutions, and to use their own language and script in the press, in public assembly and before the courts and authorities of the State, if they so choose.[27]

The Sub-Commission formally adopted this text at its 23rd meeting.[28] Unfortunately it was not maintained at the governmental level due to political reasons.

Thus far we have seen substantive ideas emanating from Asians in the early stages of the drafting of the UDHR. The next chapter sets out distinctive Asian visions for human rights that were advanced at the time of the drafting of the Declaration.

Notes

1. Proclamation of Teheran, 13 May 1968. Adopted by the UN General Assembly on 19 December 1968, by 115 votes to none, with 1 abstention, in resolution 2442 (XXIII). See Final Act of the International Conference on Human Rights, Tehran, 11 April to 13 May 1968. New York: United Nations. http://legal.un.org/avl/pdf/ha/fatchr/Final_Act_of_TehranConf.pdf.
2. See OHCHR.
3. Donnelly (2013), p. 27.
4. OHCHR, "The Core International Human Rights Instruments and their monitoring bodies," Available at https://www.ohchr.org/EN/ProfessionalInterest/Pages/CoreInstruments.aspx.
5. For debates on the customary status of the UDHR, see Vojin Dimitrijevic (2006), *Customary Law As An Instrument For The Protection Of Human Rights*, Working Paper, Milano: Istituto per gli Studi di Politica Internazionale and D'Amato, Anthony, "Human Rights as Part of Customary International Law: A Plea for Change of Paradigms." Faculty Working Papers. Paper 88, 2010.
6. W.G. Beasley, Japanese Imperialism 1894–1945. (Oxford: Oxford University Press, 2014).
7. See Mark Mazower, "An international civilization? Empire, internationalism and the crisis of the mid-twentieth century," *International Affairs* Vol. 82, Issue 3 (2006) 553–566.
8. See generally Chi Kwan Mark, *China and the World Since 1945: An International History*. (Oxon, New York: Routledge, 2012).
9. Francis. Fukuyama, *Political Order and Political Decay* (London, Profile Books, 2014), p. 360.
10. Ibid, p. 361.
11. See Dennis Dalton, *Course Guidebook on Power over People. Classical and Modern Political Theory*. (Virginia: The Teaching Company, 1998), pp. 132–134. See also, Dennis Dalton, *The Indian Idea of Freedom* (Michigan: Academic Press, 1982).
12. For a detailed outline of the drafting process, see William Schabas (2013), "Introductory Essay," xvii to cxii.
13. Commission on Human Rights (1946) 1st Meeting held on Monday, Document E/HR/6.
14. Commission on Human Rights (1946), Report Of The Commission On Human Rights To The Second Session Of The Economic And Social Council. Document E/38/Rev.1, p. 5.
15. Commission on Human Rights (1946), E/36/Eev. 1, p. 3.
16. Commission on Human Rights (1947), Report of the Commission on Human Rights, E/383 27 March 197.

17. William Schabas (2014), p. cxiiv.
18. See on this, Antony Best et al., *International History of the Twentieth Century* (London: Routledge, 2004) p. 405.
19. Ibid, p. 43.
20. GHS, p. 30.
21. See generally, Julius Stone (1932), *The League of Nations and the Protection of Minorities*. (London: Stevens. 1932).
22. Mark Mazower, "The Strange Triumph of Human Rights, 1933–1950, *The Historical Journal*, vol. 47, No. 2, (2004), pp. 379–398.
23. See, ibid., p. 388.
24. Ibid, p. 388.
25. Ibid, pp. 388–389.
26. Ibid, pp. 389–390.
27. E/CN.4/Sub.2/SR. 11, reproduced in Schabas, p. 1087.
28. E/CN.4/Sub.2/SR.23, reproduced in Schabas, p. 1098.

References

Primary Documents: United Nations Documents from Drafting Process in William Schabas:

E/36/Rev. 1, p. 3, Commission on Human Rights (1946).

E/38/Rev.1, p. 5, Commission on Human Rights (1946), Report Of The Commission On Human Rights To The Second Session Of The Economic And Social Council. Document.

E/383 27 March 197, Commission on Human Rights (1947), Report of the Commission on Human Rights.

E/CN.4/Sub.2/SR. 11, reproduced in Schabas, p. 1087.

E/CN.4/Sub.2/SR.23, reproduced in Schabas, p. 1098.

E/HR/6, Commission on Human Rights (1946) 1st Meeting held on Monday, Document.

Beasley, W.G. *Japanese Imperialism 1894–1945*. (Oxford: Oxford University Press, 2014).

OHCHR, "The Core International Human Rights Instruments and their monitoring bodies," Available at https://www.ohchr.org/EN/ProfessionalInterest/Pages/CoreInstruments.aspx

Dimitrijevic, Vojin. *Customary Law As An Instrument For The Protection Of Human Rights*, Working Paper, Milano: Istituto per gli Studi di Politica Internazionale and D'Amato, Anthony, "Human Rights as Part of Customary International Law: A Plea for Change of Paradigms". Faculty Working Papers. Paper 88, 2010.

Donnelly, Jack. *Universal Human Rights in Theory and Practice*. (Ithaca: Cornell University Press, 2013).

Mark Mazower, "An international civilization? Empire, internationalism and the crisis of the mid-twentieth century," *International Affairs* Vol. 82, Issue 3 (2006) 553–566.

Chi, Kwan Mark, *China and the World Since 1945: An International History.* (Oxon, New York: Routledge, 2012).

Fukuyama, Francis. *Political Order and Political Decay* (London, Profile Books, 2014).

Dalton, Dennis. *Course Guidebook on Power over People. Classical and Modern Political Theory.* (Virginia: The Teaching Company, 1998), pp. 132–134.

Dalton, Dennis *The Indian Idea of Freedom* (Michigan: Academic Press, 1982).

Best, Antony et al., *International History of the Twentieth Century* (London: Routledge, 2004) p. 405.

Stone, Julius. *The League of Nations and the Protection of Minorities.* (London: Stevens. 1932).

Mazower, Mark. "The Strange Triumph of Human Rights, 1933–1950, *The Historical Journal,* vol. 47, No. 2, (2004), pp. 379–398.

Proclamation of Teheran, 13 May 1968. Adopted by the UN General Assembly on 19 December 1968, by 115 votes to none, with 1 abstention, in resolution 2442 (XXIII). See Final Act of the International Conference on Human Rights, Tehran, 11 April to 13 May 1968. New York: United Nations. http://legal.un.org/avl/pdf/ha/fatchr/Final_Act_of_TehranConf.pdf

CHAPTER 3

Asian Drafters

Introduction

A short commentary, "Who wrote the Universal Declaration of Human Rights?" by Gita Seghal, was re-published on 10 December 2014 on an online forum, *open Democracy*, to rebut sceptics who argued that there were no such things as universal values. Among those she cited was Alasdair MacIntyre, whose *After Virtue*[1] incorrectly argued that "Natural rights and self evident truths proclaimed in the American declaration of independence are tantamount to belief in witches and unicorns."[2] Another work she cited, *Human Rights and Empire* by Costas Douzinas,[3] called human rights the political philosophy of cosmopolitanism and argued that human rights codified and "constitutionalised" the normative sources of Empire. Amidst the "war on terror" and the use of torture, she recalled purported attempts in the 1980s and 1990s, to limit the universality of the UDHR, citing the Cairo Declaration on Human Rights in Islam.

The UDHR as encompassing "Western" values stems in part from a narrative that places Western drafters, notably Eleanor Roosevelt from the United States and Rene Cassin from France, as key influencers. Mrs. Roosevelt, widow of Franklin Delano Roosevelt, steered the process well.[4] Rene Cassin, a French legal scholar and former adviser to General de Gaulle and the Free French, was held to have powerfully shaped the final outcome: a list of 30 rights belonging to individuals not groups and drawing on European enlightenment values. He was awarded the Nobel Peace

R. Ramcharan, B. Ramcharan, *Asia and the Drafting of the Universal Declaration of Human Rights*,
https://doi.org/10.1007/978-981-13-2104-7_3

Prize in 1968 for his contributions to the drafting of the Universal Declaration 20 years earlier and for championing the Declaration subsequently. Morsink, as noted previously, questioned this by stating that Cassin entered the room very late. Waltz supports Morsink's account by channelling John Humphrey's account, since the latter had assembled the first draft while serving as Director of the UN Division of Human Rights, from multiple sources around the world since he wished that the document would have the fullest international grounding. Waltz shows that "Cassin did eventually edit the UN Secretariat's draft, but careful comparison of the two documents shows that at least three-quarters of Cassin's text flowed directly from the UN document."[5]

Seghal's commentary channelled Waltz, who sought to expose the myth "that the mid-century human rights project was the brainchild, and a favoured project, of the Western powers."[6] As Waltz has shown, while President Franklin Roosevelt, upon advice, came to champion human rights and fundamental freedoms for the world, members of his Cabinet, including Secretary of State Cordell Hull, were not too keen on pursuing an International Bill at the time and preferred a declaratory statement rather than a legally binding instrument.[7]

A powerful counter-narrative relates the "The less known story of the men and women who wrote this foundational, emancipatory and anti-colonial document must be told in today's world."[8] Indeed, the Declaration benefitted, line by line, right by right, from the input of many delegates from newly decolonized states. John Humphrey would applaud Asian intellects in particular, Charles Malik of Lebanon and Peng Chun Chang (P.C. Chang) of China.[9]

Another Asian person was Begum Shaista Ikramullah, a member of the Constituent Assembly of Pakistan and a delegate at the UN in 1948, who noted that "It was imperative that the peoples of the world should recognize the existence of a code of civilized behavior which would apply not only in international relations but also in domestic affairs."[10]

Asian delegates spoke powerfully on emancipation and self-determination. Carlos Romulo of the Philippines argued that full rights should be given to the colonies. Article 2 thereby ensures non-discrimination (a standard clause that came to be adopted in all treaties) on the grounds of race, class property, social origin, and so on; but it also ensures that subject peoples were also endowed with rights, "no distinction shall be made on the basis of the political, jurisdictional or international status of the country or territory to which a person belongs, whether it be independent, trust, non-self-governing or under any other limitation of sovereignty."

Gender equality was ensured through the work of Hansa Mehta of India, who was a champion of women's rights and literacy for women in India.[11] Hans Mehta was a member of the Constituent Assembly who was influential in the wording of Article 1 "All human beings are equal in dignity and rights," arguing that if the word men was used, it would not be regarded as inclusive but rather taken to exclude women. She thus ensured gender equality in the document.

Asian delegates and Muslim delegates argued eloquently on marriage rights and freedom of religion or belief, for example. There were political divisions among Muslims on religion and marriage, two very contentious areas. Saudi Arabia objected to Article 16 on the right to choice in marriage. Begum Ikramullah opposed the Saudi view, making a speech against child marriage. She accepted equal rights in marriage on the grounds that equal did not necessarily mean the same. Egypt's Wahid Rafaat accepted the language on marriage, noting that marriage limitations based on race (as in the United States) were more shocking to his country than limitations based on religion or nationality. The clause on marriage, in short, was fought for by a range of opinion to form an egalitarian and adult basis for marriage which was absent then from most countries, whether eastern or western.

The exercise of freedom of religion was supported by a number of Muslim delegates. The Foreign Minister of Pakistan, Zafrallah Khan, quoted the Qur'an "Let him who chooses believe, believe and him who chooses to disbelieve, disbelieve." He believed that the right to change religion was consistent with Islam. Mohammed Habib from India supported the statement as consistent with the Constitution of India. However, Saudi Arabia objected to it and eventually abstained from voting on the Declaration itself. No one voted against the Declaration, although Saudi Arabia, South Africa, and the Soviet bloc abstained, with 50 countries voting for it.

It is widely acknowledged by those who have studied the records that Asian personalities made defining contributions to the drafting of the Universal Declaration. Some of them, such as P.C. Chang of China, Charles Malik of Lebanon, Hansa Mehta of India, and Carlos Romulo of the Philippines, participated in the Commission on Human Rights, sometimes in the Economic and Social Council, as well as in the UN General

Assembly. Others made their mark in the General Assembly, in its Social and Humanitarian Committee, and in the plenary deliberations.

Taken together, one could see Asian imprints such as the following, contributed by Asian personalities:

- The Declaration should place the focus on the centrality of the human being.
- There should be no discrimination on grounds such as race or gender.
- The Declaration should draw on the philosophical traditions of all regions of the world. P.C. Chang of China placed special emphasis on integrating Confucian values into Western values.
- The Declaration should have in view the dignity of all human beings, including the downtrodden and the oppressed.
- The importance of economic, social, and cultural rights alongside civil and political rights.
- The Declaration should have cooperative aspirations for the different peoples of the world, not imperialist ones. One sees this in the contribution of the representative of Saudi Arabia, Jamil Baroody.
- The Declaration should be accompanied by effective means of implementation nationally and internationally.
- Education should be promoted about the values of the Universal Declaration.
- The importance of solidarity and cooperation for the achievement of human rights and human progress.

The remainder of this chapter brings out these and other perspectives by looking at some of the key individuals who contributed to shaping the Universal Declaration.

Peng Chun Chang (China)

P.C. Chang of China participated from the early deliberations of the Commission on Human Rights all through to the adoption of the Universal Declaration in the plenary of the General Assembly. As a scholar and diplomat, his philosophy emphasized Confucianism values, and he thought that many influential Western thinkers on human rights had been influenced by Chinese values. While serving as a diplomat in Turkey, before he came to the UN, he lectured on the reciprocal influences and commonalities between the Islamic and Chinese cultures and on the relationship between Confucianism and Islam.

While serving in the United Nations, Dr. Chang argued strongly against what was called the "classical standard of civilization"—a standard in which certain nations or peoples were considered "civilized" or "uncivilized" and the "uncivilized" were excluded from international organizations and laws. Instead of the classical standard of civilization he advocated a new universalism of human rights. He said that "Whenever the Europeans proposed the idea of the civilized, they actually meant European rule". He sought to revise the meaning of "human" in human rights. Dr. Chang sought to bring Confucianism into the Universal Declaration of Human Rights. In some of the earlier versions, there had been no mention of "conscience." He pushed for its inclusion.

As Professor Lydia H. Liu put it in a conference at Columbia University on 8 October 2014:

> [I]n some of the earlier versions [of Article 1] there was no mention of 'conscience'. [Human beings] ..were simply endowed with 'reason'. Chang had suggested that perhaps reason alone was not adequate. He then suggested that Article One include another concept – 'ren' – that, next to reason, is also an essential human attribute. Human beings are endowed not just with reason but with something else.
>
> What is this something else? Chang came up with a literal translation of a concept from Confucian moral philosophy which he calls 'two-men-mindedness'. They decided that they would translate it as 'conscience'....[12]

Speaking in the plenary of the General Assembly as it was about to adopt the Declaration, Dr. Chang noted that "The first condition for defence of the rights of man was tolerance towards the various opinions and beliefs held throughout the world. Uncompromising dogmatism had caused much harm, by accentuating disputes, and lending them an ideological basis...If harmony was to be maintained in the human community and humanity itself was to be saved, everyone had to accept, in a spirit of sincere tolerance, the different views and beliefs of his fellow men." By pleading for tolerance of all opinions and beliefs and by insisting on precision of terminology, the Chinese delegation had striven to introduce certain improvements into the universal declaration of human rights.[13]

Mr. Chang recalled that he had worked for two years on drafting the Declaration, and he hoped that it might prosper, "nourished by the hope of mankind." He noted that in the eighteenth century, when solemn declarations of the rights of man had been made in the West, the emphasis had been laid on human rights as contrasted with divine right claimed by kings. He stressed that Chinese thought had not been without influence on the evolution of those ideas in the Western world.

He added that in the times the world was passing through, and more particularly during the years following the First World War, there had been a tendency to impose a standardized way of thinking and single way of life. With that approach, equilibrium could be reached only at the cost of moving away from the truth, or employing force. But, however violent the methods employed, equilibrium achieved in that way could never last. If harmony was to be maintained in the human community and humanity itself was to be saved, everyone had to accept, in a spirit of sincere tolerance, the different views and beliefs of his fellow man.

It was also important that conceptions should be very accurately defined; that was no purely academic question. In the modern world, it was considered clever statesmanship to confuse one's adversary; but a real statesman could not tolerate confusion. Social order and peaceful cooperation could be achieved only if people learned to express clear ideas in precise terms. The disagreements all around were only too often the result of confusion spread by the use – whether wilful or not – of inaccurate and unambiguous terms.

He concluded: "By pleading for tolerance of all opinions and beliefs and by insisting on precision of terminology, the Chinese delegation had striven to introduce certain improvements into the Universal Declaration of Human Rights."[14] At an earlier stage, speaking at the 12th meeting of the Drafting Committee of the Commission on Human Rights, Dr. Chang thought it important to take note of the cultural development of man, to include in the draft at that stage, "the better development of life itself", inasmuch as mere physical existence was not sufficient.[15]

When Dr. Chang spoke in the General Assembly, the People's Republic of China did not yet exist. It would be established only a year later. But his words could equally have been uttered by a representative of the People's Republic. It was an authentic Chinese and Asian voice, and it eloquently expressed the aspirations and passions of Asia in its quest for a new world of respect for all of humanity and its rights.

Charles Malik (Lebanon)

Charles Malik made visionary contributions to the drafting of universal values. Alongside P.C. Chang, Malik was considered the philosopher of the Universal Declaration, and, like Chang, his contribution to its drafting was legendary. He had participated intensively in the San Francisco founding conference of the United Nations, the Commission on Human Rights, the Economic and Social Council, the Social and Humanitarian Committee (which he presided over when it finalized the draft declaration), and the plenary of the General Assembly.[16] Thomas W. Jacobson, US Representative to the United Nations (2001–2010), has noted that "without Dr. Malik's leadership, diplomatic skills and perseverance, as well as his sensitivity, understanding, and respect for the input of all 58 Member Nations and their differing legal and cultural traditions, there may not have been a Universal Declaration." Further, he noted, Dr. Malik insisted that the task of creating the United Nations Charter was not complete without a formal guarantee of inherent human rights.[17] Glendon has written about Malik that "(N)o individual played a greater role in shaping and securing consensus for the UN's 1948 Universal Declaration of Human Rights, and… none of the framers reflected in greater depth on the dilemmas of human rights."[18]

At the San Francisco conference in 1945, representing Lebanon in San Francisco, 28 April 1945. Malik urged his contemporaries that "The peace, which man believes in and will spontaneously rise up to defend, is only that which is grounded in his ultimate rights and freedoms, and in the reality of justice."[19] In the Commission in February 1947, he noted that:

> The Charter speaks in the preamble of the worth and dignity of man … That is what we are called upon to promote and protect. … We here in this Commission represent and defend the individual man in his conscience and in his individual freedom, and there is no other body in the United Nations to do that. We must defend him against tyranny, against tyranny of the state and the tyranny of systems, because man has other loyalties than his loyalty to the state. He has loyalty to his family, to his religion, to his profession; he has his loyalty to science and to truth. These loyalties are as exacting on him as his loyalty to the state. And, in my opinion, the fight for freedom today consists primarily in asserting the rights of these intermediate institutions ().[20]

Early on in the drafting process, at the third meeting of the Drafting Committee, he touched on the essence of human rights when he urged, during the consideration of the Draft Outline of the International Bill of Rights prepared by the Division of Human Rights, that "The conception that the State must be a just State should also be included…."[21] At the eighth meeting of the Drafting Committee, Prof. Malik stated that in his opinion the right of property was a fundamental right which must have a place in the Bill, and certainly in the Declaration. He felt that it was self-evident that man cannot live without personal property; that this particular right was as essential and as fundamental as almost any other right. He did not see how reference to such a right could be suppressed. He pointed out that the unlimited character of the ownership of private property could not be considered a fundamental right, but that even the most socialistic constitutions refer to the fact that a man must have something which is his own.[22]

At the 12th meeting of the Drafting Committee, Prof. Malik urged that politics was one of the fundamental activities of man in which discrimination existed. He felt that the Commission on Human Rights should decide whether or not discrimination was allowable on the basis of political belief. There were excesses in some of these practices, he said, and there was no harm in stating that man is free to hold political convictions without danger of discrimination and persecution.[23]

At the 13th meeting of the Drafting Committee, Prof. Malik argued for the fundamental freedom to change one's opinions and beliefs and suggested the wording "individual freedom of thought and conscience, to hold or change beliefs, is an absolute and sacred right."[24] At the next meeting of the Drafting Committee, it was Prof. Malik who brought into the future Declaration the crucial concept of the will of the people. On his proposal, the article then under consideration was altered to read, "The State can derive its authority only from the will of the people and has a duty to conform thereto. This will is manifested particularly by democratic elections, which shall be periodic, free and fair, and by secret ballot."[25]

At the 21st meeting of the Drafting Committee of the Commission on Human Rights, Prof. Malik made the following remarkable statement:

> Mr Malik (Lebanon) declared that the discussions of the Committee would remain on the abstract plane unless the historic origin of the present concern for human rights were kept in mind. In recent years, men had arisen who embodied the worst aspects of human nature and had trampled on the dignity of the human being. That was the reason for the present desire to make the future safe against the recurrence of such monstrosities.
>
> It seemed that the basic factors of modern life should be taken into account in a recast of ideas on human rights. He could quote four main factors. First of all came the maladjustments and ills of society resulting from the impersonal working of economic and social factors. Man was cramped by the social ills of modern society and this must be taken into account.

Secondly, the world was faced with a tendency to 'statism', or the determination by the state of all relations and ideas, thus supplanting all other sources of convictions. The state insisted on the individual's obligations and duties to it. This too was a grave danger, for man was not the slave of the state, and did not exist to serve the state only. This applied to the relative position of the individual and other groups to which he belonged. There were innumerable other intermediate loyalties which the individual must respect, such as those towards his family, his profession, his friends, and also towards philosophical laws. The state could not be the exclusive arbiter of truth and beauty. Real freedom sprang from the loyalty of the individual not to the state but to these intermediate forms. These must find their place in the general social picture.

Another modern evil was the exclusive concentration on material needs. Material abundance was not everything in life, and the requirements of culture, of the intellect and of the spirit must be taken into account.

Group pressure also should be curbed. Loyalty was owed to the group to which one belonged, but the individual must not be overwhelmed by the group, or he would lose his essential freedom.

Should the [Drafting] Committee disregard these dangers, it would merely serve the trends of the age without improving it. Man might live in a perfect state, have all material security, be free from all social maladjustments, and yet not be the man which the Charter of the United nations had in mind, a man with a worth and a dignity of his own. The exact worth and dignity must be determined. Man must be able to think and choose freely and even to reject freely and to rebel freely.[26]

Malik summarized the work of the Commission thus in August 1948: "(T)he Commission faced and wrestled with these four basic issues: the nature of man; the place of the individual in society; the relation of man and state; and man's ultimate loyalties."[27] Jacobson called attention to "Charles Malik the philosopher ... [who] more than any other framer, helped to reinforce the declaration's claim to be universal. And it was Charles Malik the master diplomat who, more than any other individual, helped to assure its adoption without a single dissenting vote."[28]

In May 1948 the Commission referred its final draft to the UN General Assembly's Third Committee, where in daily sessions over a two-month period delegates scrutinized the text, article by article. Charles Malik presided over these sessions, wherein some 168 amendments were proposed and debated. Finally, the text was referred to the General Assembly for another round of oratory and debate, and amendment, before a final vote.

On 10 December 1948 it was adopted without dissenting vote (eight states abstained).

As President of the ECOSOC, he presented the draft Declaration to the General Assembly, 27 September 1948, and noted that the problem of human rights lay at the heart of the UN. When the draft declaration was presented to the plenary of the General Assembly in December 1948, he took the floor on 9 December to recapitulate the drafting work that had produced the work. He began by commenting that the declaration was destined to mark an important stage in the history of mankind. He recalled that the members of the United Nations had already solemnly pledged themselves, under the Charter, to promote respect for human rights and fundamental freedoms but that it was the first time that human rights and fundamental freedoms had been set forth in detail. Hence every government knew, henceforth, to what extent exactly it had pledged itself, and every citizen could protest to his government if the latter did not fulfil its obligations. The declaration would therefore provide a useful means of criticism and would help to bring about changes in present legal practice. A convention could subsequently be prepared, but it would rest on the rights laid down in the Declaration which was, consequently, of extreme importance.[29]

He also noted, while transmitting the Charter to the General Assembly, that "Finally, there is the question of their [human rights] origin." He asked:

> Where do they come from? Are they conferred upon me by some external visible power such as the state or the United Nations, so that what is now granted me may some day be conceivably withdrawn from me? Or do they belong to my essence so that if they are violated in any way I cease to be a human being at all? If they did belong to my essence, should they not also be grounded in a Supreme Being who, by being the Lord of history, could guarantee their meaning and stability?[30]
>
> … Everybody by now knows that the ultimate issues of today are all ideological. …
>
> Superficial people … ridiculed the classical ages of faith; they are now paying the price of their faithless superficiality …. It is dangerous to neglect the mind and spirit of man; it is dangerous to poke fun at logos ….

The most important issue in the order of truth today is what constitutes the proper worth and dignity of man. This will be the central theme of the debate in the Declaration of Human Rights. Unless this issue is rightly settled, there

> is no meaning to any other settlement. Do not tell me you are going to settle Korea, and Germany, and Palestine, and atomic energy, and leave this central issue unsettled! For what is the use of peace and a settlement in which man is left ambiguous, estranged from himself and from the truth?

Hansa Mehta (India)

Mrs. Hansa Mehta of India participated in the drafting of the Universal Declaration throughout the work of the Commission on Human Rights and in other fora of the UN. She had been a leading figure in the struggle for Indian independence and reflected a new spirit at large in the world arguing for human dignity and equality.

As we saw in the previous chapter, during the drafting of the Universal Declaration, India tabled a draft declaration that included the following statement: "Every human being has the right of equality, without distinction of race, sex, language, religion, nationality or political belief."[15] Mrs. Mehta, at the very first meeting of the Commission, supported the position that when discussing the proposed bill of rights, the status of women would have to be considered in cooperation with the Commission on the Status of Women. General Romulo of the Philippine Republic affirmed that the status of women was an integral part of whatever bill of rights would be discussed.[31]

At the very outset of the full Commission on Human Rights, when it began its deliberations, Mrs. Mehta raised the problem of discrimination in forthright terms: She

> declared that the Government and people of India attached the greatest importance to the Human Rights Commission and considered that it work would profoundly influence the future of the United Nations. She recalled that the Government of South Africa had maintained the position during recent discussions that there had been no violation of human rights in South Africa since there existed no written definition of human rights as such within the framework of the United Nations. The Government of the United Kingdom had taken a similar attitude by suggesting that the dispute between India and South Africa might be referred to the International Court of Justice. Mrs. Mehta considered it the justification of the Commission that pleas of this nature should not be allowed to be advanced within the forum of the United Nations in the future....

The Representative of India pointed out that her country faced a problem of exceptional magnitude for reasons beyond its control: during the past 100 years, four million Indians had been transplanted to various parts of the world under the aegis of the colonial governments concerned, and were now residing abroad in special communities, created at the request and for the benefit of those governments. As a result of this transplantation, numerous cases of denials of rights in law and equality and complicated questions of nationality and citizenship had arisen, due to certain administrative practices on the part of the governments concerned. Such problems had to be solved within the meaning of the terms of reference of the Commission on Human Rights and the principles of the Charter.

The Representative of India considered that an effort should be made to define in precise legal terminology the terms "discrimination" and "minority." It was also necessary to define what specific safeguards should be incorporated in the proposed bill of rights against the dangers of assimilation. Moreover, the Commission on Human Rights should compile a list from every country in the world of legal and administrative measures tending to decrease human rights within the meaning of the principles of the Charter. The most important consideration before the Commission should not be merely the enunciation of principles in terms of a bill of human rights, but the improvisation of adequate machinery to implement those principles. In fact, the proposed bill of human rights would be meaningless unless an unequivocal definition were given of the relationship which ought to exist between the individual, the community, the state, and the international organization.[32]

Speaking in the 14th meeting of the first session of the Commission on Human Rights, Mrs. Mehta made the following impassioned statement for freedom of movement:

> With regard to the right to freedom of movement, there was another freedom that I wish to mention to you. It is not freedom of migration only, but freedom of movement within the State itself. There are laws today in many States which restrict individuals from one part of the country going into the other part of the country. Therefore, there must be freedom of movement within the State itself. That is very important.[33]

Numerous similar impassioned statements were made by Mrs. Mehta as the Universal Declaration of Human Rights was being drafted.

Mrs. Laxshmi Menon (India)

When the draft declaration was considered in the plenary of the General Assembly, the Indian delegate was Mrs. Laxshmi Menon. On behalf of India she supported the declaration, which ".. provided a solid basis for the international cooperation referred to in Article 55 of the Charter, and it expressed the aspirations of peoples, who, though they had but recently attained political freedom, had always accepted and practiced the noble ideals of religious tolerance and cultural freedom."

"The full significance of the Indian delegation's attitude in the Third Committee could only be understood when considered in relation to the decision taken by the Indian Constituent Assembly to include in the Constitution of that country the same rights and freedoms as were proclaimed in the declaration.

"The Universal declaration of human rights was born from the need to reaffirm those rights after their violation during the war. It was now more than ever necessary to reaffirm those rights. The remedies to be applied to humanity had to be adapted to the seriousness of the conditions in which it lived; and when conditions deteriorated the remedy had to be all the stronger and more drastic."[34]

She continued that this was one of the reasons why the declaration was fuller and more detailed than all the other similar declarations. Earlier declarations had not mentioned rights such as the right to equal pay for equal work; the right of mothers and children to social protection, whether the children were born in or out of wedlock; the right to education; equality of rights for men and women. Those rights were the expression of a new social order, or true democracy based on social justice.

She added that in accordance with the principles of the Charter, the Declaration emphasized the equality of all human beings without any distinction whatsoever; and it proclaimed clearly, for the first time, that the rights mentioned were also applicable to Non-Self-Governing and Trust Territories. The Indian delegation stood, as always, against all forms of discrimination.

The right to hold different opinions was a sacred right and the prerogative of every truly democratic people. The Indian delegation had therefore upheld that right, though perfectly aware of the dangers inherent in it. India, like other countries, would never agree to restricting political rights in order to realize social aims, however noble those aims might be.

As regards Article 30 of the Declaration on the duties of the individual, Mrs. Menon recalled that Mahatma Gandhi had said that all rights were born of obligations, and no man could claim the right to live unless he fulfilled his duties as a citizen of the world. From the very fact that it proclaimed rights, therefore, the Declaration was a declaration of obligations.

After recalling the importance of measures of implementation, Mrs. Menon concluded by expressing the hope that the Declaration would pave the way to a new era of international solidarity, because the basis of rights was neither the state nor the individual, but the social human being, participating in social life, and striving for national and international cooperation.[35]

Speaking at the 139th meeting of the Social and Humanitarian Committee of the General Assembly as it finalized the text of the Universal Declaration, Mrs. Menon made the following impassioned plea for gender equality:

> Even in countries said to be advanced socially – for example the United States and the United Kingdom – the principle of equal pay for men and women was not fully accepted. In many countries women were still carrying on a vain fight against inequality and injustice. Moreover, in various parts of Asia and in countries elsewhere, as well as in Trust Territories and Non-Self-Governing Territories, there was still discrimination for reasons not only on sex, but of race and colour. India was opposed to discrimination which compelled women and certain coloured races to accept a lower standard of living than other groups and thought the declaration should clearly condemn this practice.[36]

Carlos Romulo (Philippines)

General Carlos Romulo participated throughout the efforts of the Commission on Human Rights, the Economic and Social Council, and the General Assembly. He made a substantial contribution to the drafting of the opening article of the Universal Declaration, as we shall see in Chap. 4. At the 41st meeting of the Commission on Human Rights, General Romulo proposed the following text for inclusion in the Declaration:

> All laws in any State shall be in conformity with the purposes and principles of the United Nations as embodied in the Charter.[37]

Speaking in the General Assembly at the time of the adoption of the Declaration, General Romulo pointed out that, during its third session, the United Nations had been on trial for its life and that it was at that very moment that it had justified its existence before an anxious world by producing the universal declaration of human rights. He noted that the new charter of human freedom was the outcome of two and a half years of painstaking work by different bodies of the United Nations. "It expressed the wish of the various peoples of the world to live together in amity, mutual co-operation and fuller freedom. That document was in reality the first in history which, from a truly universal standpoint, defined the basic rights and the fundamental freedoms to which all men were entitled. The declaration's greatest interest lay in the fact that it would prevent the recurrence of the recent atrocities by ensuring human rights the protection of the law."[38]

He then recalled all the recognized political rights of the individual. He further stated that, parallel to the list of political rights, the document contained economic and social rights. In his assessment,

> The practical implications of the economic and social provisions were the distinguishing features which really characterized the universal declaration of human rights as a charter of human freedom. The new declaration recognized rights which were perhaps not even contemplated in the Magna Carta, the 1789 Declaration of the Rights of Man, or the American Declaration of Independence. That recognition was based upon the fact that a traditional declaration of political rights would be insufficient unless buttressed by a declaration of economic and social rights.

General Romulo noted that it had been objected that the Declaration infringed upon national sovereignty. In refutation of that statement, he quoted the preamble to the Declaration. In conclusion, he stated that the General Assembly "was in duty bound to give to all mankind what it had been seeking for so long: the respect of human rights and the guarantee of human freedoms."[39]

Mr. Ghassan Ghani (Iran)

Mr. Ghassan Ghani represented Iran on the Commission on Human Rights. A physician, he "felt that freedom of expression and of opinion were possible only in countries where the standard of education was high enough to allow the masses to form a sound opinion, and so he wished the United Nations to take steps first of all to eliminate illiteracy and promote education, by such means as granting financial assistance to backward countries."[40]

Abdul Rahman Kayali (Syria)

Abdul Rahman Kayali of Syria participated actively in the Social and Humanitarian Committee of the General Assembly, and, at the time of its adoption, he lauded the work that had been done. He said that in his delegation's view the declaration set forth the principles already included in the constitution adopted and put into force in Syria five years previously ….

Throughout the discussion, the Syrian delegation had upheld three principles:

> Firstly, the declaration should deal with the rights of individuals and not with those of the State or society. It should deal with human beings as individuals because, without the security and the welfare of the individual, society could not exist. The other aspect of the question had to be covered by other declaration which would be established by means of international agreements.
>
> Secondly, the principles set forth should be harmonious, logical, clear, concise, exact and understandable to all; there were to be no ambiguities.
>
> Thirdly, there should be no contradiction between the declaration and the United Nations Charter. The declaration dealt for the most part with abstract principles and ideals the application of which had been left to future instruments of implementation. That was why the articles were short and precise.
>
> …
>
> If there were no social justice, individuals would fight against each other and there would be no peace in the world. For that reason the great reformers, thinkers and philosophers had laboured hard for many centuries to establish a declaration of human rights to fulfil the requirements of social justice by giving an equal chance to all on a basis of universal brotherhood, to which article 1 of the present declaration referred.
>
> …
>
> The nations should endeavour to work incessantly with faith and determination to honour the rights of the human being as proclaimed in the present declaration, and to ensure that they were put into effect in their legislations, their policies, their forms of government, and their education, thus bringing peace nearer.[41]

Muhammad Zafrulla Khan (Pakistan)

Mohammad Zafrulla Khan was a distinguished scholar in world religions and a member of the Ahmadiyya Movement, a missionary branch of Islam. He became Foreign Minister of Pakistan in 1947 and for many years led the Pakistan Delegation to the United Nations General Assembly. He was President of the 17th Session of the General Assembly and served two terms as Judge of the International Court of Justice in the Hague, of which he was Vice-President.

In 1967, on the eve of the International Conference on Human Rights in Tehran, Judge Khan wrote a book, *Islam and Human Rights*, which was published by The London Mosque. In it he stated that the Universal Declaration embodied the "broadest consensus of contemporary civilization on the subject of Human Rights." He saw the Declaration "as a shining milestone along the long, and often, difficult and weary, path trodden by Man down the corridors of History, through centuries of suffering and tribulation, towards the goal of freedom, justice and equality."[42]

The Declaration, he thought, was entitled to rank with the great historical documents and charters. He considered that the principal instrument which should be availed of to make the rights enforceable was the national legislature of each state, which should, through appropriate constitutional and legislative processes, invest human rights with legal sanctions enforceable through the national judicial system. A free and independent judiciary was the sine qua non for the effective safeguarding of human rights and for guaranteeing freedom, justice, and equality.[43]

This, he considered, is the "Age of Man. Man is beginning to be conscious of his own position in the universe and demands that his personality and dignity shall be accorded due recognition and respect."[44] The spirit of the Universal Declaration and of Islam was similar: the overall standard of Islam was that *ma'roof*, equity, was to be fostered and *munkar*, iniquity, is to be eschewed.[45]

At the time of the adoption of the Universal Declaration of Human Rights, Mohammad Zafrulla Khan of Pakistan spoke eloquently in favour of the Declaration and particularly its article on freedom of religion or belief. Recalling the adoption, the previous day, of the Convention on Genocide, an epoch-making event, he said that adoption of the Universal Declaration of Human Rights would also be of that character. The Pakistani delegation associated itself with what had been said in praise of the Declaration, and with the appreciation of the work accomplished by all the delegations who had taken part in drawing up the document.

He commented in particular on what is now Article 18 dealing with freedom of conscience, including freedom to change one's religion. When the latter question was discussed in the Third Committee, its whole scope had not been understood; for that reason he thought it necessary to set out very clearly his delegation's position as to that part of the article. He declared:

> Pakistan was an ardent defender of freedom of thought and belief and of all the freedoms listed in article 19. There could be no doubt on that point and, if that question only had a political aspect the declaration he had just made would have been sufficient. But for the Pakistani delegation the problem had a special significance as some of its aspects involved the honour of Islam. He therefore thought it necessary to explain his delegation's point of view on the subject to the Assembly; it was a point of view arising out of the teaching of Islam in that field.
>
> The teaching of Islam was based on the Koran which contained the oral revelations made to the prophet Mohammed; the Koran was, therefore, the very word of God for Moslems. Now it stated that neither faith, nor conscience which gave birth to it, could have an obligatory character. The Koran expressly said: 'Let he who chooses to believe, believe, and he who chooses to disbelieve, disbelieve', and it formally condemned not lack of faith but hypocrisy. The Moslem religion was a missionary religion: it strove to persuade men to change their faith and alter their way of living, so as to follow the faith and way of living it preached, but it recognized the same right of conversion for other religions as for itself.
>
> Article 1[8] had given rise to anxiety among certain delegations because of the actions of the missionaries of certain other religions. He was glad to pay tribute to the work carried out by the Christian missionaries in the East, especially in the fields of education, hygiene and medicine; nevertheless, it was undeniable that their activity had sometimes assumed a political character which had given rise to justifiable objections. In certain cases, the means employed to bring about conversion had made that conversion a worse remedy than the ill it set out to cure.
>
> There were other aspects of the problem but it was not appropriate to deal with them at that stage of the work. His delegation considered that the essential point was to repeat that for its part the Moslem religion had unequivocally proclaimed the right to freedom of conscience and had declared itself against any kind of compulsion in matters of faith or religions practices.
>
> The Pakistan delegation would therefore vote for article 1[8], and would accept no limitation on its provisions.[46]

Mr. Kemal Kural (Turkey)

Speaking in the Third Committee of the General Assembly at its 146th meeting on 19 November 1948, Mr. Kural of Turkey reiterated his delegation's position that it found the Declaration as drafted by the Commission on Human Rights satisfactory in the main and requiring amendment only in a few exceptional instances. Draft Article 23, on education, was such an exception. Two conditions were necessary for the implementation of the statement that everyone had the right to education. The first was that primary education must be compulsory and that secondary and higher education must be open to all who were able to profit by it. The second was that primary education must be free—otherwise it could not be made compulsory—and also that secondary and higher education must be free or it could not be said, as stated in Article 23, that there should be equal access to it on the basis of merit. It was at that point that draft Article 23 became inadequate.

Mr Kural would have liked to suggest that all education be free, as in fact it was in a number of countries, including his own, but since he realized that such a state of affairs could not be brought about everywhere immediately, he had contented himself with proposing that at least primary education should be free (A/C.3/273/Rev.1). He hoped that his amendment, thus redrafted, would be acceptable to the Committee.[47]

One sees here the degree of intensity of the participation of Asian delegations in the drafting of the Universal Declaration. In the eventual discussion, Mr. Kural's idea was included in the text of the article. One may note, in this connection, the equally impassioned statement of the delegation of the Philippines on this article. Speaking at the 147th meeting of the Third Committee, Mr. Aquino of the Philippines recalled that it was his delegation, together with that of Panama, which had had the honour of submitting the original text of the article on the right to education. In proposing that article, the Philippine delegation had drawn upon the experience acquired by the Philippine people in the matter of popular education during the past 40 years. The Republic of the Philippines attached considerable importance to the education of the masses. In its view, the events of recent years had shown that an enlightened and well-informed public constituted the best defence of democracy and progress. In Article 23 the United Nations should state its position unequivocally not only on certain immediate objectives on the subject of which there could be no disagreement but also on questions of principle which went beyond the question of education pure and simple and touched upon the ideological, where there was conflict between the concepts of totalitarianism and of democracy and between the principles of authority and of liberty.[48]

Jamil Baroody (Saudi Arabia)

Jamil Baroody was a legendary diplomat who represented Saudi Arabia at the United Nations. He could be profound and colourful at the same time. A Christian, he represented the Islamic Kingdom of Saudi Arabia with passion.

As the Social and Humanitarian Committee of the UN General Assembly was putting the final touches on the draft Universal Declaration, Mr. Baroody intervened passionately to oppose the text in what is now Article 18 of the Universal Declaration that an individual had the right to change his or her religion. Mr. Baroody supported the Commission's draft article on freedom of thought, conscience, and religion. However, he was surprised to find that the Commission had sponsored the draft article wherein, after stating these three freedoms, it had concentrated exclusively on freedom of religion and the right to change religious beliefs, without any mention of the right of the individual to change his general conception of things and the dictates of his conscience. He wondered whether the members of the Commission had not been afraid, in discussing the delicate matter of freedom of thought and conscience, to take a stand openly on the basis of their different political ideologies. Mr. Baroody therefore proposed an amendment to delete the words "to change his religion or belief."

Explaining the reasons behind his amendment,[49] Mr. Baroody pointed out that throughout history missionaries had often abused their rights by becoming the forerunners of political intervention, and they were many instances where peoples had been drawn into murderous conflict by the missionaries' efforts to convert them.

So it was that bloody and unjustifiable crusades organized in the name of religion had had as their real economic and political purpose the acquisition of a place in the sun for the surplus populations of Europe. Religious wars between Catholics and Protestants had caused, in Europe, the death of millions of persons of both faiths which differed but little from each other.

Mr. Baroody felt that religion was essentially a manifestation of an emotion. He did not feel he should analyse in detail the complex psychological elements which characterized religion, but he wished to point out that even at this time when, according to some, tolerance prevailed, the dangerous weapon of propaganda was being used in all parts of the world to stir up peoples' religious or other beliefs. Every section of mankind could, if so desired, make clever use of such an aim to appeal to the religious beliefs of some other section which for a given material reason might not be able to fall in with the plan proposed or which might simply want to avoid any recourse to such an aim. A man often considered himself to be superior to his neighbour merely because he was richer. Similarly, certain groups of people had claimed throughout history to be God's chosen people or to belong to a superior religion, merely because they were more powerful than their neighbours of a different faith. Those who believed in God should admit that all human beings, regardless of their religion, were equal before Him. As to those who did not believe in God, they should understand that in playing upon the religious beliefs of others they might draw the world into a new murderous crusade. For the Arab world, a good religion was one which advocated a reciprocal spirit of kindness and tolerance among mankind.

For those reasons, Mr. Baroody wished the Third Committee to make the Declaration as clear as possible and omit any provisions apt to serve as an easy pretext for exciting hatred and encouraging dangerous differences of opinion. The delegation of Saudi Arabia would be ready to accept the article in question provided the words "freedom to change his religion or belief…" were omitted.[50]

In the end, Saudi Arabia abstained in the vote to adopt the Declaration because of its disagreement with the provision on the right to change one's religion. The General Assembly had rejected the Saudi Arabian position on this point. But what is relevant for present purposes is the vigour of the participation of an Asian country, which supported the rest of the Declaration but found this particular provision unacceptable. Asia was very much present and argued its positions with force.

Mr. Mohamed Raafat (Egypt)

We include here the contribution of an Egyptian delegate because of the traditionally close relations between Egypt and Asia and the shared aspirations of the African and Asian continents, many of whose members were actively struggling for their self-determination at the time of the adoption of the Declaration.

Speaking in the plenary of the General Assembly shortly before the adoption of the Declaration, Mr Rafaat said that his delegation appreciated the high ideals which had guided the Third Committee in its work, the result of which was the declaration of human rights now before the Assembly. That declaration, together with the Convention on Genocide, already unanimously adopted by the Assembly, constituted a real step forward in the establishment of legal and humanitarian principles. He declared that "many of the principles set forth in the declaration of human rights were already established in the democratic constitutions of different countries, including Egypt". After entering some reservations to articles 17 and 1[8] of the draft declaration he continued that "having submitted those explanations…his delegation was ready to vote in favour of the declaration of human rights."[51]

Conclusion

The passion of the Asian drafters of the Universal Declaration comes out forcefully from the foregoing review of the participation of key Asian drafters. Without a doubt, the Universal Declaration has strong Asian imprints.

Notes

1. See Alasdair Macintyre, *A Study in Moral Theory* (Notre Dame Press, 2007).
2. Gita Seghal, "Who Wrote the Universal Declaration of Human Rights?" *open Democracy*, 10 December 2014.
3. Coustas Douzinas, *Human Rights and Empire. The Political Philosophy of Cosmopolitanism* Routledge-Cavendish, London, 2007.
4. See generally, John Sears, *Eleanor Roosevelt and the universal declaration Of human rights, Hyde Park:* Franklin and Eleanor Roosevelt Institute (FERI), https://drive.google.com/drive/folders/111xVhf6GvcjmhuAVJ7VIfYRhfygcxSAs.
5. Susan Waltz (2002), Reclaiming and rebuilding the history of the Universal Declaration of Human Rights," Third World Quarterly, Vol. 23, No. 3, p. 438 (pp. 437–448).
6. Ibid.
7. Ibid, p. 439. See also Paul Gordon Lauren's *The Evolution of International Human Rights* ….
8. Seghal (2014), *open Democracy.*

9. See John P. Humphrey "International Protection of Human Rights. The Annals, Vol. 255 (January 1948), pp. 15–21; John Humphrey. "Memoirs of John P. Humphrey: The First Director of the United Nations Division of Human Rights," *Human Rights Quarterly*, 5:4 (November 1983), pp. 387–439; and John Humphrey *Human Rights. A Great Adventure*. Transnational Publishers, 1984.
10. Seghal, (2014).
11. Ann Foster, "Hansa Mehta, of UN Sub-Commission, Speaks for Women of India," *Christian Science Monitor*, 18 July 1946, p. 22.
12. See weaicolumbia, P.C. Chang. October 8 [2014] Event "Around 1948: Human Rights and Global Transformation. Video, Photos, and Audio. (no paging in text).
13. A/PV. 182, reproduced in Schabas, op. cit. p. 3058. (PV means proces verbale).
14. Ibid.
15. E/CN.4/AC.1/SR.12, reproduced in Schabas, op. cit., p. 848.
16. Malik's career featured the following highlights: Signer of the United Nations Charter for Lebanon (24 October 1945); Ambassador of Lebanon to the United Nations (1945–1955); Ambassador of Lebanon to the United States (1945–1955); Member, Rapporteur, and Chairman (1951–1953), Commission on Human Rights (1946–1953); Member and Officer, Drafting Committee of the Universal Declaration (1946–1948); Member and President (1947–1948), United Nations Economic and Social Council (1946–1949); Chairman, Third Committee of the United Nations General Assembly (1948).
17. Thomas Jacobson, *Ambassador Charles Malik and The Universal Declaration Of Human Rights, Focus on the Family*. Focus on the Family – August 28, 2008. International Government Affairs Department. Quotations taken from Dr. Charles H. Malik's speeches and writings, edited by his son, Professor Habib C. Malik, Ph.D. The title of the book is: *The Challenge Of Human Rights: Charles Malik and The Universal Declaration.*
18. Glendon, Mary Ann, "Foundations of Human Rights: The Unfinished Business," *American Journal of Jurisprudence.*, Vol. 44: No. 1, 1999, p. 1 Available at: http://scholarship.law.nd.edu/ajj/vol44/iss1/1.
19. Habib C. Malik, *The Challenge Of Human Rights: Charles Malik And The Universal Declaration*, p. 1, cited in Jacobsen, Ibid.
20. Habib C. Malik, *The Challenge Of Human Rights: Charles Malik And The Universal Declaration*, p26, cited in Jacobsen,
21. E/CN.4/AC.1/ASR 3, reproduced in Schabas, op. cit. p. 734.
22. E/CN.4/AC.1/SR.8, reproduced in Schabas, op. cit., p. 807.
23. E/CN.4/AC.1/SR.12, reproduced in Schabas, op. cit. p. 847.

24. E/CN.4/AC.1/SR.13, reproduced in Schabas, op. cit., p. 863.
25. E/CN.4?AC.1/SR. 14, reproduced in Schabas, op. cit. p. 871.
26. E/CN.4/AC.1/SR.21, reproduced in Schabas op cit., pp. 1489–1490.
27. Habib C. Malik, *The Challenge Of Human Rights: Charles Malik And The Universal Declaration*, p. 110–11, cited in Jacobsen.
28. Jacobsen, op.cit.
29. A/PV.180, reproduced in Schabas, op. cit., pp. 3027–3029.
30. Habib C. Malik, *The Challenge of Human Rights: Charles Malik and The Universal Declaration*, p. 113–116, cited in Jacobsen.
31. E/CN.4/SR.1, 27 January 1947. (Schabas, 159).
32. Second meeting of the Commission on Human Rights, 27 January, 1947; E/CN.4/SR.2, 27 January, 1947, p. 1. (Schabas pp. 161–162).
33. E/CN.4/SR. 14, reproduced in Schabas, p. 391.
34. A/PV. 182, reproduced in Schabas, op. cit. P. 3056.
35. Ibid.
36. A/C.3/SR.139, reproduced in Schabas, op. cit., p. 2603.
37. E/CN.4/SR.41, reproduced in Schabas, op. cit., p. 1305.
38. A/PV.180, reproduced in Schabas, op. cit. P. 3034.
39. Ibid.
40. E/CN.0.4/SR 14, 4 February, 1947, (Schabas, 200)
41. A/PV.183, reproduced in Schabas, op. cit., pp. 3080–3081.
42. Muhammad Zafrulla Khan, Islam and Human Rights. London, The London Mosque, 1967, p. 10.
43. Ibid., p. 11.
44. Ibid., p. 12.
45. Ibid., p. 15.
46. A/PV. 182, reproduced in Schabas, op. cit. pp. 3054–3055.
47. A/C.3/SR.146, reproduced in Schabas, op. cit., p. 2673.
48. A/C.3/SR. 147, reproduced in Schabas, op. cit., p. 2685.
49. A/C.3/247).
50. A/C.3/SR. 127 (Schabas, pp. 2491–2492).
51. A/PV.183, reproduced in Schabas, op. cit. P. 3073.

References

Primary Documents: United Nations Documents from Drafting Process in William Schabas:

E/CN.4/AC.1/ASR 3, reproduced in Schabas, p. 734.
E/CN.4/AC.1/SR.8, reproduced in Schabas, p. 807.
E/CN.4/AC.1/SR.12, reproduced in Schabas, p. 847.
E/CN.4/AC.1/SR.13, reproduced in Schabas, p. 863.
E/CN.4?AC.1/SR. 14, reproduced in Schabas, p. 871.

E/CN.4/AC.1/SR.21, reproduced in Schabas, pp. 1489–1490.
A/PV.180, reproduced in Schabas, pp. 3027–3029.
E/CN.4/SR.1, 27 January, 1947a. (Schabas, 159).
E/CN.4/SR.2, 27 January, 1947b, p. 1. (Schabas pp. 161–162), Second meeting of the Commission on Human Rights, 27 January, 1947.
E/CN.4/SR. 14, reproduced in Schabas, p. 391.
A/PV. 182, in Schabas, P. 3056.
A/C.3/SR.139, reproduced in Schabas, p. 2603.
E/CN.4/SR.41, reproduced in Schabas, p. 1305.
A/PV.180, reproduced in Schabas, P. 3034.
E/CN..4/SR 14, 4 February, 1947 (Schabas, 200).
A/PV.183, reproduced in Schabas, pp. 3080–3081.
Muhammad Zafrulla Khan, Islam and Human Rights. London, The London Mosque, 1967, p. 10.
A/PV. 182, reproduced in Schabas, pp. 3054–3055.
A/C.3/SR.146, reproduced in Schabas, p. 2673.
A/C.3/SR. 147, reproduced in Schabas, p. 2685.
A/C.3/247
A/C.3/SR. 127 (Schabas, pp. 2491–2492)
A/PV.183, reproduced in Schabas, P. 3073.
A/PV.182, reproduced in Schabas, p. 3058. (PV means proces verbale).
E/CN.4/AC.1/SR.12, reproduced in Schabas, p. 848.

Douzinas, Coustas, *Human Rights and Empire. The Political Philosophy of Cosmopolitanism.* (London: Routledge-Cavendish, 2007.

Foster, Ann, "Hansa Mehta, of UN Sub-Commission, Speaks for Women of India," *Christian Science Monitor*, 18 July 1946, p. 22.

Glendon, Mary Ann, "Foundations of Human Rights: The Unfinished Business," *American Journal of Jurisprudence.*, Vol. 44: No. 1, 1999, p. 1 Available at: http://scholarship.law.nd.edu/ajj/vol44/iss1/1

Humphrey, John, "International Protection of Human Rights. The Annals, Vol. 255 (January 1948), pp. 15–21.

Humphrey, John "Memoirs of John P. Humphrey: The First Director of the United Nations Division of Human Rights," *Human Rights Quarterly*, 5:4 (November 1983), pp. 387–439.

Humphrey, John, *Human Rights. A Great Adventure.* Transnational Publishers, 1984.

Jacobson, Thomas, *Ambassador Charles Malik and The Universal Declaration Of Human Rights, Focus on the Family.* Focus on the Family – August 28, 2008. International Government Affairs Department.

Lauren, Paul G. *The Evolution of International Human Rights: Visions Seen.* 2nd ed. (Philadelphia, University of Pennsylvania Press, 2003).

Macintyre, Alasdair *A Study in Moral Theory* (Notre Dame Press, 2007).

Malik, Habib C. (Ed.), *Charles Malik and the Universal Declaration*. Published by the Charles Malik Foundation in association with the Centre for Lebanese Studies, Oxford, 2000.

Malik, Habib C. *The Challenge of Human Rights. Charles Malik and the Universal Declaration*. (Charles Malik Foundation and Centre for Lebanese Studies, 59 Observatory Street).

Schabas, William T*he Universal Declaration of Human Rights, The travaux préparatoires*, Volumes 1 and 2. October 1946 to November 1947 (Cambridge: Cambridge University Press, 2013), p. 64.

Sears, John *Eleanor Roosevelt and the universal declaration Of human rights, Hyde Park:* Franklin and Eleanor Roosevelt Institute (FERI), https://drive.google.com/drive/folders/111xVhf6GvcjmhuAVJ7VIfYRhfygcxSAs

Seghal, Gita, "Who Wrote the Universal Declaration of Human Rights?" *open Democracy*, 10 December 2014.

Susan Waltz (2002), Reclaiming and rebuilding the history of the Universal Declaration of Human Rights," Third World Quarterly, Vol 23, No 3, p. 438 (pp 437–448) weaicolumbia, P.C. Chang. October 8 [2014] Event "Around 1948: Human Rights and Global Transformation. Video, Photos, and Audio. (no paging in text)

CHAPTER 4

Asian Visions at the Time of Drafting

Introduction

At the time of the drafting of the Universal Declaration of Human Rights, distinct Asian visions were presented formally or existed in the intellectual swirl of Asia. Recalling the context of the drafting described in the preceding chapter, five visions are presented in this chapter: China, India, Lebanon, all three formally presented to the drafters, and those of Vietnam and Indonesia, then fighting for their freedom from colonial rule. It presents these very succinctly.

While seeking to refute the "myth" that the Holocaust atrocities were the spark for the UDHR, Waltz points out that non-state actors were offering universal rights well before. She noted that "non-state actors led the way in promoting the political idea of human rights". She continued,

> There was great intellectual interest in the notion of rights at the opening of the twentieth century. Movements for women's rights and minority rights flourished in the West and elsewhere. In Iran Talibov-i Tabrizi published Izahat dar Khusus-i Azadi (Explanations Concerning Freedom); in China, Kang Youwei published early segments of his Datong shu (The Book of Great Harmony), promoting individual liberty, freedom, equality and the natural rights of all humanity.[1]

As for the role of governments, Waltz also noted the irony that while the big three great powers laid plans during the war to include human

R. Ramcharan, B. Ramcharan, *Asia and the Drafting of the Universal Declaration of Human Rights*,
https://doi.org/10.1007/978-981-13-2104-7_4

rights provisions in the future UN Charter, by the end of the war, they backed away from this, and it was China that championed the inclusion of human rights. She pointed out that:

> By the time China joined the Dumbarton Oaks talks [in 1944], the Big Three had already decided to obscure mention of human rights within the text. It is ironic to learn that China alone remained deeply attached to the idea of human rights and the enforcement of justice, declaring its willingness 'to cede as much of its sovereign power as may be required'. Through the promise of human rights China hoped to promote peace and combat the international racism from which its people suffered.[2]

By the time of the 1945 San Francisco conference on the UN, it was a Panamanian jurist, Alvaro Alvarez, who came to the conference equipped with a draft human rights declaration. Small states were disappointed that the UN Charter only made minimal reference to human rights. US commitments to human rights during the Cold War were critically reviewed by Waltz.

Asians also came equipped with their ideas and plans, starting with China.

The Chinese Vision

China, from the 1840s to the 1940s, had borne the brunt of Western and Japanese aggression and racism, and its citizens were being treated as less than human in foreign enclaves even inside China as well as in countries such as the United States. But China itself was a feudal country in which notions such as democracy, the rule of law, and respect for human rights were far from being practiced. The protest movement inside China did, however, advocate for respect and protection, and, nominally, this was also the banner of KMT leaders such as Chiang Kai-shek.

China joined the "Big Four" at a later stage in the war, and it was only from the Dumbarton Oaks Conference onwards that its representatives began to make detailed proposals for the future international architecture, emphasizing the importance of the international rule of law. At Dumbarton Oaks, the Chinese head of delegation, Mr. Wellington Koo, commented on what his delegation regarded as the main weakness in the draft UN Charter as it stood at that point—its lack of a detailed statement of principles. On 3 October 1944, Mr. Koo listed seven points that he thought would strengthen the new organization and ensure its wide support among the smaller nations of the world.[3]

First, he suggested that some reference be made to a body of law or specific principles of justice as criteria for the settlement of disputes between nations. This would expedite enforcement, reinforce confidence in the new organization, and give assurance to smaller states that the world body was not intended to become merely an instrument of power politics.

Second, he thought that international law should be progressively codified and become the basis for the future decisions of the world organization. He suggested the codification of international law by the General Assembly, which would eventually provide the world organization with a kind of legislative function. The Chinese delegation advanced the idea of establishing an international law codification commission to study problems and propose conventions to ratify new laws in the future. Mr. Koo's third proposal was that a world court be granted compulsory jurisdiction over the peaceful settlement of disputes.

Mr. Koo's fourth point called for the inclusion in the Charter of a provision that would guarantee international respect for the political independence and territorial integrity of member states. "Such a statement naturally meant more to the Chinese, who had only secured abolition of the unequal treaties and regained respect for their own independence during the Second World War."[4] Fifth, Mr. Koo called for a definition of aggression. Sixth, the Chinese delegation supported the idea of an international air force. Such a force, the Chinese thought, if placed directly under the control of the Security Council, would make it possible to punish aggressors quickly while serving as a potent symbol of the Security Council's authority.

Seventh, Mr. Koo called for provisions in the Charter being drafted to enhance the new organization's role in fostering cultural cooperation as a means of preventing conflict. The Chinese had in mind the establishment of an international cultural relations office, which would prepare propaganda designed to promote worldwide understanding and friendship, encourage international peace movements, alleviate possible causes of ill-feeling among nations, and effect various kinds of cultural exchanges.

Later in the day on 3 October, because of American and British reservations, the Chinese delegation narrowed down their proposals from seven to the following: the adjustment of international disputes according to principles of justice and law, the development and revision of international law by the General Assembly, and the promotion of cultural cooperation by the new organization.

During the drafting of the Universal Declaration of Human Rights, Mr. P.C. Chang of China called for a document that would accord with the spirit and atmosphere of the post-war era and argued that the document should reflect freedom from want.

The Chinese Draft Declaration

On 3 May 1948, China submitted a Draft International Declaration on Human Rights to the Commission on Human Rights.[5] The draft declaration consisted of ten articles as follows:

Article I

Every person has the right to life.

Article II

Every person has the right to freedom of conscience and belief, to freedom of assembly and of association, and to freedom of information, speech and expression.

Article III

Every person has a right to a decent living, to work and leisure, to health, education, economic and social security.

Article IV

Every person has the right to take part in the affairs of his government directly or through his representatives.

Article V

Every person has the right to equal protection under law.

Article VI

Every person has the right to seek asylum from persecution.

Article VII

No person shall be subjected to unreasonable interference with his privacy, family, home, correspondence or reputation.

Article VIII

No person shall be subjected to arbitrary arrest or detention.

Article IX

No person shall be held in slavery or involuntary servitude or be subjected to torture or to cruel or inhuman punishment or indignity.

Article X

Every person is entitled to the human rights and fundamental freedoms set forth in this declaration without distinction as to race, sex, language or religion. The exercise of these rights requires recognition of the rights of others and the just requirements of the community in which he resides.

The Indian Vision

On 31 January 1947, the Representative of India submitted a draft resolution for consideration and adoption by the General Assembly.[6] The draft resolution recognized the fact that the United Nations had been established for the specific purpose of enthroning the natural rights of man to freedom and equality before the law, and for upholding the worth and dignity of human personality. It proposed that the General Assembly incorporate the following provisions into a "General Act of the United Nations Assembly":

I.(a) Every human being is entitled to the right of liberty, including the right to personal freedom; freedom of worship; freedom of opinion; freedom of assembly and association; and the right to access to the United Nations, without risk of reprisal, whenever there is an actual or threatened infringement of human rights.

(b) Every human being has the right of equality, without distinction of race, sex, language, religion, nationality or political belief.

(c) Every human being has the right of security, including the right to work, the right to education, the right to health, the right to participate in government, and the right to property, subject only to the over-riding consideration of public weal when the State or its appropriate organs acquire it after paying equitable compensation.

II.(a) This General Act is an obligation undertaken by Member States of the United Nations, and comes into force within twelve calendar months from the date on which it is passed by the United Nations General Assembly.

(b) Non-self-governing areas and areas under the trusteeship of the United nations automatically come under the regime of this Act.

(c) Non-member States are eligible to adhere to this Act.

III. Nothing mentioned in this Act shall be construed as not obligating the individual to his corresponding duties to his own State and to the international community under the United Nations.

IV. No state Member of the United Nations, non-selfgoverning territory, trusteeship area or nonmember of the United Nations which has adhered to this Act shall have the right to suspend it in whole or in part once it was adhered to in due form.

V. The Security Council of the United Nations shall be seized of all alleged violations of human rights, investigate them and enforce redress within the framework of the United Nations.

The Lebanese Vision

At the founding conference of the United Nations held in San Francisco, in 1945, the Representative of Lebanon, Charles Malik, offered a powerful vision of a new world built on the foundations of human dignity and rights:

As regards the fundamental purpose of the proposed Organization of the United Nations, Lebanon wishes to suggest that there be added the following purpose: 'To create a permanent Committee of Jurists whose function shall be the periodic codification or consolidation of existing principles of international law together with the modifications thereof which shall be deemed necessary from time to time.' It is obvious that the precise formulation of the law of nations, constantly updated in accordance with the development of the theory and practice of that law, will be a potent instrument for the maintenance of international peace and security.

…

Accordingly, the United Nations in this Conference must devote some time to the determination of a dynamic and positive conception of civilized existence, which will justify the organization they will set up. The peace which man believes in and will spontaneously rise up to defend, is only that which is grounded in his ultimate rights and freedoms, and in the reality of justice. There is a peace that only cloaks terrible conflicts; and there is a security that is utterly insecure.

...

It is to the spirit and mind of man, to his ideas and his attitudes, that we must devote considerable attention if the peace is going to be truly won. Unless we secure the right conditions for spiritual and intellectual health, and unless we determine the right positive ideals for which man should live, I am afraid that all our work at this conference will prove in vain.[7]

When the Commission on Human Rights began drafting the Universal Declaration in 1947, the same Charles Malik, who has been considered the philosopher of the Universal Declaration, urged that the commission base itself on the following four principles:

(a) the human person is more important than the racial, national, or other group to which he may belong;
(b) the human person's most sacred and inviolable possessions are in his mind and his conscience, enabling him to perceive the truth, choose freely, and to exist;
(c) any social pressure on the part of the state, religion, or race involving the automatic consent of the human person is reprehensible;
(d) the social group to which the individual belongs may, like the human person himself, be wrong or right. The person alone is the judge.[4]

Malik also argued that social and economic rights and the problem of discrimination were very important and should form part of the instrument.

As Rapporteur of the Third (Social and Humanitarian) Committee of the General Assembly in 1948, it was Malik who shepherded the passage of the draft declaration through the General Assembly:

> Mr Malik ... pointed out that the Third Committee had devoted 85 meetings to the discussion of the draft declaration, in addition to 20 meetings held by various sub-committees. Of the 29 articles of the present draft declaration, 18 had been adopted without any opposition. Of a total of 1,233 individual votes, 88.08 per cent had been affirmative, 3.73 per cent negative and 8.19 per cent had been abstentions. He stressed the contributions made to the drafting of the declaration by the members of the Third Committee, who had also earned the gratitude of the General Assembly.

> The Third Committee has not made any substantial alterations in the general structure of the declaration. The latter had, however, undergone certain important changes. He quoted the modifications made in article 3 on the proposal of the Yugoslav representative, in the preamble on the initiative of the representative of the Dominican Republic, in article 24 on the suggestion of the Cuban representative; article 10 had been amended as a result of a proposal of the Ecuadorean representative, and article 9 at the suggestion of the representative of Mexico. Finally, important changes had been made in the articles concerning economic and social rights.[8]

The contribution of Charles Malik to the drafting of the Universal Declaration has been recorded by his son in a book containing his key statements and writings.[9]

The Vietnamese Vision

On 2 September 1945, Ho Chi Minh issued a Declaration of Independence of the Democratic Republic of Vietnam. While he was not a "drafter" of the UDHR, the Declaration is striking for its bold historic human rights provisions at the time:

> All men are created equal. They are endowed by their Creator with certain inalienable rights, among them are Life, Liberty, and the pursuit of Happiness.
>
> This immortal statement was made in the Declaration of Independence of the United States of America in 1776. In a broader sense, this means: All peoples on the earth are equal from birth, all the peoples have a right to live, to be happy and free.
>
> The Declaration of the French Revolution made in 1791 on the Rights of Man and the Citizen also states "All men are born free and with equal rights, and must always remain free and have equal rights". Those are undeniable truths.[10]

The Declaration continued on, after admonishing the colonial powers for abusing "Liberty, Equality and Fraternity," and for acting contrary to the ideals of humanity and justice:

> Notwithstanding all this, our fellow-citizens have always manifested toward the French a tolerant and humane attitude. Even after the Japanese putsch of March, 1945, the Vietminh League helped many Frenchmen to cross the frontier, rescued some of them from Japanese jails, and protected French lives and property

From the autumn of 1940, our country had in fact ceased to be a French colony and had become a Japanese possession

After the Japanese had surrendered to the Allies, our whole people rose to regain our national sovereignty and to found the Democratic Republic of Vietnam.

The truth is that we have wrested our independence from the Japanese and not from the French.

The French have fled, the Japanese have capitulated, Emperor Bao Dai has abdicated. Our people have broken the chains which for nearly a century have fettered them and have won independence for the Fatherland. Our people at the same time have overthrown the monarchic regime that has reigned supreme for dozens of centuries. In its place has been established the present Democratic Republic.

For these reasons, we, members of the Provisional Government, representing the whole Vietnamese people, declare that from now on we break off all relations of a colonial character with France; we repeal all the international obligations that France has so far subscribed to on behalf of Vietnam and we abolish all the special rights the French have unlawfully acquired in our Fatherland.

The whole Vietnamese people, animated by a common purpose, are determined to fight to the bitter end against any attempt by the French colonialists to reconquer their country.

We are convinced that the Allied nations which at Tehran and San Francisco have acknowledged the principle of self-determination and equality of nations, will not refuse to acknowledge the independence of Vietnam.

A people who have courageously opposed French domination for more than eighty years, a people who have fought side by side with the Allies against the Fascists during these last years, such a people must be free and independent.

For these reasons, we, members of the Provisional Government of the Democratic Republic of Vietnam, solemnly declare to the world that Vietnam has the right to be a free and independent country and in fact it is so already. The entire Vietnamese people are determined to mobilise all their physical and mental strength, to sacrifice their lives and property in order to safeguard their independence and liberty.[11]

The Indonesian Vision (Pancasila)

Like Vietnam, Indonesia did not participate in the drafting of the Universal Declaration of Human Rights because neither country had yet secured its independence. However, the Indonesians vision of Pancasila was part of the Asian ethos at the time. Pancasila was the vision of the Indonesian independence struggle and is the political philosophy of the Indonesian state since independence was proclaimed in 1945. Pancasila was first introduced by nationalist leader and first president, Ir. Sukarno, on 1 June 1945, and enshrined in the Jakarta Charter of 22 June 1945.[12] The Preamble of the Constitution of 1945 enshrined Pancasila as its guiding principle and it has remained so since then. Pancasila is composed of five principles that are considered interrelated and inseparable: a divinity that is an ultimate unity, a just and civilized humanity, the national unity of Indonesia, democracy predicated on the inherent wisdom of unanimity arising from deliberation among popular representatives, and social justice for all Indonesian people. One should note the emphasis on a just and civilized humanity and on democracy. The 1945 Constitution, adopted three years before the UDHR on 18 August, contained provisions on human rights, without calling them as such.

Conclusion

There can be no doubt that Asian visions inspired the drafting of the Universal Declaration of Human Rights. The five visions outlined above were concrete and inspiring. The quest for freedom was prevalent throughout Asia: political, economic, and social freedom grounded in respect of human dignity and rights. Asian drafters of the Universal Declaration, as we shall see in the next chapter, played a leading role in shaping the text of this historic document.

In the next chapter we look at some of the prominent drafters who contributed to shaping the Declaration.

Notes

1. Susan Waltz, "Reclaiming and rebuilding the history of the Universal Declaration of Human Rights," p. 438.
2. Susan Waltz (2002), p. 440.
3. See Robert C. Hildebrand, Dumbarton Oaks. The Origins of the United Nations and the Search for Postwar Security. Chapel Hill and London, The University of North Carolina Press, 1990, pp. 237–240.
4. Ibid, p. 238.
5. E/CN.4/AC.1/18, 3 May 1948. reproduced in Schabas, op. cit. pp. 1475–76.
6. E/CN.4/11., 31 January 1947, reproduced in Schabas, op. cit., pp. 175–176.

7. Address by Dr Charles Malik, Minister Plenipotentiary of Lebanon in the United States, on behalf of Mr. Wadi Naim, Chairman of the Delegation of Lebanon, at the Third Plenary Session of the Conference at San Francisco on Saturday 28 April 1945. Reproduced in *The Challenge of Human Rights. Charles Malik and the Universal Declaration*. Edited by Habib C. Malik with a Foreword by Mary Anne Glendon. Published in 2000 by the Charles Malik Foundation in association with the Centre for Lebanese Studies, 59 Observatory Street, p. 38.
8. A/PV.180, reproduced in Schabas, op. cit, p. 3028.
9. Charles Malik and the Universal Declaration. Edited by Habib C. Malik with a Foreword by Mary Anne Glendon. Published in 2000 by the Charles Malik Foundation in association with the Centre for Lebanese Studies, 59 Observatory Street.
10. Source: Ho Chi Minh, *Selected Works*. (Hanoi, 1960–1962), Vol. 3, pp. 17–21.
11. Ibid.
12. Herlambang, "Understanding Pancasila Position as the Fundamental Norms (Grundnorm) of Indonesian Law," *Southeast Asian Journal of Contemporary Business, Economics and Law*, Vol. 13, No. 4, August 2017, p. 145 (pp. 145–155).

References

Primary Documents: United Nations Documents from Drafting Process in William Schabas:

E/CN.4/AC.1/18, 3 May 1948. reproduced in Schabas, pp. 1475–76.

E/CN.4/11., 31 January 1947, reproduced in Schabas, pp. 175–176.

A/PV.180, reproduced in Schabas, p. 3028.

Herlambang, "Understanding Pancasila Position as the Fundamental Norms ("Grundnorm") of Indonesian Law," *Southeast Asian Journal of Contemporary Business, Economics and Law*, Vol. 13, No. 4, August 2017, p. 145 (pp. 145–155).

Hildebrand, Robert C. *Dumbarton Oaks. The Origins of the United Nations and the Search for Postwar Security* (Chapel Hill and London: The University of North Carolina Press, 1990), pp. 237–240.

Ho, Chi Minh, *Selected Works*. Vol. 3 (Hanoi, 1960–1962).

Malik, Charles, Minister Plenipotentiary of Lebanon in the United States, Address on behalf of Mr Wadi Naim, Chairman of the Delegation of Lebanon, at the Third Plenary Session of the Conference at San Francisco on Saturday 28 April 1945.

Malik, Habib C. (Ed.), *Charles Malik and the Universal Declaration*. Published by the Charles Malik Foundation in association with the Centre for Lebanese Studies, Oxford, 2000.

Schabas, William, T*he Universal Declaration of Human Rights*, *The travaux préparatoires*, Volumes 1 and 2. October 1946 to November 1947 (Cambridge: Cambridge University Press, 2013), p. 64.

Waltz, Susan (2002), Reclaiming and rebuilding the history of the Universal Declaration of Human Rights," Third *World Quarterly*, Vol 23, No 3, 1 June 2002, p. 438 (pp 437–448).

CHAPTER 5

Asian Foundations

Introduction

Thus far, this work has adduced evidence of the Asian quest for a new humanism, presented five Asian visions of human rights that were advanced at the time of the drafting of the Universal Declaration, and discussed the role of ten key Asian drafters who pleaded for a world of human dignity, social justice, international solidarity, and cooperation.

This chapter, following a brief exploration of constitutionalism and human rights in post-Second World War Asia, presents stunning evidence of Asian roots of the Universal Declaration in the form of Asian constitutional provisions upon which the UN Division of Human Rights drew when it prepared the first, Secretariat draft for a universal declaration.

Constitutionalism and Rights in Post-war Asia

A burgeoning literature on constitutions and constitutionalism in Asia over the last century has highlighted the increasing human rights component in Asian constitutions, especially since the Second World War as many post-colonial states emerged and crafted new, independent nation-states. In their book on *Constitutionalism in Southeast Asia* (2009),[1] Hill and Menzel in noting the rise of constitutionalism in Asia remarked that most countries, including Asian, are constitutional states that function according to the constitutions, that provide the basic and supreme laws of each

R. Ramcharan, B. Ramcharan, *Asia and the Drafting of the Universal Declaration of Human Rights*,
https://doi.org/10.1007/978-981-13-2104-7_5

country, that guarantee rules for the political process and the rule of law, and often guarantee individual rights and fundamental policies.

In this regard, the adoption of the ASEAN Charter in 2007 was an important moment. Angeles and Yusingco have commented that while the Charter is not the founding document of ASEAN, its importance lies in its "functional supremacy" over prior binding documents. The "real constituent power is not the peoples of the Southeast Asia region but the people of each member country as represented by their respective heads of state." While non-interference and respect for sovereignty remain cornerstones, the preamble "impresses upon all member states a commitment of compliance with 'the principles of democracy, the rule of law and good governance, respect for and protection of human rights and fundamental freedoms.'"[2] They note that these constitutional values "are not exactly new ideas in Southeast Asia," even if constitutionalism in the region has been a turbulent process.[3]

It is true, as A.H.Y Chen has noted, that "non-Western world [countries] were not enacted after a revolution in order to constitute a new state and a new political order, nor inspired by the liberal doctrine of the protection of individuals rights against possible violations by the government."[4] Indeed, constitutions tended to be drafted to bolster the new regimes that came to power, such as the constitution promulgated by the Meiji Emperor of Japan in 1889 and that of the Qing Empire in China in 1908, also attempted to move towards a constitutional monarchy in the early twentieth century, but was overthrown by the 1911 Revolution.[5] New constitutions across Northeast, South, and Southeast Asia experienced similar vicissitudes. Nevertheless, they incorporated aspects of former colonial states,[6] such as parliaments and elections, that would serve as checks on absolute power, and many states would come to adopt institutions, according to Beer,[7] that emerged with the creation of the United States in the late eighteenth century. By the mid-twentieth century, according to Chen, fascism in Europe and Japan and the terror and atrocities of the Second World War "prompted deeper reflections on constitutionalism, what it requires and how it can be sustained." This resulted in a "post-War constitutional paradigm… in which respect for human dignity and equality came to be recognised as the core value of the modern constitutional state."[8] India's post-war constitution-making process is a shining example of this. Domenico Amerante argues that India's path to modernity "has followed a very peculiar path, resulting in an original blend of tradition and innovation and challenging the mainstream assumption which considers traditional culture and democracy to be substantially incompatible."[9] Most constitutions in the region today provide for checks on power and the fundamental rights of citizens and contestation within each state for respect for those rights continues today. Beer has noted that:

> Although Asian nations can boast of a richness of cultural heritage equal to that of countries in any world area, all Asian legal systems are, at least in important part, of relatively recent origin. The legal impact of the Western world on Asia has been great. Indigenous legal institutions and ideas have developed alongside of or been deftly integrated or replaced with newer concepts, forms, and processes derived from the Western world. One aspect of these Asian legal developments has been an explosion of innovative, significant, and fascinating constitutional thinking as Asian nations have made, amended, and occasionally remade their constitutions. This phenomenon has been part of a worldwide pattern. The period since World War II has seen more constitution-making and legal change than any comparable time span in world history.[10]

Strong traces of the new humanism were already found in many Asian constitutions at the time of the drafting of the UDHR.[11] Bearing in mind the list of substantive rights enshrined in the International Bill of Human Rights provided in Table 2.1, Chap. 2, this chapter proceeds to outline the various provisions in Asian constitutions at that time that influenced drafting of the UDHR. They are grouped according to substantive rights as found in international human rights law. The evidence speaks for itself.

Asian Constitutional Sources Used in Drafting the Universal Declaration

On 4 June 1947, the United Nations Secretariat, led by Professor John Humphrey, Director of the Division of Human Rights, submitted to the Drafting Committee of the Commission on Human Rights, at its request, "A Draft Outline of International Bill of Rights (prepared by the Division of Human Rights" (E/CN.4/AC.1/3/Add.1). This draft outline consisted of a preamble and 48 articles. For each article, the Secretariat referred to the sources that it had taken into account in formulating them. These included, prominently, constitutional provisions from 55 states, including the following Asian States: Afghanistan, China, India, Iran, Iraq,

Lebanon, Saudi Arabia, Siam (now Thailand), the Philippines, Syria, and Turkey.

At the time, India was engaged in the process of drafting an independence constitution and the text that was used from India was the Government of India Act of 1935, which had been enacted by the British administration.[12] In many instances there were no provisions in this Act corresponding to the headings of the 48 articles of the Secretariat draft, but India, as was seen in Chap. 2, submitted a text of a proposed universal declaration. The Indian delegation, which was very active, made numerous proposals in respect of the issues treated in the Secretariat draft.

In the following section, we present the Asian constitutional foundations that the UN Division of Human Rights drew upon in preparing its draft. They are all found in document E/CN.4/AC.1/3/Add.1, the compilation prepared by the UN Secretariat. Recalling Table 2.1 in Chap. 2, it will be seen how dynamic and far-reaching some of these constitutional provisions were. They are as follows.

Right to Existence

Article 15 of the Constitution of China contained the inspirational provision that "The right to existence, the right to work and the right of property shall be guaranteed to the people."

Self-Determination and Justice

Article 141 of the Constitution of China provided that "The foreign policy of the Republic of China shall, in a spirit of independence and initiative and on the basis of the principles of equality and reciprocity, cultivate good neighbourliness with other nations and respect treaties and the United Nations Charter in order to protect the rights and interests of overseas Chinese nationals, promote international cooperation, advance international justice and ensure world peace."

Equality

Article 5 of the Constitution of China provided that "All racial groups of the Republic of China shall enjoy equality." Article 7 added that "All citizens of the Republic of China, irrespective of sex, religion, race, class or party affiliation shall be equal before the law."

Article 298 of the Constitution of India provided as follows:

1. No subject of His Majesty domiciled in India shall on grounds only of religion, place of birth, descent, colour or any of them be ineligible for office under the Crown in India, or be prohibited on any such grounds from acquiring, holding or disposing of property or carrying on any occupation, trade, business or profession in British India.
2. Nothing in this section shall affect the operation of any law which (a) prohibits, either absolutely or subject to exceptions, the sale or mortgage of agricultural land situated in any particular area, and owned by a person belonging to some class recognized by the law as being a class of persons engaged in or connected with agriculture in the area, to any person not belonging to any such class; or (b) recognizes the existence of some right, privilege or disability attaching to members of a community by virtue of some personal law or custom having the force of law.
3. Nothing in this section shall be construed as derogating from the special responsibility of the Governor-General or of a Governor for the safeguarding of the legitimate interests of minorities.

Article 8 of the Supplementary Fundamental Laws of Iraq provided that "The people of the Persian Empire are to enjoy equal rights before the law."

Article 6 of the Constitution of Iraq provided that "there shall be no differentiation in the rights of Iraqis before the law, whatever differences may exist in language, race or creed." Article 18 added that "Iraq nationals are equal in the enjoyment of civil and political rights and the performance of public duties and obligations. No distinction shall be made between them on account of origin, language or religion."

Article 7 of the Constitution of Lebanon provided that "All Lebanese shall be equal in the eyes of the law. They shall enjoy civil and political rights and shall also be liable to public charge and obligations without any distinction whatsoever being made."

Protection of Motherhood and of Children

Article 156 of the Constitution of China provided that "The State, in order to secure the foundation of national existence and development, shall protect motherhood and carry out the policy of promoting the welfare of women and children."

Prohibition of Slavery

Article 11 of the Constitution of Afghanistan provided that "The practice of slavery is forbidden in Afghanistan. No male or female may keep any person as a slave."

Freedom

Article 8 of the Constitution of China provided that "Freedom of person shall be guaranteed to the people."

Article 4 of Egypt's Royal Prescript provided that "The freedom of the individual is guaranteed."

Article 8 of the Constitution of Lebanon provided that "Personal freedom shall be guaranteed and protected."

Article 8 of the Constitution of Lebanon provided that "No offence may be established and no penalty imposed except by law."

Iran's Supplementary Fundamental Laws provided in its Article 9 that "All individuals are protected and safeguarded in respect to their lives, property, homes, and honour, from every kind of interference, and none shall molest them save in such case and in such a way as the laws of the land shall determine."

Article 8 of China's Constitution provided that "Freedom of person shall be guaranteed to the people." Article 9 provided that "No person may, except those in active military service, be subject to trial by a military court." Article 22 of the Chinese Constitution provided that "All other liberties and rights of the people that are not inimical to social order or public interest shall be guaranteed under the Constitution."

Article 4 of Egypt's Royal Prescript No. 42 provided that "The freedom of the individual is guaranteed."

Article 72 of the Constitution of Turkey provided that "No individual shall be seized or arrested under any other circumstance or manner than that provided by law."

Article 8 of the Constitution of Iraq provided that "Personal freedom shall be guaranteed and protected."

Article 8 of the Constitution of Lebanon provided that "No person may be arrested or kept in custody except in accordance with the law."

Article 10 of the Supplementary Fundamental Law of Iran provided that "No one can be summarily arrested, save *flagrante delicto* in the commission of some crime or misdemeanour, except on the written authority of the President of the Tribunal of Justice, given in conformity with the law. Even in such case the accused must immediately or at the latest in the course of the next twenty-four hours, be informed and notified of the nature of his offence."

Article 7 of the Constitution of Syria provided that "Personal Freedom shall be guaranteed. No person may be arrested or kept in custody, except in cases determined by the law and in observance of the forms prescribed by it." Article 8 added that "Every person who is arrested or detained in custody shall be informed within twenty-four hours of the g rounds for such detention or arrest, and of the authority at whose instance it has been carried out, and such persons shall, within the same period, be accorded all possible facilities for preparing their defence."

Article 14 of the Syrian Constitution provided "Subject to the provisions of the law, every person enjoys full liberty of person, abode, property, speech, writing, publication, education, public meeting, association and vocation."

Article 70 of the Constitution of Turkey provided that "Personal immunity, freedom of conscience, of thought, of speech and press, the right to travel, to make contracts, to work, to own and dispose of property, to meet and associate and to incorporate, form part of the rights and liberties of Turkish citizens."

Article 16 of the Fundamental Principles of the Government of Afghanistan provided that "The residence of every Afghan subject is safe from every sort of interference. No official or other person may enter a private residence without an order under Sharia law or the law of the land."

Article 12 of the Constitution of China provided that "The people shall have the freedom of secrecy of correspondence."

The Supplementary Fundamental Laws of Iran contained the following extensive provisions on personal freedom:

Article 9: "All individuals are protected and safeguarded in respect to their lives, homes, from every kind of interference, and none shall molest them save in such case and in such way as the laws of the land shall determine."

"All individuals are protected and safeguarded in respect of their…honour, from every kind of interference, and none shall molest them save in such a case and in such a way as the laws of the land shall determine."

Article 13: "Every person's house and dwelling is protected and safeguarded, and no dwelling place may be entered save in such case and in such a way as the law has decreed."

Article 22: "Correspondence passing through the post is safeguarded and exempt from seizure or examination, save in such exceptional cases as the law lays down."

Article 23: "It is forbidden to disclose or detain telegraphic correspondence without the express permission of the owner, save in such cases as the law lays down."

Article 8 of the Constitution of Iraq provided that "The inviolability of all places of residence is guaranteed. They may not be entered or searched except in such circumstances and in such a manner as may be prescribed by law." Article 15 added, "All postal and telegraphic correspondence and all telephonic communications shall be secret and free from censorship or detention, except in such circumstances and in such manner as may be prescribed by law."

Article 14 of the Constitution of Lebanon provided that "Dwellings shall be inviolable. No one may enter therein except in the circumstances and in the manner prescribed by law."

Article 111, Section 1, of the Constitution of the Philippines provided: "(3) The right of the people to be secure in their persons, houses, papers, and effects against unreasonable searches and seizures shall not be violated, and no warrants shall issue but upon probable cause, to be determined by the judge after examination under oath, or affirmation of the complainant and the witnesses he may produce, and particularly describing the place to be searched, and the persons or things to be seized....(5) The privacy of communications and correspondence shall be inviolable except upon lawful order of the court or when public safety and order require otherwise."

Article 12 of the Constitution of Syria provided that "Dwellings shall be inviolable; no one may enter therein, except in the circumstances and in the manner prescribed by law." Article 18 added that "Postal, telegraphic and telephonic communications shall be inviolable and may not be delayed or censored, except as provided by law."

Article 70 of the Constitution of Turkey provided that "Personal immunity, freedom of conscience, of thought, of speech and press, the right to travel, to make contracts, to work, to own and dispose of property, to meet and associate and to incorporate, form part of the rights and liberties of Turkish citizens."

Article 71 of the Constitution of Turkey provided that "The life, property, honour and residence of each individual are inviolable." Article 76 added that "No one's domicile may be entered or his person searched except as in the manner and under the conditions stipulated by law." Article 81 further stated that "Documents, letters, and all kinds of parcels delivered to the postal authorities may not be opened without a decision by a competent examining magistrate and tribunal. Likewise the secrecy of telegraphic and telephonic conversations may not be violated."

Article 14 of the Constitution of Siam provided that "Subject to the provisions of the law, every person enjoys full liberty of person, abode, property, speech, writing, publication, education, public meetings, association and vocation."

Article 11 of the Fundamental Principles of the Government of Afghanistan provided that "There is no interference with personal liberty. No one is imprisoned or punished without an order in accordance with the Shariat or the appropriate laws. The practice of slavery is forbidden in Afghanistan. No male or female may keep any person as a slave."

Right to Liberty

Article 68 of the Constitution of Turkey provided that "Every Turk is born free and free he lives. Liberty consists of any action which is not detrimental to others. The limits of an individual's liberty, which is his natural right, extend only to the point where they infringe on the liberties enjoyed by his fellow-citizens. The said limits are defined solely by law." Article 71 added that "The life, property, honour and residence of each individual are inviolable."

Article 7 of the Constitution of Iraq provided that "There shall be no violation of, or interference with, the personal liberty of any of the inhabitants of Iraq. None of them shall be arrested, detained, punished or obliged to change their place of residence, or be placed in bonds, or compelled to serve in the armed forces, except in conformity with law."

Article 14 of the Constitution of Siam provided that "Subject to the provisions of the law, every person enjoys full liberty of person, abode, property, speech, writing, publication, education, public meeting, association and vocation."

Article 11 of the Constitution of Afghanistan provided that "There is no interference with personal liberty. No one is imprisoned or punished without an order in accordance with the Shariat or the appropriate laws. The practice of slavery is forbidden in Afghanistan. No male or female may keep any person as a slave."

Article 11 of the Fundamental Principles of the Government of Afghanistan provided that "There is no interference with personal liberty. No one is imprisoned or punished without an order in accordance with the Shariat or the appropriate laws. The practice of slavery is forbidden in Afghanistan. No male or female may keep any person as a slave."

Democratic Rights

The Constitution of China provided as follows:

Article 1: "The Republic of China, funded on the San Min Chu I (Three People's Principles) is a democratic republic of the people, for the people and governed by the people."

Article 3: "Persons possessing the nationality of the Republic of China are citizens of the Republic of China."

Article 17: "The people shall have the right of election, recall, initiative and referendum."

Article 18: "The people shall have the right to take public examinations and to hold public offices."

Article 129: "The election stipulated in the Constitution, except when otherwise provided for by the Constitution, shall be universal, equal and direct suffrage and by secret ballot."

Article 130: "Any citizen of the Republic of China having attained the age of twenty years shall have the right of election in accordance with law. Unless otherwise provided by the Constitution and laws, any citizen having attained the age of twenty-three years shall have the right of being elected in accordance with law."

Article 14 of the Fundamental Principles of the Government of Afghanistan provided that "Any Afghan subject, according to his ability and capacity, is taken into Government service as required."

Accountability

Article 25 of the Supplementary Fundamental Laws of Iran provided that "No special authorization is required to proceed against government officials in respect of shortcomings connected with the discharge of their public functions, save in the case of Ministers, in whose case the special laws on this subject must be observed."

Prohibition of Torture

On the prohibition of torture, Article 19 of Afghanistan's Fundamental Principles of the Government provided that "The rack and other kinds of torture are absolutely abolished. No punishment can be inflicted which is not prescribed by the law of the land and the sacred Sharia Law!". Iraq's Constitution provided in its Article 7 that "Torture and the deportation of Iraqis from the Kingdom of Iraq are absolutely forbidden. Article 11 of the Syrian Constitution provided that "Corporal punishment is forbidden," while Article 73 of the Turkish Constitution stated that "Torture, bodily mistreatment, confiscation and forced labour are prohibited."

Article 13 of the Constitution of Turkey provided that "Torture, bodily mistreatment, confiscation and forced labour are prohibited."

Article 7 of the Constitution of Iraq provided that "Torture and the deportation of Iraqis from the Kingdom of Iraq are absolutely forbidden."

The Rule of Law

Article 8 of the Constitution of China provided that "No person may be tried or punished except by a law court in accordance with legal procedure. Any arrest, detention, trial or punishment, if conducted not in accordance with legal procedure may be refused." Article 16 provided that "The people shall have the right to file complaints or institute legal proceedings."

Article 12 of the Supplementary Fundamental Laws of Iran provided that "No punishment can be decreed or executed save in conformity with the law."

Article 9 of the Constitution of Syria provided that "No offence shall be punished and no conviction may be pronounced, except in conformity with the law." Article 10 provided that "No person shall be tried except before the courts prescribed by law."

Article 3, Section 1, of the Constitution of the Philippines provided as follows:

"(1) No person shall be deprived of life, liberty, or property without due process of law, nor shall any person be denied the equal protection of the laws."
"(11) No ex post facto law or bill of attainder shall be enacted."
"(15) No person shall be held to answer for a criminal offence without due process of law."
"(17) In all criminal prosecutions the accused shall be presumed to be innocent until the contrary is proved, and shall enjoy the right to be heard by himself and counsel, to be informed of the nature and cause of the accusation against him, to have a speedy and public trial, to meet the witnesses face to face, and to have compulsory process to secure the attendance of witnesses in his behalf."
"(18) No person shall be compelled to be a witness against himself."

Article 24 of the Fundamental Principles of the Government of Afghanistan provided that "The settlement of personal disputes and other matters between subjects falls within the province of the courts of justice and other official departments connected therewith, and such persons as are not satisfied with a decision and order of a court may appeal to higher authorities up to the Ministry concerned and, if still not satisfied, to the prime Minister and His Majesty the King."

"(20) No person shall be twice put in jeopardy of punishment for the same offence. If an act is punished by a law and an ordinance, conviction or acquittal under either shall constitute a bar to another prosecution for the same act."

Article 9 of the Constitution of Iraq provided that "No person shall be prevented from having recourse to the Courts, or be obliged to have recourse to a Court other than the Court competent to deal with his case, except in accordance with law."

Article 83 of the Constitution of Turkey provided that "No one may be summoned before or taken to a court other than to that curt having jurisdiction in the question in accordance with the law."

Article 11 of the Supplementary Fundamental Laws of Iran provided that "No one can be forcibly removed from the tribunal which is entitled to give judgment on his case to another tribunal."

Right to Nationality

Article 9 of the Fundamental Principles of the Government of Afghanistan provided that "All persons residing in the Kingdom of Afghanistan are called Afghan subjects without any distinction of creed and religion. Afghan nationality is acquired or lost in accordance with the nationality laws."

Article 3 of the Constitution of China provided that "Persons possessing the nationality of the Republic of China are citizens of the Republic of China."

Article 5 of the Constitution of Iraq provided that "Iraq nationality and the rules applicable thereto will be prescribed by law."

Article 6 of the Constitution of Lebanon provided that "Lebanese nationality and the manner in which it is acquired, retained and lost shall be determined in accordance with the law."

Article 4 of the Philippine Constitution provided as follows:

The following are citizens of the Philippines:

1. Those who are citizens of the Philippine Islands at the time of the adoption of this Constitution.
2. Those born in the Philippine Islands of foreign parents who, before the adoption of this Constitution, had been elected to public office in the Philippine Islands.
3. Those whose fathers are citizens of the Philippines.
4. Those whose mothers are citizens of the Philippines and, upon reaching the age of majority, elect Philippine citizenship.
5. Those who are naturalized in accordance with law.

"Philippine citizenship may be lost or reacquired in the manner provided by law."

Article 5 of the Constitution of Syria provided that "The conditions under which Syrian nationality may be acquired or forfeited shall be laid down by law."

Article 88 of the Constitution of Turkey provided that "Any person born of a Turkish father in Turkey, or elsewhere, as well as any person born of an alien father domiciled in Turkey and who, residing in Turkey, formally assumes Turkish citizenship upon attaining majority, as well as any person granted Turkish citizenship by law are Turks. Turkish citizenship may be lost under circumstances defined by law."

Article 24 of the Supplementary Fundamental Laws of Iran provided that "Foreign subjects may become naturalized as Persian subjects, but their acceptance or continuance as such, or their deprivation of this status, is in accordance with a separate Law."

Minority Rights

Article 168 of the Constitution of China provided that "The state shall accord legal protection to the status of the racial groups in the border regions, and shall render special assistance to their undertakings of local self-government." Article 169 added, "The State shall positively undertake and foster the development of education, culture, communications, river conservancy, public health and other economic and social enterprises of the racial groups in the border region."

Article 298 of the Constitution of India provided as follows:

1. No subject of His Majesty domiciled in India shall on grounds only of religion, place of birth, descent, colour or any of them be ineligible for office under the Crown in India, or be prohibited on any such grounds from acquiring, holding or disposing of property or carrying on any occupation, trade, business or profession in British India.

...

3. Nothing in this section shall be construed as derogating from the special responsibility of the Governor-General or of a Governor for the safeguarding of the legitimate interests of minorities.

Article 16 of the Constitution of Iraq provided that "The various communities shall have the right of establishing and maintaining schools for the instruction of their members in their own tongues, provided that such instruction is carried out in conformity with such general programmes as may be prescribed by law." Article 17 added that "Arabic shall be the official language, except as may be prescribed by a special law."

Article 10 of the Constitution of Lebanon provided that "There shall be no interference with public instruction as long as it is not contrary to public order and morals and does not affect the dignity of the various creeds. The communities shall be entitled to maintain their own schools, provided that they conform to the general requirement relating to public instruction laid down by the State." Article 11 added, "Arabic shall be the official national language in all Government departments. French shall also be an official language; the cases in which it is to be used shall be determined by a special law."

Article 24 of the Constitution of Syria provided that "Arabic shall be the official language in all the public services, except in so far as other languages may be used in addition, in virtue of a law or an international agreement." Article 28 specified that "the rights of the different religious communities shall be guaranteed, and [the relevant] bodies may found schools for the education of children in their own language, provided always that they conform to the principles laid down by the law."

Freedom from Arbitrary Arrest or Detention

Article 8 of the Constitution of China provided that "No person may, except in case of *flagrante delicto* as otherwise provided for by law, be arrested or detained except through a judicial or a police organ in compliance with legal procedure."

Article 8 of the Chinese Constitution added that "When a person is arrested or detained on suspicion of having committed a crime, the organ responsible therefor shall in writing inform the said person and his designated relatives or friends of the reason for the arrest or detention, and shall, within twenty-four hours, turn him over to a competent court for trial. The said person, or any other person may petition the competent court to demand from the organ concerned the surrender, within twenty-four hours, of the said person to the court for trial."

Article continued: "The Court may not reject the petition mentioned in the preceding section, nor shall lit order the organ concerned to make an investigation and report first. The organ concerned may not refuse to execute or delay in executing the writ of the court for surrender of the said person for trial." Furthermore, "When a person is arrested or detained illegally hey or any other person may petition the court for investigation. The court may not reject such petition, and shall, within twenty-four hours, make the investigation with the organ concerned, and proceed with the case in accordance with law."

Freedom of Thought, Conscience, Religion, or Belief

The Fundamental Principles of the Government of Afghanistan provided as follows:

Article 1: "The faith of Afghanistan is the sacred faith of Islam and the official religion and that of the population in general is Hanafi religion.

The King of Afghanistan should be a follower of this religion. Followers of other religions such as Hindus and Jews, who live in Afghanistan, provided they do not infringe the ordinary rules of conduct and propriety, also enjoy protection."

Article 9: "All persons residing in the Kingdom of Afghanistan are called Afghan subjects without distinction of creed and religion. Afghan nationality is acquired or lost in accordance with the nationality laws."

Article 10: "All Afghan subjects, although required to observe the injunctions and prohibitions of their Government in religious and political matters, are free to enjoy all right conferred by Shariat Law."

Article 13: "All Afghan subjects have equal rights and duties under the Shariat law and the law of the State."

Article 9 of the Constitution of Lebanon provided that "There shall be complete freedom of conscience. While acknowledging the Most High, the Government shall respect all creeds and safeguard and protect the free exercise of all forms of worship on condition that public order is not interfered with. It is also guaranteed that the personal status and religious interests of the populations, to whatever creed they belong, shall be respected."

Article 111 of the Constitution of the Philippines provided in Section 1.(7) that "No laws shall be made respecting an establishment of religious profession and worship, without discrimination or preference, shall forever be allowed."

Article 13 of the Constitution of Siam provided that "Every person is entirely free to profess and religion or creed and to exercise the form of worship in accordance with his own belief, provided that it is not contrary to the duties of a national or to public order or public morals."

Article 15 of the Constitution of Syria provided that "There shall be absolute liberty of conscience; the State shall respect all creeds and religions established in the country; it shall guarantee and protect the free exercise of all forms of worship consistent with public order and good morals; it shall also guarantee for all peoples, of whatever creed they may belong, the respect of their religious interests and their personal rights."

Article 75 of the Constitution of Turkey provided that "Personal immunity. Freedom of conscience, of thought, of speech and press, the right to travel, to make contracts, to work, to own and dispose of property, to meet and associate and to incorporate, form part of the rights and liberties of Turkish citizens."

Article 1 of the Fundamental Principles of the Government of Afghanistan provided that "The faith of Afghanistan is the sacred faith of Islam, and the official religion and that of the population in general is the Hanafi religion. The King of Afghanistan should be a follower of this religion. Followers of other religions such as Hindus and Jews, who live in Afghanistan, provided they do not infringe the ordinary rules of conduct and propriety, also enjoy protection."

Article 13 of the Constitution of China provided that "The people shall have the freedom of religion or belief."

Article 13 of the Constitution of Iraq provided that "Islam is the official religion of the State. Freedom to practise the rites of the different sects of that religion, as observed in Iraq is guaranteed. Complete freedom of conscience and freedom to practise the various forms of worship, in conformity with accepted customs, is guaranteed to all inhabitants of the country, provided such forms of worship do not conflict with the maintenance of order and discipline or public morality."

Article 16 of the Constitution of Syria provided that "Freedom of thought shall be guaranteed; all persons shall be entitled to express their views verbally, in writing, in speeches or graphically, subject to the limitations provided by law." Article 17 added that "Freedom of the press, and of printing shall be guaranteed, subject to the conditions laid down by the law."

Article 70 of the Constitution of Turkey provided that "Personal immunity, freedom of conscience, thought, of speech and press, the right to travel, to make contracts, to work, to own and dispose of property, to meet and associate and to incorporate, form part of the rights and liberties of Turkish citizens." Article 17 added that "The press shall enjoy freedom within the framework of the law and shall not be subject to any censorship or control prior to publication."

Freedom of Opinion and of Expression

Article 12 of the Constitution of Iraq provided that "Freedom of expression of opinion is guaranteed to all Iraqis within such limits as may be prescribed by law."

Article 11 of the Constitution of China provided that "The people shall have the freedom of speech, academic instruction, writing land publication."

Article 20 of the Supplementary Fundamental Laws of Iran provided that "All publications, except heretical books and matters hurtful to the perspicuous religion of Islam are free and are exempt from censorship. If, however, anything should be discovered in them contrary to the Press law, the publisher or writer is liable to punishment according to that law. If the writer be known, and be resident in Persia, then the publisher, printer and distributor shall not be liable to prosecution."

Freedom of Assembly

Article 14 of the Constitution of China provided that "The people shall have freedom of assembly...."

Article 12 of the Constitution of Iraq provided that "Freedom...of meeting together...is guaranteed to all Iraqis within such limits as may be prescribed by law."

Article 13 of the Constitution of Lebanon provided that "...[F]reedom to assemble...shall be guaranteed within the limits laid down by the law."

Article 111, Section 1(8) of the Constitution of the Philippines provided that "No law shall be passed abridging the right of the people peaceably to assemble."

Article 14 of the Constitution of Siam provided that "Subject to the provisions of the law, every person enjoys full liberty of person, abode, property, speech, writing, publication, education, public meeting, association and vocation."

Article 25 of the Constitution of Syria provided that "Freedom of assembly and association shall be guaranteed in the manner prescribed by the law."

Article 79 of the Constitution of Turkey provided that "The limits imposed on the liberty of making contracts, of labour, of ownership, meeting and associating and of incorporation shall be determined by law."

Freedom of Association

Article 14 of the Constitution of China provided that "The people shall have freedom of ...association."

Article 21 of the Supplementary Fundamental Laws of Iran provided that "Societies (anjumans) and associations (ijtimalat) which are not productive of mischief to Religion of the State, and are not injurious to good order, are free throughout the whole Empire, but members of such associations must not carry arms, and must obey the regulations laid down by the Law on this matter. Assemblies in the public thoroughfares and open spaces must likewise obey the police regulations."

Article 12 of the Constitution of Iraq provided that "Freedom of forming and joining associations is guaranteed to all Iraqis within such limits as may be prescribed by law."

Article 13 of the Constitution of Lebanon provided that "...[Freedom] of association shall be guaranteed within the limits laid down by the law."

Article 3, Section 1, of the Constitution of the Philippines provided that "(6) The right to form associations or societies for purposes not contrary to law shall not be abridged."

Article 14 of the Constitution of Siam provided that "Subject to the provisions of the law, every person enjoys full liberty of person, abode, property, speech, writing, publication, education, public meeting, association and vocation."

Article 25 of the Constitution of Syria provided that "Freedom of assembly and association shall be guaranteed in the manner prescribed by the law."

Article 70 of the Constitution of Turkey provided that "Personal immunity, freedom of conscience, of thought, of speech and press, the right to travel, to make contracts, to work, to own and dispose of property, to meet and associate and to incorporate, form part of the rights and liberties of Turkish citizens." Article 79 added that "The limits imposed on the liberty of making contracts, of labour, or ownership, of meeting and associating and of incorporating shall be determined by law."

Economic, Social, and Cultural Rights

Article 15 of the Constitution of China provided that "The right of existence, the right of work and the right of property shall be guaranteed to the people." Article 142 provided that "National economy shall be based on the Principle of the People's livelihood for equitable distribution of land ownership and control of capital in order to obtain a well-balanced development of public economy and private livelihood."

Article 153 added that "All land within the territory of the Republic of China shall in principle belong to the whole body of citizens. Private ownership of land, acquired by the people in accordance with law, shall be protected and restricted by law. Privately owned land shall be liable to taxation according to its value and the government may buy such land according to its value."

"If any land has an increase in its value, not through the exertion of labour and the employment of capital, the state shall levy thereon an increment tax, the proceeds of which shall be enjoyed by the people in common."

"In the distribution and adjustment of land, the state shall, as a principle, assist self-farming landowners and persons who make use of the land by themselves, and shall also regulate their appropriate areas of operation."

Article 299 of the Constitution of India provided as follows:

1. No person shall be deprived of his property in British India save by authority of law.
2. Neither the Federal nor a Provincial legislature shall have power to make any law authorizing the compulsory acquisition for public purposes of any land or any commercial or industrial undertaking, or any interest in, or in any company owning, any commercial or industrial undertaking, unless the law provides for the payment of compensation for the property acquired and either fixes the amount of the compensation, or specifies the principles on which and the manner in which, it is to be determined.
3. No Bill or amendment making provision for the transference to public ownership of any land or for the extinguishment or modification of rights therein, including rights or privileges in respect of land revenue, shall be introduced or moved in either Chamber of the Federal Legislature without the previous sanction of the Governor-General in his discretion, or, in a Chamber of a Provincial Legislature without the previous sanction of the Governor in his discretion.
4. Nothing in this section shall affect the provisions of any law in force at the date of the passing of this Act.
5. In this section 'land' includes immovable property of every kind and any rights in or over such property, and 'undertaking' includes part of an undertaking.

Article 17 of the Supplementary Fundamental Laws of Iran provided that "To deprive owners or possessors of the properties or possessions controlled by them on any pretext whatever is forbidden, save in conformity with the law." Article 16 provided that "The confiscation of the property or possessions of any person under the title of punishment or retribution is forbidden, save in conformity with the law." Article 15 provided that "No property shall be removed from the control of its owner save by legal sanction, and then only after its fair value has been determined and paid."

Article 19 provided that "All individuals are protected and safeguarded in respect to their...property...from every kind of interference, and none shall molest them save in such case and in such a way as the laws of the land shall determine."

Article 10 of the Constitution of Iraq provided that "...[T]he general confiscation of movable property are absolutely forbidden. 1. Rights of ownership shall be safeguarded. No person's goods or property shall be expropriated except for the public benefit, and in the circumstances and in the manner prescribed by law, and on condition that just compensation is paid. 2. Forced loans may not be imposed, nor may goods or property be seized or prohibited goods confiscated, except in accordance with law."

Article 15 of the Constitution of Lebanon provided that "Rights of ownership shall be protected by law. No person may be expropriated except on g rounds of public utility, in the circumstances defined by law and on condition that fair compensation is paid beforehand."

Article 13 of the Constitution of the Philippines provided as follows:

Section 1. "All agricultural, timber and mineral lands of the public domain, waters, minerals, coal, petroleum, and other mineral oils, all forces of potential energy, and other natural resources of the Philippines belong to the State, and their disposition, exploitation, development, or utilization shall be limited to citizens of the Philippines or to corporations or associations at least sixty *per centum* of the capital of which is owned by such citizens, subject to any existing right, grant, lease, or concession at the time of the inauguration of the Government established under this Constitution. Natural resources, with the exception of public agricultural land, shall not be alienated, and no license, concession, or lease for the exploitation, development, or utilization of any of the natural resources shall be granted for a period exceeding twenty-five years, renewable – for another twenty-five years, except as to water rights for irrigation, water supply, fisheries, or industrial uses other than the development of water power, in which cases beneficial use may be the measure and the limit of the grant."

Section 2. "No private corporation or association may acquire, lease or hold public agricultural lands in excess of one thousand and twenty-four hectares, nor may any individual acquire such lands by purchase in excess of one hundred and forty-four hectares, or by lease in excess of one thousand and twenty-four hectares or by homestead in excess of twenty-four hectares. Lands adapted to grazing, not exceeding two thousand hectares, may be leased to an individual, private corporation, or association."

Section 3. "The National Assembly may determine by law the size of private agricultural land which individuals, corporations, or associations may acquire and hold, subject to rights existing prior to the enactment of such law."

Section 4: "The National Assembly may authorize, upon payment of just compensation, the expropriation of lands to be subdivided into small lots and conveyed at cost to individuals."

Section 5: "Save in cases of hereditary succession, no private agricultural land shall be transferred or assigned except by individuals, corporations or associations qualified to acquire or hold lands of the public domain of the Philippines."

Section 6: "The State may, in the interest of national welfare and defence, establish and operate industries and means of transportation and communication, and, upon payment of just compensation, transfer to public ownership utilities and other private enterprises to be operated by the Government."

Article 14 of the Constitution of Siam provided that "Subject to the provisions of the law, every person enjoys full liberty of person, abode, property, speech, writing, publication, education, public meeting, association and vocation."

Article 13 of the Constitution of Syria provided that "Rights of ownership shall be protected by law, no person may be expropriated, except on grounds of public utility and in the circumstances defined by law, and on condition that fair compensation is paid beforehand."

The Constitution of Turkey provided as follows:

Article 70. "Personal immunity, freedom of conscience, of thought, of speech, and press, the right to travel, to make contracts, to work, to own and dispose of property, to meet and associate and to incorporate, form part of the rights and liberties of Turkish citizens."

Article 71. "The life, property, honour and residence of each individual are inviolable."

Article 73. "Torture, bodily mistreatment, confiscation and forced labour are prohibited."

Article 74. "No person may be deprived of his possession and property or have them expropriated unless he has first been indemnified in case for the value of the property in accordance with the pertinent laws."

"The expropriation indemnity and the manner of payment of such indemnity and land or forest to be expropriated in order to make the farmer proprietor of land and to place administration of forests under the State, shall be determined by special laws."

"No person shall be constrained to make any sort of sacrifice except such as may be imposed in kind, or money, in the form of labour in extraordinary circumstances and in conformity with the law."

Right to Health

Article 157 of the Constitution of China provided that "The State, in order to improve national health, shall extensively establish sanitations and infant health protection enterprises and a system of socialized medical service."

The Right to Education

Article 21 of the Fundamental Principles of the Government of Afghanistan provided that "In Afghanistan, instruction in the knowledge of Islam is unrestricted. Every Afghan subject is permitted to impart Islamic religious instruction. Foreigners, however, with the exception of those engaged to teach arts, industries and foreign languages, are not permitted to open and conduct schools in the Kingdom of Afghanistan." Article 22 added that "The public schools of Afghanistan are under the supervision of the Government, so that the education and culture imparted by these institutions may, without infringing the articles of the Islamic faith, provide the benefits which accrue from the study of literature, art and science. But there will be no interference with principles of education which are concerned with the faith and religion of the 'Ahl-i-Zimma.'"

The Chinese Constitution provided as follows:

Article 21: "The people shall have the right and duty of receiving citizen's education."

Article 158: "Education and culture shall have as its aim the development among citizens of national spirit, a democratic spirit, national morality, sound and healthy physique, of sciences and of the knowledge and ability to earn a living."

Article 159: "Citizens shall have equal opportunity to receive education."

Article 160: "All children of the school age from six to twelve years shall receive primary education free and those who are poor shall be supplied with textbooks by the Government. All citizens beyond the school age who have not received primary education shall receive supplementary education free, and shall also be supplied with textbooks by the Government."

Article 164: "Expenditure for educational, scientific and cultural purposes shall be, in case of the Central Government, not less than fifteen percent of the total national budget, in case of the provinces, not less than 25 percent of the total national budget."

Article 11 of the Constitution of China provided that "The people shall have the freedom of speech, academic instruction, writing and publication."

Article 18 of the Supplementary Fundamental Laws of Iran provided that "The acquisition and study of all science, arts and crafts is free, save in the case of such as may be forbidden by the ecclesiastical law." Article 19 added that "The foundation of schools at the expense of the government and the nation, and compulsory instruction, must be regulated by the Ministry of Sciences and Arts, and all schools and colleges must be under the supreme control and supervision of the Ministry."

Article 10 of the Constitution of Lebanon provided that "There shall be no interference with public instruction as long as it is not contrary to public order and morals and does not affect the dignity of the various creeds."

Article 14 of the Constitution of the Philippines provided "Section 4. The State shall promote scientific research and invention. Arts and letters shall be under its patronage. The exclusive right to writings and inventions shall be secured to authors and inventors for a limited period." Section 5 added: "All educational institutions shall be under the supervision of and subject to regulation by the State. The Government shall establish and maintain a complete and adequate system of public education and shall provide at least free public primary instruction, and citizen training for adult citizens. All schools shall aim to develop moral character, personal discipline, civil conscience, and vocational efficiency, and to teach the duties of citizenship. Optional religious instruction shall be maintained in the public schools as now authorized by law. Universities established by the State shall enjoy academic freedom. The State shall create scholarships, in arts, science and letters for special gifted citizens."

Article 23 of the Constitution of Saudi Arabia of 29 August 1926 provided that "Higher education comprises the diffusion of science, education and the arts, and the opening of libraries, schools and religious institutes, great care and attention being taken to act in accordance with the foundations of religions in all the Kingdom of the Hejaz." Article 25 added that "A law for public education shall be decreed and shall be brought into force gradually. Elementary education shall be free of cost throughout the Kingdom of the Hejaz."

Article 21 of the Constitution of Syria provided that "Primary education shall be compulsory for all Syrians of both sexes, and shall be given free of charge in the public schools."

Article 14 of the Constitution of Siam provided that "Subject to the provisions of the law, every person enjoys full liberty of person, abode, property, speech, writing, publication, education, public meeting, association and vocation."

Article 19 of the Constitution of Syria provided that "Education shall be free, in so far as it is not contrary to public order and good morals and is not detrimental to the dignity of the country or of religion." Article 20 added that "Education shall be directed to raising the moral and intellectual standard of the people on lines best suited to the national characteristics, and the promoting concord and a fraternal spirit among all citizens."

Article 80 of the Constitution of Turkey provided that "Instruction of any kind is free within the limits laid down by law under the supervision and control of the State." Article 87 provided that "Primary education is compulsory for all Turks and is free in public schools."

Right to Work

Article 152 of the Constitution of China provided that "The State shall provide opportunity of employment to people who are capable of work." Article 155 added that "The State, in order to promote social welfare, shall enforce a social insurance system. To the aged, the infirm and crippled among the people who are unable to earn a living, and to victims of unusual calamities, the State shall extend appropriate assistance and relief."

Article 18 of the Constitution of Iraq provided that "…To them alone (i.e., to Iraq nationals) shall public appointments, civil or military, be entrusted, and foreigners may not hold such appointment except in the exceptional circumstances to be prescribed by law."

Article 12 of the Constitution of Lebanon provided that "All forms of public employment shall also be open to all Lebanese citizens in accordance with the conditions laid down by law, preference being given solely to merit and capacity. The conditions applicable to State officials shall be embodied in a special Statute, according to the department to which they belong."

Article XIV, Section 6, of the Constitution of the Philippines provided that "The State shall afford protection to labour, especially to working women and minors, and shall regulate the relations between landowner and tenant, and between labour and capital in industry and in agriculture. The State may provide for compulsory arbitration."

Article 26 of the Syrian Constitution provided that "All Syrians shall have access to public employment, without any other distinction than that due to their qualifications or capacity, subject to the conditions laid down by the law."

Article 70 of the Constitution of Turkey provided that "Personal immunity, freedom of conscience, of thought, of speech and press, the right to travel, to make contracts, to work, to own and dispose of property, to meet and associate and to incorporate, form part of the rights and liberties of Turkish citizens."

No Imprisonment for Debt and Prohibition of Forced Labour

Article 18 of the Constitution of Afghanistan provided that "Levies of money and forced labour are prohibited, except during time of war."

Article III, Section 1. (12) of the Philippine Constitution provided that "No person shall be imprisoned for debt or non-payment of debt."

Article 18 of the Fundamental Principles of the Government of Afghanistan provided that "Levies of money and forced labour are prohibited, except during time of war."

Article 10 of the Constitution of Iraq provided that "Unpaid forced labour…are absolutely forbidden."

Article 111 of the Constitution of the Philippines (Bill of Rights) provided that "No involuntary servitude in any form shall exist except as a punishment for crime whereof the party shall have been duly convicted."

States of Emergency

Article 120 of the Constitution of Iraq provided as follows: "Should disturbances occur, or should anything happen indicating the likelihood of the occurrence of events of such a character in any part whatsoever of Iraq, or should there be a menace of hostile attack upon any part whatsoever of Iraq, the King shall have power, subject to the approval of the Council of Ministers, to proclaim martial law provisionally in these districts of Iraq exposed to the danger of disturbances or attacks. The application of the existing laws and regulations may be suspended by the proclamation declaring martial law in force, in such places and to such extent as may be prescribed in such proclamation, provided that those charged with the execution of the proclamation shall be subject to any legal consequences of their acts, until a special law has been PASSED BY Parliament exempting them therefrom. The method of administration of the places in which martial law has been declared to be in force shall be prescribed by Royal Irada."

"Upon the occurrence of danger or rebellion or anything which disturbs the peace, in any part of Iraq, the King may, with the consent of the Council of Ministers, notify a state of emergency in the whole of Iraq, or in any part thereof. The districts affected by the notification shall provide for trial by Special Courts, of those who commit specified offences, and prescribe the administrative measures to be taken by specified authorities."

Article 86 of the Constitution of Turkey provided that "In the event of a war, rebellion or in case of convincing evidence of a positive and serious conspiracy against the country and the Republic, the Council of Ministers may proclaim partial or general martial law on condition that this does not exceed one month and that this measure is submitted without delay to the Grand National Assembly for approval. The Assembly may, if deemed necessary, extend or reduce the duration of martial law. Should the Assembly not be in session, it shall be convened immediately."

"The prolongation of Martial Law is subject to the decision of the Grand National Assembly. Martial Law implies the temporary restriction or suspension of personal and residential immunity, of inviolability of correspondence, of the freedom of the press, and of the right of assembling and associating. The area over which Martial Law may be proclaimed, the application of the provisions of this regulation over the said area, as well as the mode of restriction or suspension of immunity, and freedom in time of war is determined by law."

Freedom of Abode and of Travel

Article 14 of the Supplementary Fundamental Laws of Iran provided that "No Persian can be ... prevented from residing in any part thereof, or compelled to reside in any specified part thereof, save in such cases as the Law may explicitly determine."

Article 78 of the Constitution of Turkey provided that "Travel is subject to no restriction whatsoever except in cases of general mobilization, martial law, or legislative restrictions of a hygienic nature necessitated by epidemics."

Article 111, Section 1, of the Constitution of the Philippines provided that "(4) The liberty of abode and of changing the same within the limits prescribed by law shall not be impaired."

Article 11 of the Constitution of Syria provided that "It is...forbidden to deport Syrians from their national territory or to compel them, or forbid them, to reside in any other place, except as provided by law."

Article 7 of the Constitution of Iraq provided that "[D]eportation of Iraqis from the Kingdom of Iraq are absolutely forbidden."

Freedom of Domicile

Article 10 of the Constitution of China provided that "The people shall have the freedom of domicile and of change of domicile."

Freedom from Exile

Article 14 of the Supplementary Fundamental Laws of Iran provided that "No Persian can be exiled from the country, ... save in such cases as the Law may explicitly determine."

Duties

Performance of Military Service
Article 20 of the Constitution of China provided that "The people shall have the duty of performing military service in accordance with law."

Taxes Article 19 of the Constitution of China provided that "The people shall have the duty of paying taxes in accordance with law."

Article 11 of the Constitution of Iran provided that "No tax or duty shall be imposed except by law, the provisions whereof shall include all the persons liable to pay the tax."

Article 84 of the Constitution of Turkey provided that "Taxes shall be understood to be the participation of the people in the general expenditures of the State. The collection of toll, tithes, or any kind of taxes in a manner incompatible with the aforesaid principle by individuals or corporations or on their behalf is prohibited."

Article85 of the Constitution of Turkey provided that "Taxes may be levied and collected only by virtue of a law. However, the collecting of such taxes as have been customarily levied by the State or by provincial and municipal administrations shall be continued pending the enactment of new laws."

Right to Petition

Article 32 added that "Any individual may submit in writing to the petition Department of the Archives of the Assembly a statement of his own case, or of any criticisms or complaints. If the matter concerns the Assembly itself, it will give him a satisfactory answer; but if it concerns one of the Ministries, it will refer it to that Ministry, which will enquire into the matter and return a sufficient answer."

Article 14 of the Constitution of Iraq provided that "Iraq nationals have the right to present petitions of complaints and memorials, in matters concerning themselves personally, or in public matters, to the King and to Parliament and to the public authorities, in the manner and in the circumstances to be prescribed by law."

"It is not permitted, except to official bodies and juristic persons, to address the authorities in the name of a number of persons."

Article 111, Section 1.(8) of the Constitution of the Philippines provided that "No law shall be passed abridging...the right of the people to assemble and petition the Government for redress of grievances."

Article 27 of the Constitution of Syria provided that "All Syrians shall be entitled to submit requests or petitions, in conformity with the law, to the authorities or to Parliament, whether collectively or individually, and in regard to business, personal or general matters."

Article 82 of the Constitution of Turkey provided that "Turkish citizens shall have the right, should they notice any instances which are in contravention to the laws and regulations in force, to report such cases or complaints, individually or collectively, either in their own interest or in the interest of the Assembly. The reply to a personal application must be communicated to the petitioner in written form."

Brief Comments on the Evidence

The evidence speaks for itself. From the preceding extracts taken from John Humphrey's compilation from the constitutional provisions of ten Asian States used in the drafting of the UDHR, the following observations can be made: First, the states involved were spread over Asia and included countries with the largest populations, such as China and India, as well as historic powers such as Iran and Turkey. Second, the ten Asian countries concerned were of varied philosophical and religious persuasions: Buddhist, Christian Confucian, Hindu, and Muslim. Third, each country had extensive constitutional provisions on human rights. Fourth, the constitutional provisions of the various countries bear close resemblance to the articles eventually adopted in the Universal Declaration of Human Rights. Fifth, some of the constitutional provisions were stronger than those in the Universal Declaration.

In their right-by-right, quantitative analysis of the historical influences on the UDHR, Zachary Elkins, Tom Ginsburg, and James Melton have noted that:

> …we compared the content of the UDHR to that of a large sample of constitutions written since 1789. We tested hypotheses that the constitutions of larger, wealthier, and politically important countries had served as models for the UDHR's drafters. We found no support for any of these hypotheses, which corroborated the characterization of the process as an inclusive one. The only robust predictor of dyadic similarity was the age of the referenced constitution: more recent constitutions were considerably more similar to the UDHR than were those drafted in earlier eras. The UDHR, we concluded, was very much a product of its time.[13]

It should be reiterated that the existence of these impressive constitutional provisions does not mean that they were necessarily observed in practice.[14] But that is not the point for present purposes. What is of importance is that in terms of policy and intellectual content, the key Asian countries were already committed to the notion of respect for the dignity and rights of human beings. Asia had a strong intellectual tradition of human rights.

Conclusion

The constitutional provisions of Asian countries used in the drafting of the Universal Declaration leave no doubt whatsoever that Asia contributed integrally to the drafting of the Universal Declaration. The Universal Declaration was very much an Asian declaration as it was a world declaration.

Notes

1. Clauspeter Hill and Joerg Menzel, *Constitutionalism in Southeast Asia*. Vol. 1. National Constitutions/ASEAN Charter. (Singapore: Konrad Adenauer Stiftung, 2009).
2. Marford Angeles and Michael Yusingco, "ASEAN Charter: deepening constitutionalism in Southeast Asia," *Asian Currents*. (Association of Asian Studies of Australia. 1 September 2017) http://asaa.asn.au/asean-charter-deepening-constitutionalism-southeast-asia/.
3. Angeles and Michael Yusingco, Ibid.
4. Chen, Albert H.Y. (Ed.) "The achievement of constitutionalism in Asia: moving beyond 'constitutions without constitutionalism.'" In *Constitutionalism in Asia in the Early Twenty-First Century* (Cambridge: Cambridge University Press, 2014) p. 1–32.
5. Chen, Ibid.
6. See, for example, Harshan Kumarasingham, Ed., *Constitution-making in Asia: Decolonisation and State-Building in the Aftermath of the British Empire*. (London and New York: Routledge, 2016).
7. Lawrence Beer Ed. "Preface," *Constitutionalism in Asia: Asian Views of the American Influence*. in Occasional Papers/Reprint Series on Contemporary Asian Studies, NUMBER 6–1988 (89). Beer noted by 1988 that "Asian nation-states now share adoption of a government institution invented by the United States in the eighteenth century, the single-document constitution setting forth a country's public principles, its governmental structures, and the relationships between its leaders and governed" (p. iii).
8. Hongyi Chen, *Constitutionalism in Asia in the Early Twenty-First Century* (Cambridge: Cambridge University Press, 2014) p. 7.
9. Domenico Amerante, "Post-modern Constitutionalism In Asia: Perspectives From The Indian Experience," *NUJS Law Review*, April to June 2013, p. 215. pp. 213–228.
10. Lawrence Beer, "Introduction: Constitutionalism in Asia and the United States," *Constitutionalism in Asia: Asian Views of the American Influence*. in Occasional Papers / Reprint Series on Contemporary Asian Studies, NUMBER 6–1988 (89) p. 8.

11. See, generally, Albert H.Y. Chen (2014) *Constitutionalism in Asia in the Early Twenty-first century.* (Cambridge: Cambridge University Press, 2014).
12. See generally Ramachandra Guha, *India After Gandhi: A History of the World's Largest Democracy* (PanMacmillan, 2017).
13. Zachary Elkins, Tom Ginsburg and James Melton, "Imagining a world without the Universal Declaration of Human Rights," 6 September 2017, available online at http://www.law.nyu.edu/sites/default/files/upload_documents/Zachary%20Elkins%20Paper%20September%202017%20v.2.0%20%282%29.pdf
14. For recent developments in constitutionalism and rights in Asia, see Wen-Chen Chang, Li-ann Thio, Kevin YL Tan, Jiunn-rong Yeh, *Constitutionalism in Asia: Cases and Materials* (West Sussex, UK: Hart Publishing, 2014); Kevin YL Tan and Li-ann Thio (Eds.) (forthcoming). *Constitutionalism in Southeast Asia.* (West Sussex, UK: Hart Publishing, n.d.).

References

Amerante, Domenico. "Post-modern Constitutionalism In Asia: Perspectives From The Indian Experience," *NUJS Law Review*, April to June 2013, p. 215. pp. 213–228.

Angeles, Marford and Michael Yusingco, "ASEAN Charter: deepening constitutionalism in Southeast Asia," *Asian Currents.* (Association of Asian Studies of Australia. 1 September, 2017) http://asaa.asn.au/asean-charter-deepening-constitutionalism-southeast-asia/

Beer, Lawrence Ed. "Preface," *Constitutionalism in Asia: Asian Views of the American Influence.* in Occasional Papers / Reprint Series on Contemporary Asian Studies, NUMBER 6–1988 (89).

Chang, Wen-Chen, Li-ann Thio, Kevin YL Tan, Jiunn-rong Yeh, *Constitutionalism in Asia: Cases and Materials* (West Sussex, UK: Hart Publishing, 2014); Kevin YL Tan and Li-ann Thio (Eds.) (forthcoming). *Constitutionalism in Southeast Asia.* (West Sussex, UK: Hart Publishing, n.d.).

Chen, Albert H.Y. "The achievement of constitutionalism in Asia: moving beyond 'constitutions without constitutionalism'." In *Constitutionalism in Asia in the Early Twenty-First Century*, Chen, Albert H.Y. Ed. (Cambridge: Cambridge University Press, 2014) p. 1–32.

Elkins, Zachary, Tom Ginsburg and James Melton, "Imagining a world without the Universal Declaration of Human Rights," 6 September 2017, available online at http://www.law.nyu.edu/sites/default/files/upload_documents/Zachary%20Elkins%20Paper%20September%202017%20v.2.0%20%282%29.pdf

Guha, Ramachandra. *India After Gandhi: A History of the World's Largest Democracy* (PanMacmillan, 2017).
Hill, Clauspeter and Joerg Menzel, *Constitutionalism in Southeast Asia*. Vol. 1. National Constitutions/ASEAN Charter. (Singapore: Konrad Adenauer Stiftung, 2009)
Kumarasingham, Harshan Ed., *Constitution-making in Asia: Decolonisation and State-Building in the Aftermath of the British Empire*. (London and New York: Routledge, 2016).

CHAPTER 6

The Principle of Humanity

Introduction

"There existed now a new humanism," declared the Chinese delegate P.C. Chang in the Economic and Social Council on 31 May 1946, "as otherwise there would be no incentive for the efforts that were [being] made. Those incentives must be the ideals of human freedom and human dignity."[1]

Speaking at the 69th meeting of the ECOSOC on 14 March 1947, the Rapporteur of the Commission on Human Rights, Charles Malik, declared:

> The Bill of Human Rights would be the United Nations' answer to the question: 'What is man?' and would give meaning to the phrase, 'dignity and worth of the human person', which was to be found in the Preamble of the Charter. The elaboration of the bill of rights was fraught with three grave dangers. The first was that of legalism or getting lost in legalistic distinctions and niceties. The second danger was that of instrumentalism, namely allowing the instrumental things of life to obscure the essence of man. The last and most important danger was that of totalitarianism. It was not to be feared that the rights of the State would not be properly represented. But the danger existed that the individual human person might be forgotten. Unless the Bill of Rights embodied man as he really was, the declaration would merely express the dominant forces of the age, which did not respect man sufficiently.[2]

R. Ramcharan, B. Ramcharan, *Asia and the Drafting of the Universal Declaration of Human Rights*,
https://doi.org/10.1007/978-981-13-2104-7_6

In what follows we shall first look at the vision of the drafters; discuss the legal and philosophical significance of Articles 1 and 2, elucidating the contents of eight concepts that appear in the two articles (human beings, free, equal, dignity, rights, reason, conscience, brotherhood); and then look at policy and normative developments undertaken in implementation of the two articles since the Universal Declaration was adopted 70 years ago.[3]

Vision of the Drafters

Writing in 1967, on the eve of the International Year for Human Rights, and looking to the 1968 International Conference on Human Rights, Rene Cassin recalled that when the Drafting Committee of the Commission on Human Rights met in June 1947,

> it commended its Rapporteur who, following the principles of the French Revolution of 1789 and in strong reaction to Hitler's totalitarian oppression, had not begun [the draft declaration] by enumerating individual freedoms, nor even by stating the most fundamental rights, as the right to life, but had placed first *a categorical affirmation of a higher value* which makes life itself worthwhile: that all human beings are endowed with an inherent dignity and a common heritage of liberty, equality of rights and full membership in the brotherhood of man.[4]

The Rapporteur was, of course, Cassin himself!

In the same publication, the eminent Harvard Professor of International Law, Louis Sohn, concluded that the constant and consistent practice of the United Nations had imbued the Declaration with a status almost equal to that of the Charter itself. The Declaration derived its strength from being an authoritative interpretation of the Charter. It strengthened the obligations of the Charter by giving a more precise meaning to the general phrases of the Charter. Step by step, the United Nations had proceeded to enforce more vigorously the obligations of member states to observe human rights and fundamental freedoms, and almost all members had accepted the gradual extension of United Nations powers in this area. Many traditional rules of international law may have been changed through these developments. In a relatively short period, the Universal Declaration had thus become a part of the constitutional law of the world community, and, "together with the Charter of the United Nations, it has achieved the character of a world law superior to all other international instruments and to domestic laws." Prof. Sohn added that the rules of international law relating to sources of international law were flexible enough to allow, as had been suggested by Dr. Bin Cheng, "instant creation of new rules of law by unanimous, or nearly unanimous, consent."[5]

Articles 1 and 2 of the Universal Declaration, building on the human rights provisions of the UN Charter, laid the foundations of the contemporary international legal order and are of the greatest importance legally, philosophically, and from the perspectives of international public policy. Even though the Universal Declaration, as such, was professedly considered a moral rather than a legal document, Articles 1 and 2 had implicit legal status and made "instant international customary law" because of the "higher value" of the self-evident truths contained in Article 1, the fact that the non-discrimination provisions in Article 2 reiterated and expanded on the Charter's non-discrimination legal obligations, and because of the consensus that flowed into these articles. The General Assembly was effectively announcing to the world that the future governance of humanity must be on the basis of the principles contained in these two articles.

This point can be made in another way: is it conceivable that the world could be governed on any other basis than that provided in Articles 1 and 2? Morsink, referring to Article 1, put the matter thus: "These are not mere Enlightenment reflexes; they are deep truths rediscovered in the midst of the Holocaust and put on paper again shortly thereafter."[6]

The clarity and force of the provisions of Articles 1 and 2 bear out their historic legal, philosophical, and policy significance. All human beings, Article 1 proclaimed, are born free and equal in dignity and rights. They are endowed with reason and conscience and should act towards one another in a spirit of brotherhood. Everyone, Article 2 proclaimed, is entitled to all the rights and freedoms set forth in the Declaration without distinction of any kind such as race, colour, sex, language, religion, political or other opinion, national or social origin, property, birth or other status. Furthermore, no distinction shall be made on the basis of the political, jurisdictional or international status of the country or territory to which a person belongs, whether it be independent, trust, non-self-governing or under any other limitation of sovereignty. In tracing the drafting of Article 2, Morsink highlighted three points: the article reiterated the Charter's non-discrimination principle; the prohibited grounds of discrimination were expanded; and a strong effort was made to extend the principles of equality and non-discrimination to the peoples of non-self-governing territories.

The General Assembly adopted these provisions cognizant that dignity, equality, and non-discrimination were lacking in many parts of the world.

At one point the Saudi Arabian representative, Jamil Baroody, had "pointed out that to say that all human beings were endowed with reason and conscience was too broad a statement, one that was not, and had never been true. Moreover, the words 'dignity and rights' ... were ambiguous and had different meanings in different countries." Mrs. Eleanor Roosevelt did acknowledge that "In the current period it was obviously not true that human beings always remained free and equal in dignity and rights."[7] Nevertheless, the General Assembly wanted to lay down new ground rules for the conduct of governance throughout the world. Norms of international law and public policy thus entered international law through the provisions of Articles 1 and 2. The Lebanese delegate, Mr. Azkoul, pointed out that the lengthy discussions on Article 1 indicated that:

> that article was more than a mere summary of the detailed rights listed in the following articles; it was an important enunciation of the basic principle which was the source of all the later affirmations, and as such should lay a solid foundation for all that followed. Article 1 should not simply proclaim a common desire but should clearly state a universally recognized truth based on reason. In affirming the equality of all human beings, it should express a rational conviction, a decision that men were, in fact, to be equal.[8]

The Egyptian delegate, Mr. Bagdadi, " thought that article 1 should set forth man's inherent right to freedom and equality."[9]

The Human Rights Ethic of Asian Drafters

Asia contributed substantially to shaping the foundation articles of the Universal Declaration, Articles 1 and 2, as will be seen below. Charles Malik, P.C. Chang, and Carlos Romulo were at the heart of this process. Charles Malik of Lebanon advocated that the Commission base itself on four principles:

(a) The human person is more important than the racial, national, or other group to which he may belong;
(b) The human person's most sacred and inviolable possessions are in his mind and his conscience, enabling him to perceive the truth, choose freely, and to exist;
(c) Any social pressure on the part of the state, religion, or race involving the automatic consent of the human person is reprehensible;

(d) The social group to which the individual belongs may, like the human person himself, be wrong or right. The person alone is the judge.[4] Speaking later in the General Assembly, Malik underlined that the declaration had been constructed on a firm international basis wherein no regional philosophy or way of life was permitted to prevail.[10]

P.C. Chang of China advocated a declaration that would accord with the spirit and atmosphere of the post-war era and submitted that the document should reflect freedom from want.[14]

Legal and Philosophical Significance of Articles 1 and 2

It may be recalled that on the basis of a path-breaking report by Professor Charles de Visscher, the Institute of International Law had adopted, at its Lausanne session in 1947, a resolution calling for the restoration of the authority of international law on the foundations of fundamental human rights.[11] Hersch Lauterpacht had also argued along these lines. It will also be recalled that in the year following the adoption of the Universal Declaration, the International Court of Justice, in the *Corfu Channel case*, recognized the existence of "elementary considerations of humanity," basically echoing the rationale of Article 1 of the Universal Declaration and the Nuremberg Principles adopted on the margins of the San Francisco conference.[12] Let it be clear: at least in relation to Articles 1 and 2, the United Nations was in effect recognizing the existence of new legal obligations for the future governance of humanity. The normative obligations of governments henceforth would be:

- To recognize in their constitutional, legal, and governance systems the freedom, dignity, equality, and fundamental human rights of every person on the planet.
- To legislate for, and uphold, the principle of equality and non-discrimination for every human being.
- To recognize and apply the foregoing normative precepts to the inhabitants of non-self-governing territories.
- To govern on the basis of the principles of international solidarity and cooperation.

In arguing that Articles 1 and 2 contained instant international customary law, we are aware that, as pointed out by Morsink, "The view that the Declaration had no legal and only moral force was the nearly unanimous view of the delegations involved in the drafting."[13] Morsink also noted that Cassin, who often stressed that the Declaration was "an authoritative interpretation of the Charter of the United Nations," admitted that it "would not have coercive legal force."[14]While views such as these may apply to the integral Declaration, they do not preclude that individual provisions had immediate legal status.

While recognizing that the Declaration as such was meant to be a moral rather than a legal document, the issue of the legal status of specific provisions is one for objective determination, item by item, in light of the provisions of international law regarding the formation of international customary law as articulated in the decision of the International Court of Justice in the *North Sea Continental Shelf Cases.*[15] Cassin, cited earlier, argued that the Universal Declaration was an authoritative interpretation of the Charter of the United Nations. The non-discrimination principle of the Charter contained binding legal obligations on governments. In short, even while adopting a document meant to be a moral rather than a legal one, the General Assembly was, by virtue of the provisions of general international law on treaty and customary obligations, in fact implicitly recognizing norms of instant international customary law contained in Articles 1 and 2.

On the philosophical significance of the provisions of Articles 1 and 2, it may be recalled that, as a contribution to the drafting of the Declaration, the UNESCO had approached a group of philosophers to help think through the philosophical aspects of a future declaration. In the end result, the Commission on Human Rights did not pay any attention to the report of the UNESCO on this matter. But it may be alluded to here from a historical perspective.

The UNESCO group concluded that it was possible to achieve agreement across cultures concerning certain rights that "may be seen as implicit in man's nature as an individual and as a member of society and to follow from the fundamental right to live." A leading French philosopher in the group, Jacques Maritain,[16] advised that the only feasible goal was to achieve agreement not on the basis of common speculative ideas, but on common practical ideas, not on the affirmation of one and the same conception of the world, of man, and of knowledge, but upon the affirmation of a single body of beliefs for guidance in action. If there were some things so terrible in practice that virtually no one will publicly approve them, and some things so good in practice that virtually no one will oppose them, a common project can move forward without agreement on the reasons for those positions. He argued that an international declaration of rights would provide a framework within which the divergent philosophies, religions, and even economic, social, and political theories might be entertained and developed. He stated on 11 October 1948 during General Assembly debates that "...nations should try to reach agreement on a declaration of human rights, but that it was useless to try to reach agreement on the origin of those rights."[17]

On this same occasion, Mrs. Menon (India) agreed that, although different countries had different beliefs and political systems, "they shared the same ideals of social justice and freedom" and that the purpose of the declaration was "to set forth those ideals and to find a basis of agreement acceptable to all." She continued, "as far as article 1 was concerned, there was general agreement that all men should live together in freedom and brotherhood. In that connexion lessons could be learnt from the democracies of both the East and the West."[18]

At the first meeting of the Drafting Committee of the Commission on Human Rights, when it considered the opening draft prepared by John Humphrey, Col. Hodgson (Australia) asked "what was the 'philosophy' behind the paper? What principles did they adopt; what method did they follow? Is it their own idea; is it a collection of various principles." Humphrey replied that he could not oblige Colonel Hodgson "for the simple reason that [the draft] is based on no philosophy whatsoever." He had been asked to compile a list of rights for discussion purposes, and that was what he had done.[19]

During the discussions, the Chinese representative, P.C. Chang, commented that Article 1 rested on the basis of eighteenth-century philosophy. That philosophy was based on the innate goodness of man. Other schools of thought had said that man's nature was neutral and could be made good or bad, or again that his nature was all bad. The eighteenth-century thinkers, whose work had led to the proclamation of the principles of liberty, equality, and fraternity in France and in the United States, to the Declaration of Independence, had realized that although man was largely animal, there was a part of him which distinguished him from animals. That part was the real man and was good, and that part should therefore be given greater importance. There was no contradiction between the eighteenth-century idea of goodness of man's essential nature and the idea of a soul given to man by God, for the concept of God laid particular stress on the human, as opposed to the animal, part of human nature. Mr. Chang urged that the Committee should not debate the question of the nature of man but should build on the work of the eighteenth-century philosophers.[20]

In declaring human rights for human beings, the drafters sought to protect everyone with human attributes: a thinking being capable of consciousness (experience of thoughts and sensations), with memory, beliefs, hopes, and emotions, able to perform actions, which makes them moral agents responsible for what they do.[21] The drafters were influenced by the Holocaust grounded in theories of racial superiority, of superior and inferior human beings, and of a genocidal campaign against the latter. Atrocities across Asia also were committed for similar reasons. Protection of peoples from genocide had featured in resolution 96(I) adopted a year before the Universal Declaration and then repeated in the Convention on the Prevention and Punishment of Genocide adopted a day before the Universal Declaration.

Resolution 96(I) had declared genocide a denial of the right of existence of entire human groups, as homicide was the denial of the right to live of individual human beings. Denial of the right to existence had shocked the conscience of mankind and resulted in great losses to humanity, and was contrary to moral law. Many instances of genocide had occurred when racial, religious, political and other groups had been destroyed, entirely or in part. The Convention recognized that at all periods of history genocide had inflicted great losses on humanity. The General Assembly therefore expressed the conviction that in order to liberate mankind from such an odious scourge, international cooperation was required.

Concept of "Human Being"

On the concept of a "human being," the eminent philosopher, Prof. Simon Blackburn, has written that from Plato to Aristotle, "our capacities for reason have been seen as the crowning glory of humanity: the bit that sets us apart from other, 'lower' animals, and is even a special mark of divine favour."[22] It was expressly recognized during the drafting of the declaration that the words "all human beings" had been used precisely in order that both men and women might be included.[23]

When Cassin's embellishment of the first draft by Humphrey was considered by the Drafting Committee, he told it that he had taken two leading ideas as "fundamental": that every human being has a right to be treated like every other human being and the concept of solidarity and fraternity among men. Cassin reiterated the point upon which he had insisted since the Commission's very first meeting: the declaration should base universal rights on the "great fundamental principle of the unity of all the races of mankind." Cassin later wrote that the main difficulty in framing the introductory "General Principles" was "to find a formula that did not require the Commission to take sides on the nature of man and society, or to become immured in metaphysical controversies, notably the conflict among spiritual, rationalist, and materialist doctrines of the origin of human rights."[24] The Egyptian delegation, for example, in a submission on Article 1, proposed that "the fundamental rights of man ...constitute inherent attributes of his person."[25]

The affirmation of human rights for human beings would come to inspire efforts for the protection of minorities, indigenous peoples, children, women, and persons with disabilities, among others. The project of the Universal Declaration was one of mutual respect and solidarity for every human being on the planet. This perspective would come to extend recognition of the humanity of tribes and indigenous peoples of all stripes.

Concept of "Being Free"

On the concept of being free, it may be recalled that at the time when the United Nations Charter and the Universal Declaration were being drafted, there had been popular movements for freedom and independence in places such as India, Indonesia, South Africa, Vietnam, and elsewhere. The concept of freedom was undoubtedly linked with the Charter's concept of self-determination, which would give rise to the momentous decolonization movement and which would lead to a transformation of the world through recognition of the rights of all colonial and dependent peoples to freedom and self-determination.

The drafters of Articles 1 and 2 sought to register that human beings, by their very nature, in the words of Iraqi proposal on Article 1, "should be free"[26] to develop to the fullness of their potential, with freedom to think, being in charge of themselves, without being subjected to slavery or subjection, without being in bondage to another, having personal rights and social and political liberty. The concept of freedom was universal, applying to all countries and peoples across the globe, to minority as well as majority populations, to women as well as men, to children, to minorities and indigenous peoples. A Chinese delegation proposal on Article 1 by October 1948 emphasized that "All human beings *are* free and equal…," though it objected to the word "born."[27] Likewise, Mr. Akzoul of Lebanon proposed "that article 1 should be amended to read: 'All human beings are free and equal …' There should be no implication that people, though born equal, might lose that equality for any reason."[28]

Concept of Equality

On the concept of equality, the factual claim is that human beings are equal; and the normative claim is that human beings should be treated equally. The factual and normative claim, combined, leads to the claim that human beings ought to be treated as the equal beings that they in fact are. Bernard Williams has noted of the idea of equality, "It is their common humanity that constitutes their equality."[29] While the idea of equality has been challenged by some prominent philosophers such as Robert Nozick,[30] the international community, in the UN Charter, the Universal Declaration, and subsequent normative instruments, has, as a matter of international public policy, elevated the principle of equality into a norm of *jus cogens* in international law.

Kantian ethics had laid stress on the equal right of all human beings to treatment as ends in themselves as a foundation of all morality.[31] During the drafting Santa Cruz (Chile) considered that Article 2 aimed above all at giving expression to one of the basic provisions of the Charter. The United Nations had been founded principally to combat discrimination in the world. It was essential to set forth in a separate article the basic postulates of the declaration, namely, the principles of liberty, equality, and fraternity.[32] Mr. Ramirez-Moreno (Columbia) recognized that the philosophical basis of the phrase "all human beings are free and equal" was fragile …. It could be alleged that no equality existed, as men were not equally gifted or talented. Human equality, however, should be considered at a deeper level.[33] In other words, this was a matter of international public policy for the future.

P.C. Chang, commenting on a Cuban proposal to fuse Articles 1 and 2, stressed only after "mature consideration" had the Commission on Human Rights decided:

> to state the principles of equality and liberty in two separate articles of the draft declaration of human rights which it was submitting to the General Assembly. Article 2 did, in fact, aim at ensuring that everyone, without distinction of any kind, should enjoy all the rights and freedoms set forth in the declaration
>
> The Chinese delegation was in whole-hearted agreement with the Commission on Human Rights and hoped that the Third Committee would make a point of retaining article 2 in its existing form.[34]

Concept of Dignity

The concept of dignity signifies worth, estimation. In modern moral philosophy, especially that of Kant, dignity is considered as a universal attribute, an offshoot of the capacity for self-consciousness and practical reason. The entrenchment of human dignity as a universal human rights norm was one of the great normative cascades of the 1940s. The UN Charter makes several references to the principles of the dignity and equality of all human beings. In the Preamble of the Charter, the Peoples of the United Nations reaffirmed their faith in fundamental rights, in the dignity and worth of the human person, and in the equal rights of men and women.

During the drafting, dignity as a right had been challenged by the representative of South Africa. Mrs. Roosevelt recalled that the word dignity had been considered carefully by the Human Rights Commission, which had included it in order to emphasize that every human being is worthy of respect.[35] The Commission had decided to include it in order to emphasize the inherent dignity of all mankind.[36]

Concept of a Right

Turning to the concept of a right, Kant thought that the fundamental moral right is to be treated as an end in oneself, and reason alone justifies and grounds this right.[37] The Charter and the Universal Declaration began a process whereunder human rights norms are discussed, distilled, and proclaimed in consensual processes in authoritative international organs such as the UN General Assembly. The International Bill of Human Rights and the broader collection of United Nations human rights instruments are the outcomes of this process. This, in the stirring words of the late Louis Henkin, is an Age of Rights.

Concept of Reason

The concept of reason signifies the intellectual faculty characteristic of human beings by which conclusions are drawn from premises. Among philosophers the concept of reason has attracted a variety of positions. Brand Blanshard's definition of reason, in *Reason and Analysis*,[38] as "the faculty and function of grasping necessary connections" has been considered too narrow.[39] Some consider reason as being the faculty by the exercise of which we can perceive, or arrive, at truths of some particular kind. Reason may signify the careful weighing of arguments and evidence.

In General Assembly debates on Article 1, on 11 October 1948, the Syrian delegate, Mr. Kayali, noted that:

> He agreed with the representative of China that the words "endowed with reason and conscience" should be retained as they served to differentiate man from the animals. In his opinion, most of the evils apparent in the world and most international misunderstandings were due to the fact that man's reason and conscience had been impaired.[40]

Mr. Akzoul proposed Lebanon's formulation as follows: "Since all human beings are endowed by their nature with reason and conscience, they are free [120] and equal in dignity and rights and in their duty to act towards one another in a spirit of brotherhood."[41]

Concept of Conscience

The concept of conscience signifies a moral sense of right or wrong as regards things for which one is responsible; a faculty or principle pronouncing upon moral quality of one's own actions or motives; reason or fairness: "The consciousness humans have that an action is morally required or forbidden."[42] As Mr Chang put it at one point,

> The first condition for defence of the rights of man was tolerance towards the various opinions and beliefs held throughout the world. Uncompromising dogmatism had caused much harm, by accentuating disputes, and lending them an ideological basis…If harmony was to be maintained in the human community and humanity itself was to be saved, everyone had to accept, in a spirit of sincere tolerance, the different views and beliefs of his fellow men.

By pleading for tolerance of all opinions and beliefs and by insisting on precision of terminology, the Chinese delegation had striven to introduce certain improvements into the universal declaration of human rights.[43]

Concept of Brotherhood

The concept of brotherhood signifies fraternal ties. During the drafting process, Mr. Kayali (Syria) commented that the word brotherhood was an expression of the ideal moral relationship which should exist between men and meant that all men should behave to others as they would wish others to behave to them.[44] Mr. Anze Matienzo (Bolivia) thought that there was no intention of claiming that human beings were perfect. The draft declaration was designed to set a goal for mankind. It should inspire men to transform into realities the principles it proclaimed.[45]

Mr. Chang (China) commented that the second sentence of Article 1 called upon men to act towards one another in a spirit of brotherhood. That attitude was perfectly consistent with the Chinese attitude towards manners and the importance of kind and considerate treatment of others. It was only when man's social behaviour rose to that level that he was truly human. Decorum was an ideal which should not be lost sight of—as unfortunately it was—in the struggle to uphold noble principles.[46]

Normative and Policy Implementation

The United Nations has done a great deal for the normative and policy implementation of the two articles and their eight concepts, which remain the foundations of the international legal and political order, in the face of grievous threats and challenges. First, on the centrality of human beings, the International Court of Justice has emphasized the principle of humanity in peacetime as well as during armed conflicts. The United Nations has sought to improve the conditions of life for children, women, indigenous peoples, minorities, indigenous populations, those living under slavery or at risk of enslavement of being trafficked. Caring for humanity is the rationale for all these activities.

Unfortunately, humanity today is buffeted by climate change, extensive poverty, conflicts, terrorism, bad governance, inequality, gross violations of human rights, mass movements, and trafficking of people. In whatever governments and society do, respect and caring for fellow human beings must be the inevitable starting point. There are movements and people that deliberately dehumanize and even decapitate people. Some of this is done in the name of religion. It will be essential, in the future, to uphold the principle that while religion or belief may influence the private sphere, it is the international law of human rights that governs the public sphere.

Second, on the concept of humans being born free, colonialism has been eradicated save for some remaining vestiges, self-determination is a fundamental principle of international law, *apartheid* is no more, and there is growing recognition that people may live their lives as they choose and according to their orientations.

Third, on human beings born equal, the inherent dignity and the "equal and inalienable rights of all members of the human family" were recognized in the UDHR's opening lines as the "foundation of freedom, justice and peace in the world." The UN Charter was the first international instrument to mention equal rights of men and women in specific terms. The claim to equality, the late Sir Hersch Lauterpacht held, "is in a substantial sense the most fundamental of the rights of man. It occupies the first place in most written constitutions. It is the starting point of all other liberties."[2]

The International Convention on the Elimination of All Forms of Racial Discrimination, the Convention on the Elimination of All Forms of Discrimination Against Women (CEDAW), and the Convention on the Rights of the Child, among others, are sentinels in the defence of equality. The jurisprudence of the Human Rights Committee, the CEDAW, and the Committee on the Rights of the Child reinforces the edifice of equality. With more and more people commingling worldwide, the principle of non-discrimination will have an even greater role in the future.

The prohibition of discrimination has become a norm of positive law, as has been recognized by the International Court of Justice, which has declared that to establish and to enforce distinction, exclusions, restrictions, and limitations exclusively based on grounds of race, colour, descent, or national or ethnic origin which constitute a denial of fundamental human rights is a flagrant violation of the purposes and principles of the Charter.

Fourth, on human beings born equal in dignity, the proclamation of the right to development, the launching of successive development decades, the Millennium Development Goals, the Sustainable Development Goals, and other efforts have been essentially focused on the quest for the vindication of human dignity worldwide. Norms and machinery for the protection of minorities and indigenous populations are also premised on the protection of human dignity.

Fifth, on human beings born free and equal in rights, the International Bill of Human Rights, the broader international human rights code, Charter-based and treaty-based machineries all attest to the continuing quest for the universal realization of human rights. Numerous problems of implementation still exist but the quest for universal realization and protection continues. Seven decades later, one may ask about the fate of the human rights project launched in the 1940s.

Beginning with the three parts of the International Bill of Human Rights, one may say that the moral authority of the Universal Declaration is high and that even if an era of cultural and religious contestation poses challenges to the universality of human rights, the authority of the Universal Declaration has been repeatedly reaffirmed in solemn consensual international statements of the world community, including the UN Millennium Declaration. Some parts of the Universal Declaration have attained the status of international customary law.

On the second part of the International Bill of Human Rights, numerous additional human rights treaties and other normative instruments have been adopted since 1948, elaborating on the provisions of the Universal Declaration. We thus have today a veritable international code of human rights, with instruments such as the Convention on the Rights of the Child attaining near universal ratification.

Sixth, human beings should act towards one another with reason. The continuing quest is to uphold this principle. Its validity is as important as when it was proclaimed. It will be crucial, in the future, to emphasize the principle we put forward earlier, that religion or belief is a matter for the private sphere and that the public domain must be governed by the reasoning of international human rights.

Seventh, human beings should act towards one another in conscience. Amnesty International made its name campaigning for prisoners of conscience and against torture. Conscience must guide the world in the decisions that are made in respect of people fleeing for their safety and people being persecuted in the name of religion or belief.

Eighth, people should act towards one another in a spirit of brotherhood. Caring for millions of refugees and displaced persons has been a concrete manifestation of the spirit of brotherhood and sisterhood. The quest to eliminate extreme poverty in many parts of the world is a continuing challenge to the spirit of brotherhood and sisterhood. The principle of human solidarity, which Rene Cassin so faithfully championed, remains a stirring call to human brotherhood and sisterhood.

Conclusion

Articles 1 and 2 of the Universal Declaration of Human Rights laid the foundations for a new world order grounded in respect of the human person and his or her inalienable rights. As we have seen in this chapter, Asian drafters played a seminal role in the drafting of these articles.

Notes

1. E/SR.20, 31 May, 1946. (Schabas, 65–66).
2. E/422 (Schabas, 245).
3. See, generally, Glendon, Mary A., *A World Made New: Eleanor Roosevelt and the Universal Declaration of Human Rights* (New York, Random House, 2001); Paul G. Lauren, *The Evolution of International Human Rights: Visions Seen.* 2nd ed. (Philadelphia, University of Pennsylvania Press, 2003). Habib C. Malik (Ed.), *Charles Malik and the Universal Declaration.* Published by the Charles Malik Foundation in association with the Centre for Lebanese Studies, Oxford, 2000. Johannes Morsink, *The Universal Declaration of Human Rights. Origins, Drafting and Intent.* (Philadelphia, University of Pennsylvania Press, 1999); Roger Normand, and Sarah Zaidi, *Human Rights at the UN. The Political History of Universal Justice.* (Bloomington, Indiana University Press, 2008).
4. R. Cassin, "Twenty Years After the Universal Declaration. Freedom and Equality", *Journal of the International Commission of Jurists*, December 1967, Special Issue 1968, *International Year for Human Rights*, pp. 1–16, at. P.1. Italics added.
5. L.B. Sohn, "The Universal Declaration of Human Rights", in *Journal of the International Commission of Jurists*, loc. cit. I, pp. 17–26, at - pp. 25–26.
6. J. Morsink, *The Universal Declaration of Human Rights. Origins, Drafting and Intent.* (Philadelphia, University of Pennsylvania Press, 1999) p. 39.
7. A/C.3/SR 100, reproduced in Schabas, op. cit., p. 2190.
8. Ibid., pp. 2184–2185.
9. Ibid.
10. Glendon, op. cit., p. 165.
11. See the Report of the Institute of International Law on its Lausanne session, 1947.
12. I.C.J. Report 1949.

13. Morsink, op. cit., p. 295.
14. Morsink, op. cit., p. 295.
15. North Sea Continental Shelf, Judgement of 20 February 1969, *International Court of Justice Reports*, 1969.
16. See generally, Andrew Woodcock, "Jacques Maritain, Natural Law and the Universal Declaration of Human Rights," *Journal of the History of International Law*, Vol., 8, pp. 2006, pp. 245–266.
17. A/C.3/SR.9930 11 October 1948, in Schabas, p. 2181.
18. Ibid.
19. Glendon op. cit., p. 58.
20. A/C.3/ SR 98, reproduced in Schabas, op. cit., p. 2173.
21. See on this S. Mumford, Metaphysics. A Very Short Introduction. Oxford, University Press, 2012, Chapter 7: What is a Person, esp. pp. 65–66.
22. S. Blackburn, What Do We Really Know. The Big Questions of Philosophy. (London, Quercus, 2009), p. 53.
23. A/C.3/SR. 98, reproduced in Schabas, op. cit., p. 2169.
24. Glendon, op.cit., pp. 67–68.
25. A/C.3/264 12 October 1948, in Schabas, pp. 2206.
26. A/C.3/237 7 October 1948, in Schabas, p. 2144.
27. A/C.3/243 7 October 1948, in Schabas, p. 2147.
28. Ibid., p. 2151.
29. Bernard Williams, "The idea of Equality," in Contemporary Political Philosophy: An Anthology, Robert Goodin and Philip Pettit, Eds. (Malden, MA; Oxford; Victoria, Australia: Blackwell 2006), p. 451. Originally published in Peter Laslett and W.G. Runciman, *Philosophy, Politics and Society* (Oxford: Blackwell, 1962).
30. See Robert Nozick, "Justice Does Not Imply Equality," in Louis Pojman and Robert Westmoreland, *Equality: Selected Readings* (Oxford: Oxford University Press, 1997).
31. S. Blackburn, *Oxford Dictionary of Philosophy* (Oxford: Oxford U. Press, Third Edition, 2016).
32. A/C.3/SR 100, reproduced in Schabas, op. cit. p. 2196.
33. A/C.3/SR 98, reproduced in Schabas, op. cit., p. 2171.
34. A/C.3/SR.10032 12 October 1948, in Schabas, p. 2191.
35. Glendon, op. cit., p. 146.
36. A/C.3/SR 98, reproduced in Schabas, op. cit., p. 2169.
37. Oxford Dictionary of Philosophy, op. cit.
38. Brand Blanshard, *Reason and Analysis*. London, 1962.
39. G.J. Warnock, "Reason", in *The Encyclopedia of Philosophy*. Paul Edwards, Editor in Chief, London, Macmillan, 1967, Vol. 7, pp. 83–85.
40. A/C.3/SR.9930 11 October 1948, in Schabas, p. 2184.
41. Ibid.

42. Oxford Dictionary of Philosophy, op. cit.
43. A/PV. 182, reproduced in Schabas, op. cit. p. 3058.
44. A/C.3/SR 99, reproduced in Schabas, op. cit., p. 2184.
45. A/C.3/SR 98, reproduced in Schabas, op. cit., p. 2173.
46. A/C.3/SR 96, reproduced in Schabas, op. cit., p. 2152.

References

Primary Documents: United Nations Documents from Drafting Process in William Schabas:

A/C.3/SR 98, reproduced in Schabas, op. cit., p. 2173.
A/C.3/237 7 October 1948, in Schabas, p. 2144.
A/C.3/243 7 October 1948, in Schabas, p. 2147.
A/C.3/264 12 October 1948, in Schabas, pp. 2206.
A/C.3/SR 100, reproduced in Schabas, op. cit., p. 2190.
A/C.3/SR 100, reproduced in Schabas, op. cit. p. 2196.
A/C.3/SR 96, reproduced in Schabas, op. cit., p. 2152.
A/C.3/SR 98, reproduced in Schabas, op. cit., p. 2169.
A/C.3/SR 98, reproduced in Schabas, op. cit., p. 2171.
A/C.3/SR 99, reproduced in Schabas, op. cit., p. 2184.
A/C.3/SR.10032 12 October 1948, in Schabas, p. 2191.
A/C.3/SR.9930 11 October 1948a, in Schabas, p. 2181.
A/C.3/SR.9930 11 October 1948b, in Schabas, p. 2184.
A/PV. 182, reproduced in Schabas, op. cit. p. 3058.
E/422 (Schabas, 245).
E/SR.20, 31 May, 1946. (Schabas, 65–66).

Blackburn, S. *What Do We Really Know. The Big Questions of Philosophy.* (London, Quercus, 2009).

Blackburn, S. *Oxford Dictionary of Philosophy* (Oxford: Oxford U. Press, Third Edition, 2016).

Blanshard, Brand. *Reason and Analysis.* London, 1962.

Cassin, R. "Twenty Years After the Universal Declaration. Freedom and Equality", *Journal of the International Commission of Jurists*, December 1967, Special Issue 1968, *International Year for Human Rights*, pp. 1–16, at. P.1. Italics added.

Glendon, Mary A., A World Made New: Eleanor Roosevelt and the Universal Declaration of Human Rights (New York, Random House, 2001).

ICJ, North Sea Continental Shelf, Judgement of 20 February 1969, *International Court of Justice Reports*, 1969.

Institute of International Law, Report on Lausanne session, 1947.

International Court of Justice (ICJ), *Report* 1949.

Lauren, Paul G. *The Evolution of International Human Rights: Visions Seen.* 2nd ed. (Philadelphia, University of Pennsylvania Press, 2003).

Malik Habib C. (Ed.), *Charles Malik and the Universal Declaration.* Published by the Charles Malik Foundation in association with the Centre for Lebanese Studies, Oxford, 2000.

Morsink, Johannes. *The Universal Declaration of Human Rights. Origins, Drafting and Intent.* (Philadelphia, University of Pennsylvania Press, 1999).

Mumford, s. *Metaphysics. A Very Short Introduction.* (Oxford, University Press, 2012).

Normand, Roger and Sarah Zaidi, *Human Rights at the UN. The Political History of Universal Justice.* (Bloomington, Indiana University Press, 2008).

Nozick, Robert "Justice Does Not Imply Equality," in Louis Pojman and Robert Westmoreland, *Equality: Selected Readings* (Oxford: Oxford University Press, 1997).

Sohn, Louis B. "The Universal Declaration of Human Rights", in *Journal of the International Commission of Jurists*, pp. 17–26.

Warnock, G.J. "Reason", in *The Encyclopedia of Philosophy.* Paul Edwards, Editor in Chief, London, Macmillan, 1967, Vol. 7, pp. 83–85.

Williams, Bernard. "The idea of Equality," in *Contemporary Political Philosophy: An Anthology*, Robert Goodin and Philip Pettit, Eds. ((Malden, MA; Oxford; Victoria, Australia: Blackwell 2006), p. 451. Originally published in Peter Laslett and W.G. Runciman, *Philosophy, Politics and Society* (Oxford: Blackwell, 1962).

Woodcock, Andrew "Jacques Maritain, Natural Law and the Universal Declaration of Human Rights," *Journal of the History of International Law*, Vol., 8, pp. 2006, pp. 245–266.

CHAPTER 7

Dignity, Equality, and Equitable Life Chances

Introduction

Asian delegates participating in the drafting of the Universal Declaration of Human Rights made eloquent pleas that the Declaration should lay the basis for human dignity and equitable life chances for all the peoples of the world. Human dignity and equitable life for all, regardless of race, colour, sex, language, religion, political or other opinion, national or social origin, property, birth or other status, were advanced by Asian drafters.

At the first meeting of the "Nuclear" Commission on Human Rights on 29 April 1946, Mr. Henri Laugier, Assistant Secretary-General in charge of Social Affairs, opened the first meeting by stating to the members of the Commission, including. Dr. C.L. Hsia (China) and Mr. K.C. Neogi (India):

> You know that the United Nations organization is happy to see you here and you know also that all men of all the free peoples and of all the people liberated from slavery, put in you their confidence and their hope, so that everywhere the authority of *these rights, respect of which is the essential condition of the dignity of the human person,* be respected.... Do not measure the importance of your commission on the basis of its present dimensions. We are only at the starting point of a very great enterprise, the volume of which and the action of which will have to grow, day after day.[1] (emphasis added)

R. Ramcharan, B. Ramcharan, *Asia and the Drafting of the Universal Declaration of Human Rights*,
https://doi.org/10.1007/978-981-13-2104-7_7

The Preamble of the first draft of the Declaration, prepared by John Humphrey and issued as an official document on 4 June 1947, made a link between human rights and peace and life of dignity as a requirement for peace.[2] The draft document of the Secretariat stated:

> In Resolution 290(IV), "Essentials of Peace," adopted in 1949, the General Assembly noted that the UN Charter "lays down basic principles for an enduring peace," and it called upon all nations "[t]o promote, in recognition of the paramount importance of preserving the dignity and worth of the human person, ...and full respect for all the other fundamental rights expressed in the Universal Declaration of Human Rights."[3]

This chapter briefly outlines Asian propositions on human dignity, equality, and non-discrimination in the drafting process and subsequent content in international human rights law and policy.

Asians and the Concept of Dignity

As the Commission debated an International Bill of Rights at its seventh session, on 31 January 1947, P.C. Chang stated the necessity "to affirm and enlarge the difference existing between man and animal" and called for a standard to be established "with a view to elevating the concept of man's dignity and emphasizing the respect of man: that principle should be embodied in a preamble to the International Bill of Rights."[4] Hansa Mehta, who replaced Neogi by then, considered that "this bill should eventually become an integral part of the Charter and a fundamental law of the United Nations."[5] A draft declaration submitted by India at this time included in the preamble "Recognizing the fact that the United Nations has been established for the specific purpose of enthroning the natural rights of man to freedom and equality before the law, and for upholding the worth and dignity of human personality."[6] It continued, in draft Article 1, "(b) Every human being has the right of equality, without distinction of race, sex, language, religion, nationality or political belief."

In discussions on the Commission on Human Rights' report to the Economic and Social Council, in March and April 1947, Charles Malik stated that the proposed Declaration was a chance for the UN to answer the question "What is man?" and that the declaration give meaning to the phrase "dignity and worth of the human person" that was found in the preamble of the Charter of the United Nations.[7] In treating the problem of personal liberty at the 14th session of the Commission on 4 February 1947, Malik urged the Commission to adopt the following four principles, which were in danger of being repudiated:

1. The human person is more important than the racial, national, or other group to which he may belong;
2. The human person's most sacred and inviolable possessions are his mind and his conscience, enabling him to perceive the truth, to choose freely, and to exist;
3. Any social pressure on the part of the State, religion or race, involving the automatic consent of the human person is reprehensible;
4. The social group to which the individual belongs, may, like the human person himself, be wrong or right: the person alone is the judge.

Malik stressed the fact that he had not used the word "individual" but the expression "human person" in his previous intervention. Coming back to the Charter's reference to the dignity and worth of the human person, he explained that he wished to give greater meaning to this expression. It would indeed be a dead letter if they refused to admit that the human person had the right to choose in full liberty, that is, without being exposed to reprisals or persecutions.[8]

In considering the draft Declaration on 11 June 1947, at the second session of the Drafting Committee, Malik opined that:

> the Secretariat document did not contain a sufficient reference to the dignity of man. This, he felt, ought to be made the basic woof of the Preamble. He stated that the four points enumerated in the suggestions for Preamble made by the Secretariat were excellent ones but that even when all were considered together they somehow failed to bring out what is distinctive, fundamental and human about man. If these points were not included he felt the Preamble would lose its fundamental point.[9]

Lebanon's proposal in June 1947, for draft of the Preamble for the future Declaration stated: "Whereas recognition of the inherent dignity and the equal and inalienable rights of all persons is the foundation of peace, freedom and justice in the world."

> Now therefore the General Assembly recognizes in the following solemn Declaration the essential rights and freedoms which, constituting the dignity and worth of the human person, should form a common standard of achievement for all nations, and calls upon every individual and every organ of society, national and international, to strive by teaching and education to promote their respect and by progressive measures to secure their universal recognition and observance.[10]

In considering Article 1 of the draft declaration, General Romulo (Philippines) on 5 December 1947 proposed the following draft "All men are brothers. Being endowed with reason and conscience, they are free and possess equal dignity and rights." In order to overcome illogical connection between the two parts of the original sentence "Being endowed with reason and conscience, they are members of one family."[11]

General Romulo of the Philippine Republic, referring to the principles which should appear in the proposed International Bill of Human Rights, said at the 15th meeting of the Commission on 5 February 1947 that the task of the Commission was to prepare the way for a general bill of rights for all conditions of men.[12] This Bill would prescribe rights and freedoms; it would also establish their inviolability from tyranny. "In addition, it would determine the objectives to be attained on behalf of backward populations. He was in favour of a Bill on a sufficiently broad basis to cover the needs of free men and of men still to be freed."[13]

In May 1948, amidst detailed discussions at the 21st meeting of the Drafting Committee on a draft declaration as opposed to a convention, Malik reminded his colleagues of the reasons for considering an International Bill: "In recent years, men had arisen who embodied the worst aspects of human nature and had trampled on the dignity of the human being. That was the reason for the present desire to make the future safe against the recurrence of such monstrosities." He cautioned that:

> Man might live in a perfect state, have all material security, be free from all social maladjustments, and yet not be the man, which the Charter of the United Nations had in mind, a man with a worth and a dignity of his own. This exact worth and dignity must be determined. Man must be able to think and choose freely and even to reject freely and to rebel freely.[14]

In the General Assembly debates on 27 September 1948, as the Declaration was being debated, Malik stated:

> The most important issue in the order of truth today is what constitutes the proper worth and dignity of man. This will be the central theme in the debate of the Declaration of Human Rights. Unless this issue is rightly settled, there is no meaning to any other settlement. Do not tell me that you are going to settle Korea, and Germany, and Palestine, and atomic energy, and leave this central issue unsettled. For what is the use of a peace and a settlement in which man is left ambiguous, estranged from himself and from the truth?[15]

At this same meeting, General Romulo stated:

> [General Romulo (Philippines):] Through the Human Rights Commission and the Conference on Freedom of Information, progress has been made in defining and enlarging the scope of the rights and freedoms of man. The text of a proposed Declaration on Human Rights and the various conventions and resolutions guaranteeing freedom of information await final action by the General Assembly. They constitute a vital portion of the pattern of peace and freedom, to which I have referred, whose validity does not depend on the conflicts and prejudice of the moment. They call for immediate action, and, on no pretext whatever should they be made to await a prior political settlement.

In the debates on the draft submitted for debate in E/800, various countries made proposals as follows. As of October 1948, these included the following proposals to the Third Committee[16]:

China (A/C.3/236)
Delete: – the word "born" in the first sentence, – the words "by nature" in the second sentence, [3] – the comma between the words "conscience" and "and" in the second sentence, to read this article as follows: "All human beings are free and equal in dignity and rights. They are endowed with reason and conscience and should act towards one another in a spirit of brotherhood."

Lebanon (A/C.3/235)
In the first line of this article, replace the words "are born" by the word "are."

Iraq (A/C.3/237)
Amend this article to read: "All human beings should be free and equal in dignity and worth, and should be entitled to similar treatment and equal opportunities."

Mr. Abadi of Iraq proposed a phrasing of Article 1 that would place it on an ethical plane: "All men should be free and equal in dignity and worth and should be entitled to similar treatment and equal opportunities."[17]

Egypt (A/C.3/264) proposed an amendment to the Preamble in November which stated that after the third paragraph of the Preamble, the following text should be added: "Whereas the fundamental rights of man are not derived from his status as a national of a particular State, but constitute inherent attributes of his person."[18]

Elements of a Life of Dignity: Development, Democracy, and the Rule of Law

The link between development and human rights has been prominent ever since the establishment of the United Nations. Article 55 of the United Nations Charter set out the interdependence and interrelatedness of peace, development, and human rights. The Charter provided that with a view to the creation of conditions which are necessary for peaceful and friendly relations among nations based on respect for the principle of equal rights and self-determination of peoples, the United Nations shall promote:

(a) higher standards of living, full employment, and conditions of economic and social progress and development,
(b) solutions of international economic, social, health, and related problems, and international cultural and educational cooperation;
(c) universal respect for, and observance of, human rights and fundamental freedoms for all without distinction as to race, sex, language, or religion.

Freedom from want, as the late President Roosevelt had termed it, was featured in proposals from civil society and governments in the drafting process.[19] The American Federation of Labor noted that "No peaceful, democratic, world order can be built on a foundation of fear and famine, on a basis of poverty and pestilence." It continued, "Only by removing the political, economic, and social ills and maladjustments afflicting humanity, will mankind be able to reach that long hoped for stage of civilization in which peace and plenty shall truly prevail."[20] In January 1947, the Commission recalled the International Labour Organization's "Declaration of Philadelphia" which considered that "poverty anywhere constitutes a danger to prosperity everywhere" and that "all human beings, irrespective of race, creed or sex, have the right to pursue both their material well-being and their spiritual development in conditions of freedom and dignity, of economic security and equal opportunity."[21]

The plan of the draft outline of an International Bill of Rights, prepared by the Secretariat,[22] listed in Chapter II, "Social rights" for deliberation:

Chapter II—Social rights
Article 35—Right to health
Article 36—Right to education
Article 37—Right to work
Article 38—Right to good working conditions
Article 39—Right to an equitable share of the national income
Article 40—Compensation for family responsibilities [6–7]
Article 41—Right to social security
Article 42—Right to food and housing
Article 43—Right to rest and leisure
Article 44—Right to participate in cultural, scientific, and artistic life

Asian delegations made substantive contributions to establishing the linkage between human rights and development. At the 14th meeting of the Commission on Human Rights, on 4 February 1947, Mr. Chang stated that he wished to see the expression "freedom from want" appear somewhere, either in the preamble or in the text itself.[23]

At this same meeting, the Iranian representative, Mr. Ghassan Ghani, expressed the view at the 14th meeting of the Commission on Human Rights, on 4 February 1947, "that freedom of expression and of opinion were possible only in countries where the standard of education was high enough to allow the masses to form a sound opinion, and so he wished the United Nations to take steps first of all to eliminate illiteracy and promote education, by such means as granting financial assistance to backward countries."[24]

Ms. Hansa Mehta, in considering the question of implementation of human rights, discussed in the next chapter, offered a draft General Assembly Resolution which stated in Article 1 that:

> (c) Every human being has the right of security, including the right to work, the right to education, the right to health, the [2] right to participate in government, and the right to property, subject only to the over-riding consideration of public weal when the State or its appropriate organs acquire it after paying equitable compensation[25]

In deliberations in December 1947, General Romulo (Philippines) proposed the following Article to replace Article 30 of the Drafting Committee's text: "Everyone has the right to receive pay commensurate with his ability and skill, to work under just and favourable conditions, and to join trade unions for the protection of his interests. The State shall take necessary measures within its power to ensure full employment. Women shall have the right to work under the same conditions as men and to receive equal pay for equal work."[26]

Asians and other representatives from the Global South debated and adopted a number of provisions in the final text of the UDHR, including a number of economic and social rights required for a life of dignity.

> Article 22: Everyone, as a member of society, has the right to social security and is entitled to realization, through national effort and international cooperation and in accordance with the organization and resources of each State, of the economic, social and cultural rights indispensable for his dignity and the free development of his personality.
>
> Article 23: (1) Everyone has the right to work, to free choice of employment, to just and favourable conditions of work and to protection against unemployment. (2) Everyone, without any discrimination, has the right to equal pay for equal work. (3) Everyone who works has the right to just and favourable remuneration ensuring for himself and his family an existence worthy of human dignity, and supplemented, if necessary, by other means of social protection. (4) Everyone has the right to form and to join trade unions for the protection of his interests.
>
> Article 24: Everyone has the right to rest and leisure, including reasonable limitation of working hours and periodic holidays with pay.
>
> Article 25: (1) Everyone has the right to a standard of living adequate for the health and well-being of himself and of his family, including food, clothing, housing and medical care and necessary social services, and the right to security in the event of unemployment, sickness, disability, widowhood, old age or other lack of livelihood in circumstances beyond his control. (2) Motherhood and childhood are entitled to special care and assistance. All children, whether born in or out of wedlock, shall enjoy the same social protection.
>
> Article 26: (1) Everyone has the right to education. Education shall be free, at least in the elementary and fundamental stages. Elementary education shall be compulsory. Technical and professional education shall be made generally available and higher education shall be equally accessible to all on the basis of merit. (2) Education shall be directed to the full development of the human personality and to the strengthening of respect for human rights and fundamental freedoms. It shall promote understanding, tolerance and friendship among all nations,

racial or religious groups, and shall further the activities of the United Nations for the maintenance of peace. (3) Parents have a prior right to choose the kind of education that shall be given to their children.

Article 27: (1) Everyone has the right freely to participate in the cultural life of the community, to enjoy the arts and to share in scientific advancement and its benefits. (2) Everyone has the right to the protection of the moral and material interests resulting from any scientific, literary or artistic production of which he is the author.

Article 28: Everyone is entitled to a social and international order in which the rights and freedoms set forth in this Declaration can be fully realized.

In the subsequent development of international human rights law and practice in a series of general comments, the Committee on Economic, Social and Cultural Rights has expounded on the duty to respect, protect, and fulfil particular rights in the Covenant on Economic, Social and Cultural Rights and on violations of these obligations. In General Comment No. 14, for example, dealing with the right to the highest attainable standard of health,[27] the Committee reaffirmed what it had stated in General Comment No. 3[28] that states parties had a core obligation to ensure the satisfaction of, at the very least, minimum essential levels of each of the rights contained in the Covenant, including essential primary health care. The Committee proceeded to deal with violations of the obligations to respect, to protect, and to fulfil in the following terms:

- Violations of the obligation to respect: Violations of the obligation to respect are those State actions, policies or laws that contravene the standards set out in article 12 of the Covenant and are likely to result in bodily harm, unnecessary morbidity and preventable mortality.
- Violations of the obligation to protect: Violations of the obligation to protect follow from the failure to take all necessary measures to safeguard persons within their jurisdiction from infringements of the right to health by third parties.
- Violations of the obligation to fulfill: Violations of the obligation to fulfill occur through the failure of States parties to take all necessary steps to ensure the realization of the right to health.[29]

The violations approach should also be made applicable to the national implementation of the right to development. It is at the national level that the right to development must take on meaning and practical application. International cooperation and assistance are important. But even with them, action must still take place nationally. In this chapter we have sought to indicate concrete areas where national action is needed and is indeed obligatory if the right to development is to count for the peoples of the world. In the next section, we look at the regional dimensions of the right to development.

Right to Development

These enunciations of the UDHR and subsequent law surrounding the ICESCR have informed the advancement of a right to development, which had been championed by developing states, including Asian members of the UN. Asian States attached particular importance to the adoption and implementation of the International Covenant on Economic, Social and Cultural Rights. An examination of the substantive articles of the Covenant shows the concept of development performing six roles. First, development comes closest to being recognized as a right in Article 11 of the Covenant, which refers to the right of everyone to an adequate standard of living "and to the continuous improvement of living conditions." The Covenant follows a deliberate scheme in which many articles define the right recognized and then proceed to indicate the steps to be taken, nationally and internationally, with a view to promoting the realization of an element of the right of everyone to an adequate standard of living.

Second, development is cast, in some instances, as a derivative of a recognized right. This is the case, for example, in Article 1 of the Covenant, dealing with the right to self-determination. After stating that all peoples have the right to self-determination, the article proceeds to add that by "virtue of that right" they fully pursue their economic, social, and cultural development.

Third, development is in some instances cast in the role of a goal to be pursued in going about the realization of a right recognized in the Covenant. One may see this, for example, in Article 15 on the right to take part in cultural life. This article specifies that the steps to be taken by the states parties to the Covenant shall include "the development and the diffusion of science and culture." Another example is Article 13, paragraph 2(e), which includes, among the steps to be taken to implement the right of everyone to education, "the development of a system of schools at all levels."

Fourth, in some instances, development is cast in the role of a guide in the implementation of a right recognized in the Covenant. For example, Article 12 on the right to the enjoyment of the highest attainable standard of physical and mental conditions requires states parties to take steps "for the healthy development of the child." Likewise, Article 13, after recognizing the right of everyone to education, adds that "education shall be directed to the full development of the human personality." One might have thought that this element, namely, the "full development of the human personality" should have featured explicitly in the core definition of the right to development contained in the Declaration adopted by the United Nations General Assembly in 1986.

Fifth, the concept of development also finds itself in the Covenant as a means for enabling the realization of rights recognized in the Covenant. One sees this, for example, in Article 6, which recognizes the right to work and then specifies that the steps to be taken by the state party to achieve full realization of this right should include "policies and techniques to achieve steady economic, social and cultural development." One also sees this in Article 11, paragraph 2 (a) which refers to "the need for developing or reforming agrarian systems in such a way so as to achieve the most efficient development and utilization of natural resources."

Sixth, one sees the concept of development being employed as a factor which may be taken into account in determining the extent of the obligations of a state party to guarantee economic rights recognized in the Covenants to non-nationals.

The abovementioned instances of the utilization of the concept of development indicate that the Asian drafters of the Covenant definitely had at the forefront of their minds development issues when drafting the Covenant. However, they did not consider it necessary, at that stage, to include expressly the right to development. This has now been done in the Declaration on the right to development and at the World Conference on Human Rights (1993).

This development at the World Conference drew on the UN General Assembly adopted a Declaration on the Right to Development in December 1986, which considered that "under the provisions of the Universal Declaration of Human Rights everyone is entitled to a social and international order in which the rights and freedoms set forth in that Declaration can be fully realized." The right to development is simultaneously of great importance to the suffering masses of the world. The UN Declaration on the Right to Development (1987) affirmed in its Article 1(1) that:

> the right to development is an inalienable human right by virtue of which every human person and all peoples are entitled to participate in, contribute to, and enjoy economic, social, cultural and political development, in which all human rights and fundamental freedoms can be fully be realized.

Article 8, added that:

1. States should undertake, at the national level, all necessary measures for the realization of the right to development and shall ensure, inter alia, equality of opportunity for all in their access to basic resources, education, health services, food, housing, employment and the fair distribution of income. Effective measures should be undertaken to ensure that women have an active role in the development process. Appropriate economic and social reforms should be made with a view to eradicating all social injustices.

   States should encourage popular participation in all spheres as an important factor in development and in the full realization of all human rights.

Article 9 of the Declaration on the Right to Development adopted by the GA in 1986[30] states that all the aspects of the right to development set forth in the Declaration are indivisible and interdependent and each of them should be considered in the context of the whole.[31] Is an "aspect" the same as an "element of the definition" of a right? The content of the Declaration may help to answer this question. The nearest that the Declaration comes to providing a definition of the right to development is in Article 1(1) which states that: "the right to development is an inalienable human right by virtue of which every human person and all peoples are entitled to participate in, contribute to, and enjoy economic, social, cultural and political development, in which all human rights and fundamental freedoms can be fully be realized." One could possibly include as definitional elements also Article 8, which provided that:

1. States should undertake, at the national level, all necessary measures for the realization of the right to development and shall ensure, inter alia, equality of opportunity for all in their access to basic resources, education, health services, food, housing, employment and the fair distribution of income. Effective measures should be undertaken to ensure that women have an active role in the development process.

Appropriate economic and social reforms should be made with a view to eradicating all social injustices.

2. States should encourage popular participation in all spheres as an important factor in development and in the full realization of all human rights.

The remaining articles of the Declaration proceed to make a number of statements that serve different purposes. There are collateral statements such as the one in Article 6(2) that all human rights and fundamental freedoms are indivisible and interdependent. It identifies the subjects and beneficiaries of the right to development in Article 1(1), which refers to the right to development as one by virtue of which "every person and all peoples are entitled(…)." Article 2(1) specifies that the human person is the central subject of development and should be the active participant and beneficiary of the right to development. Paragraph 3 of the same article adds that states have the right and the duty to formulate appropriate national development policies. The possible subjects and beneficiaries are therefore the individual, the state, and all peoples.

The Declaration states what the right to development implies. Article 1 paragraph 2 states that the right to development implies the full realization of the right of peoples to self-determination (as was seen above, development is cast, in Article 1 of ICESCR as a derivative of the right to self-determination). It indicates what the right to development requires. This is mentioned in places such as Article 3(2) which states that the right to development requires full respect for the principles of international law concerning friendly relations and cooperation among states. Article 4(2) adds that sustained action is required to promote more rapid development of developing countries. As a complement, effective international cooperation is also essential.

The Declaration indicates responsibilities. Article 2(2) states that all human beings have a responsibility for development. Article 3 (1) adds that states have the primary responsibility for the creation of national and international conditions favourable to the realization of the right to development. It also indicates duties of the subjects and beneficiaries of the right to development, namely: in Article 2(2) that individuals should promote and protect an appropriate political, social, and economic order for development; Article 2(3), states have the right and duty to formulate appropriate national development policies; Article 3(3), states have the duty to cooperate with each other in ensuring development and eliminating obstacles to development; Article 4, states have the duty to take steps, individually and collectively, to formulate international development policies with a view to facilitating the full realization of the right to development. Sustained action is required to promote more rapid development of developing countries. Effective international cooperation is essential: Article 5, states shall take resolute steps to eliminate massive and flagrant violations of human rights; Article 6, all states should cooperate with a view to promoting, encouraging, and strengthening universal respect for and observance of all human rights and fundamental freedoms; states should take steps to eliminate obstacles to development resulting from failure to observe civil and political rights as well as economic, social, and cultural rights; Article 7, all states should promote the establishment, maintenance, and strengthening of international peace and security; Article 8, states should undertake, at the national level, all necessary measures for the realization of the right to development. States should encourage popular participation in all spheres as an important factor in development and in the full realization of all human rights; Article 10, steps should be taken to ensure the full exercise and progressive enhancement of the right to development.

Although all of the abovementioned "aspects" are contained in a document entitled "Declaration on the Right to Development," they surely cannot all be part of the definition of the right to development. The elements that seem to be new, the normative statements that appear to have been added to the prior stock of human rights norms, are in Article 1, paragraph 1, which rests on the notions of participation in, contribution to, and enjoyment of development. The Declaration adds or consolidates a specific new right. ("The right to development is an inalienable human right by virtue of which every human person and all peoples are entitled to participate in, contribute to, and enjoy economic, social, cultural and political development, in which all human rights and fundamental freedoms can be fully realized.") This is the first time that such an explicit statement has been made in an authoritative international instrument.

The Declaration insists that development has to be of such a nature that "all human rights and fundamental freedoms can be fully realized." This point is further emphasized in Articles 5 and 6. In other words, when there is gross violation of human rights and fundamental freedoms, development is vitiated.

The Declaration insists on the indivisibility and interdependence of all human rights. It urges full respect for principles of international law and calls upon all states to promote the establishment, maintenance, and strengthening of international peace and security. These are essentially statements about inter-relationships and inter-linkages. The right to development cannot therefore be considered what some claim that it is: namely, a "synthesis right" encompassing, englobing, and subsuming other rights. Peace, disarmament, respect for human rights, and fundamental freedoms are required for development to take place. They are not, however, miraculously subsumed in an overarching right, "the right to development."

Development is conceptually employed in the Declaration in the following senses: more narrowly in the legal sense of a right (Article 1(1)), broadly as a goal, relatively as a guide, and practically as a means. The first sense (a new right) represents an advance upon the ICESCR which does not contain a specific affirmation of the right to development although there may be some traces of the notion in the Covenant. The Declaration on the Right to Development and the International Covenant also cover very much similar ground in calling for national and international measures for the realization of economic, social, and cultural rights.

Professor Oscar Schachter, one of the greatest international lawyers of the twentieth century, writing in 1992 on the implementation of the right to development, argued that the concentrated target of implementation should be alleviation of the mass poverty and the plight of vulnerable peoples. "In the state of the world today," he submitted, "mass poverty and deprivation require international action in more massive and sustained way than ever before."[32] He put forward a programme of action that included the following: mitigating the social costs of adjustment and privatization, monitoring of human needs, country reports to international agencies on measures to alleviate poverty, enhancing the "Constructive Dialogues" under the ICESCR, measures to encourage environmentally sustainable development, and measures to improve the condition of women in developing countries.

Sadly, international efforts on implementation of the right to development would not focus on practical issues such as these but, would, rather, concentrate on the issue of transfer of resources and technology from the rich to the poor countries. It is with some justification that Yash Ghai has written:

> The right to development has had remarkably little impact on constitutional lawyers, political scientists, or human rights activists. It has remained, with negative consequences, where it germinated, within the provenance of diplomats and international lawyers. It has become the focus of contention

> between diplomats of the North and the South, generating more heat than light. The North suspects, perhaps correctly, that the South wants to use the right to development to extract resources from the North and has no intention of implementing the domestic obligations expressed in the right to development. The South may think that the lukewarm, if not outright negative, attitude on the part of the west, toward the right to development is a manifestation of bad intentions – the North's determination to preserve the present unequal economic and political order and the libertarian resistance to the social justice agenda of the right to development.
>
> …
>
> In order to explore and exploit the potential of the right to development, it is necessary to locate it within the domain of national politics and constitutions. It is surprising that almost no attempt has been made at this approach….I believe that significant further intellectual developments of the concept and implications of the right to development can occur only when the right to development is related to the domestic obligations of the state and to the design of its institutions. I also believe that real gains for the people from the right to development will take place only when it is implemented in the laws and institutions of individual states – for the impact of assistance from the North, however generous, will (be) *sic* limited as well as problematic.[33]

Prof. Ghai's arguments are compelling and the need for national implementation is considered next.

An Indian UN Independent Expert on the Right to Development, the late Professor Arjun Sengupta, in a series of reports to the then UN Commission on Human Rights, argued that the right to development was, inter alia, the right to a process of development.[34] In different reports, he distinguished between the right to development, human development, human rights and development, and the human rights approach to development. He insisted that the human rights approach to development was not the same as realizing the right to development—even though at times he himself seemed to use these terms interchangeably. But his idea of the right to development as the right to a process of development is an important one and bears exploration.

In a report dated 27 July 1999, he submitted, basing himself on the language of the UN Declaration on the Right to Development, that "the right to development is that human right by virtue of which 'every human person and all peoples' are entitled to 'participate in, contribute to and enjoy' that process of development."[35] Striving to give content to the right to development as a process, he argued that:

> (I)t is basically centered around the concept of equity and justice, with the majority of the population who are currently poor and deprived to be brought upwards in their living standards and capacity to improve their position. It also implies that the well-being of 'the entire population' is to be improved. The concept of well being in that context extends well beyond the conventional notions of economic growth to the expansion of opportunities and capabilities to enjoy those opportunities.[36]

In a report to the UN General Assembly on 17 August 2000, he returned to the theme of the right to development as the right to a process and submitted that "It is only a process of development in which all human rights and fundamental freedoms can be fully realized which can be the entitlement of every human person as universal human right."[37]

He added that the process of development was one which, according to the language of the UN Declaration, would seek "the constant improvement of the well being of the entire population and of all individuals, on the basis of their actions, free and meaningful participation in development, and in the fair distribution of the benefits resulting there from." Furthermore, realizing the right to development would ensure equality of opportunity for all in their access to basic resources, education, health services, food, housing, employment, and the fair distribution of income as well as appropriate economic and social reforms and the eradication of all social injustices. Women should have an active role in the development process. He again reiterated that the concept of a process of development was rooted in the realization of the principles of equity and social justice.[38]

As he had done in his 1999 report, he again insisted in his 2000 report to the General Assembly that "one of the benefits of using a human rights approach to development is that it focuses attention on those who lag behind others in enjoying their rights and requires that positive actions be taken on their behalf."[39] One may note that he was using a human rights approach to development interchangeably with the right to development.

The Independent Expert emphasized that poverty reduction was the most important contribution that could be made to the improvement of equity and justice. The right to development, viewed as a right to a process, would require looking at the elements that contribute to the dynamics of sustained poverty reduction and human development. GDP, education, and health, the three basic variables in the human development indices, would also be the three most important variables for the sustained reduction of poverty and realization of the right to development as a process of development.[40] The right to development, he continued, was the right to a process that expands the capabilities or freedom of individuals to improve their well-being and to realize what they value.[41]

In other reports the Independent Expert provided additional elements on the content of the right to development as a process. He noted that the primary responsibility for implementing the right to development belonged to the nation-state. In order to fulfil these obligations, all levels of government and public sector organizations must coordinate their actions.[42] National actions should be aimed at the implementation of each of the constituent rights of the right to development individually as well as in combination with each other and as a part of the development process.

A right to development approach in a development programme, he continued, would be concerned with the most efficient provision of goods and services and changes in the institutions and social arrangements to realize a set of targeted objectives as human rights, identified as expansion of capabilities and freedoms. It would be concerned with the increase of both the availability of, and the access to, those goods and services. It would entail a programme aimed at the eradication of poverty. The principle of equality would be essential to any programme aimed at implementing the right to development. The principle of non-discrimination was fundamental. Preventive measures would be crucial. Measures to bring up those who lagged behind should be accorded priority. Legislative and constitutional changes would be required. The role of women must be highlighted, and NGOs could play a role in the realization of the right to development at the national level.

The Independent Expert, a macro-economist, made a valiant effort, in good faith, to give content to the notion of the right to development as a process of development. It is not readily apparent that he succeeded but, nevertheless, his advocacy of the concept of the right to development as a process was important and each country would indeed need to demonstrate that it had in place a process of development that conformed to the requirements of the UN Declaration. Professor Yash Ghai came near to the mark when he observed, "It is…my belief…that a national-oriented analysis of the right to development and modalities for its implementation will alert us to the dynamics of the right to development and political difficulties inherent in it."[43]

Democracy

The UDHR proudly proclaims that the will of the people shall be the basis of the authority of governments. The Vienna Declaration and Programme of Action of 1993 recognized "that democracy, development and respect for human rights and fundamental freedoms are interdependent and mutually reinforcing."[44] Indeed democracy, human rights, and the rule of law are inseparable in order to achieve a life of dignity for all.

On 16 September 1997, the Council of the Inter-Parliamentary Union, meeting in Cairo, adopted a Universal Declaration on Democracy in which it expressed its conviction that the strengthening of the democratization process and representative institutions would greatly contribute to the achievement of peace and development in the world. The Universal Declaration contained principles of democracy, the elements of democratic government, and the international dimension of democracy.

On the principles of democracy, the Declaration on Democracy stated that democracy is a universally recognized ideal as well as a goal, which is based on common values held by peoples throughout the world community irrespective of cultural, political, social, and economic differences. It is thus a basic right of citizenship to be exercised under conditions of freedom, equality, transparency, and responsibility, with due respect for the plurality of views, and in the interest of the polity.

Democracy, the Declaration continued, is both an ideal to be pursued and a mode of government to be applied according to modalities which reflect the diversity of experiences and cultural particularities without derogating from internationally recognized principles, norms, and standards. It is thus a constantly perfected and always perfectible state or condition whose progress will depend upon a variety of political, social, economic, and cultural factors.

As an ideal, democracy aims essentially to preserve and promote the dignity and fundamental rights of the individual, to achieve social justice, foster the economic and social development of the community, strengthen the cohesion of society, and enhance national tranquillity, as well as to create a climate that is favourable for international peace. As a form of government, democracy is the best way of achieving these objectives; it is also the only political system that has the capacity for self-correction.

The achievement of democracy presupposed a genuine partnership between men and women in the conduct of the affairs of society between men and women in the conduct of the affairs of society in which they work in equality and complementarity, drawing mutual enrichment from their differences.

A state of democracy ensured that the processes by which power is acceded to, wielded and alternates allow for free political competition and are the product of open, free and non-discriminatory participation by the people, exercised in accordance with the rule of law, in both letter and spirit.

Democracy was inseparable from international human rights. Those rights must therefore be applied effectively, and their proper exercise must be matched with individual and collective responsibilities. Democracy was founded on the primacy of the law and the exercise of human rights. In a democratic state, no one is above the law and all are equal before the law. Peace and economic, social and cultural development were both conditions for and fruits of democracy. There was thus interdependence between peace, development, respect for and observance of the rule of law and human rights.

On the elements and exercise of democratic government, the Declaration added that democracy was based on the existence of well-structured and well-functioning institutions, as well as on a body of standards and rules and on the will of society as a whole, fully conversant with its rights and responsibilities. It was for democratic institutions to mediate tensions and maintain equilibrium between the competing claims of diversity and uniformity, individuality, and collectivity, in order to enhance social cohesion and solidarity.

Furthermore, democracy was founded on the right of everyone to take part in the management of public affairs; it therefore requires the existence of representative institutions at all levels and, in particular, a parliament in which all components of society are represented and which has the requisite powers and means to express the will of the people by legislating and overseeing government action.

The key element in the exercise of democracy was the holding of free and fair elections at regular intervals enabling the people's will to be expressed. These elections must be held on the basis of universal, equal and secret suffrage so that all voters can choose their representatives in conditions of equality, openness and transparency that stimulate political competition. To that end, civil and political rights are essential, and more particularly among them, the rights to vote and to be elected, the rights to freedom of expression and assembly, access to information and the right to organize political parties and carry out political activities. Party organization, activities, finances, funding and ethics must be properly regulated in an impartial manner in order to ensure the integrity of the democratic processes.

It was an essential function of the state to ensure the enjoyment of civil, cultural, economic, political, and social rights to its citizens. Democracy thus goes hand in hand with an effective, honest, and transparent government, freely chosen and accountable for its management of public affairs.

Public accountability, which was essential to democracy, applied to all those who held public authority, whether elected or non-elected, and to all bodies of public authority without exception. Accountability entails a public right of access to information about the activities of government, the right to petition government and to seek redress through impartial administrative and judicial mechanisms.

Public life as a whole must be stamped by a sense of ethics and by transparency, and appropriate norms and procedures must be established to uphold them. Individual participation in democratic processes and public life at all levels must be regulated fairly and impartially and must avoid any discrimination, as well as the risk of intimidation by state and non-state actors.

Judicial institutions and independent, impartial, and effective oversight mechanisms are the guarantors for the rule of law on which democracy is founded. In order for these institutions and mechanisms fully to ensure respect for the rules, improve the fairness of the processes, and redress injustices, there must be access by all to administrative and judicial remedies on the basis of equality as well as respect for administrative and judicial decisions both by the organs of the state and representatives of public authority and by each member of society.

While the existence of an active civil society was an essential element of democracy, the capacity and willingness of individuals to participate in democratic processes and make governance choices could not be taken for granted. It was therefore necessary to develop conditions conducive to the genuine exercise of participatory rights, while also eliminating obstacles that prevent, hinder or inhibit this exercise. It was therefore indispensable to ensure the permanent enhancement of, inter alia, equality, transparency, and education and to remove obstacles such as ignorance, intolerance, apathy, the lack of genuine choices and alternatives, and the absence of measures designed to redress imbalances or discrimination of social, cultural, religious, and racial nature, or for reasons of gender.

A sustained state of democracy thus required a democratic climate and culture constantly nurtured and reinforced by education and other vehicles of culture and information. Hence, a democratic society must be committed to education in the broadest sense of the term, a more particularly civic education and the shaping of a responsible citizenry.

Democratic process was fostered by a favourable economic environment; therefore, in its overall effort for development, society must be committed to satisfying the basic economic needs of the most disadvantaged, thus ensuring their full integration in the democratic process. The state of democracy presupposed freedom of opinion and expression; this right implies freedom to hold opinions without interference and to seek, receive, and impart information and ideas through any media and regardless of frontiers.

The institutions and processes of democracy must accommodate the participation of all people in homogenous as well as heterogeneous societies in order to safeguard diversity, pluralism and the right to be different in a climate of tolerance. Democratic institutions and processes must also foster decentralized local and regional government and administration, which is a right and a necessity, and which makes it possible to broaden the base of public participation.[45]

Rule of Law

Ever since its inception, the International Commission of Jurists has elaborated a series of principles that provided guidance on the practical meaning of the rule of law. These included the following:

Essential Requirements of a Society Under the Rule of Law:

- The legislative power must be effectively exercised by an appropriate organ, freely elected by the citizens. The laws and other legal measures taken by the legislative cannot be abolished or restricted by a governmental measure.
- The Rule of Law can only reach its highest expression and fullest realization under representative government. By representative government is meant a government deriving its power and authority from the people, which power and authority are exercised through representatives freely chosen and responsible to them. Free periodic elections are therefore important to representative government.

The Legislature and the Rule of Law

- The function of the legislature in a free society under the Rule of Law is to create and maintain the conditions which will uphold the dignity of the human being as an individual. This dignity requires not only the recognition of his or her civil and political rights but also the establishment of the social, economic, educational and cultural conditions which are essential to the full development of his personality. Every legislature in a free society under the Rule of Law should endeavour to give full effect to the principles enunciated in the Universal Declaration of Human Rights.

The Executive and the Rule of Law

- In general, the acts of the executive which directly and injuriously affect the person or property or rights of the individual should be subject to review by the courts.
- It will further the Rule of Law if the executive is required to formulate its reasons when reaching its decisions of a judicial or administrative character and affecting the rights of individuals and at the request of a party concerned to communicate them to him.

The Criminal Process and the Rule of Law

- It is always important that the definition and interpretation of the law should be as certain as possible, and this is of particular importance in the case of the criminal law, where the citizen's life or liberty may be at stake.

The Judiciary and the Rule of Law

- An independent judiciary is an indispensable requisite of a free society under the Rule of Law.

The Legal Profession and the Rule of Law

- It is essential to the maintenance of the Rule of Law that there should be an organized legal profession free to manage its own affairs. But it is recognized that there may be general supervision by the courts and that there may be regulations governing the admission to and pursuit of the legal profession.

- Lawyers should refuse to collaborate with any authority in any action which violates the Rule of Law. Lawyers should endeavour to promote knowledge of and to inspire respect for the Rule of Law, and an appreciation by all people of their rights under the law.

Economic and Social Development

- It is essential to economic and social development to overcome inequality arising from birth or wealth and discrimination.

Equality and Non-discrimination

At the very outset of the full Commission on Human Rights, when it began its deliberations, Mrs. Hansa Mehta of India raised the problem of discrimination in forthright terms: Mehta declared that the government and people of India attached the greatest importance to the Human Rights Commission and considered that it work would profoundly influence the future of the United Nations.[46] She recalled that the Government of South Africa had maintained the position during recent discussions that there had been no violation of human rights in South Africa since there existed no written definition of human rights as such within the framework of the United Nations. The Government of the United Kingdom had taken a similar attitude by suggesting that the dispute between India and South Africa might be referred to the International Court of Justice. Mrs. Mehta considered it the justification of the Commission that pleas of this nature should not be allowed to be advanced within the forum of the United Nations in the future.

The Representative of India pointed out that her country faced a problem of exceptional magnitude for reasons beyond its control: during the past one hundred years, four million Indians had been transplanted to various parts of the world under the aegis of the colonial governments concerned, and were now residing abroad in special communities, created at the request and for the benefit of those governments. As a result of this transplantation, numerous cases of denials of rights in law and equality and complicated questions of nationality and citizenship had arisen, due to certain administrative practices on the part of the governments concerned. Such problems had to be solved within the meaning of the terms of reference of the Commission on Human Rights and the principles of the Charter.

The Representative of India considered that an effort should be made to define in precise legal terminology the terms “discrimination” and “minority.” It was also necessary to define what specific safeguards should be incorporated in the proposed bill of rights against the dangers of assimilation. Moreover, the Commission on Human Rights should compile a list from every country in the world of legal and administrative measures tending to decrease human rights within the meaning of the principles of the Charter. The most important consideration before the Commission should not be merely the enunciation of principles in terms of a bill of human rights, but the improvisation of adequate machinery to implement those principles. In fact, the proposed bill of human rights would be meaningless unless an unequivocal definition were given of the relationship which ought to exist between the individual, the community, the state, and the international organization.[47]

During the drafting of the Universal Declaration, India tabled a draft declaration that included the following statement: “Every human being has the right of equality, without distinction of race, sex, language, religion, nationality or political belief.”[15] Mrs. Mehta, at the very first meeting of the Commission, had supported the position that when discussing the proposed bill of rights, the status of women would have to be considered in cooperation with the Commission on the Status of Women. General Romulo of the Philippine Republic affirmed that the status of women was an integral part of whatever bill of rights would be discussed.[48]

General Carlos Romulo would recall later in his memoirs:

> At one point, while we were writing the Declaration of Human Rights the Russians proposed a provision against racial discrimination. And I can understand the feelings of Mrs Roosevelt representing a government that was divided by the serious problem of racism, and having, I suppose, received instructions from Washington. She had to act in a manner that was, I am sure, contrary to her own personal feelings. When the Russian began to speak on their proposal, Mrs Roosevelt sent her adviser James P. Hendrick to me and he whispered to me ‘Mrs Roosevelt would like to suggest if it is possible for you to answer the Russians and be against their proposal.
>
> Unfortunately, I could not. I was convinced that the Russian proposal was the correct proposal. I had studied it the night before. I had discussed it with my advisers, and we decided to take a stand in favour of the Russian

proposal. So I whispered to Mr Hendrick, 'Please tell Mrs Roosevelt I'm very sorry but we've taken a different stand on this question. We are writing a declaration not for today but for all ages, not for Alabama or Tennessee or Kentucky, but for the entire world, and so please tell her that I regret that I will have to defend and support the proposal'.

So he left me and went around the table and whispered to Mrs Roosevelt and suddenly I saw Mrs Roosevelt look at me and motion to me, 'Okay, okay'[49]

The inherent dignity and the "equal and inalienable rights of all members of the human family" were recognized in the UDHR's opening lines as the "foundation of freedom, justice and peace in the world." The claim to equality, the late Sir Hersch Lauterpacht held, "is in a substantial sense the most fundamental of the rights of man. It occupies the first place in most written constitutions. It is the starting point of all other liberties."[50]

The prohibition of discrimination has become a norm of positive law, as has been recognized by the International Court of Justice which has declared that to establish and to enforce distinction, exclusions, restrictions, and limitations exclusively based on grounds of race, colour, descent, or national or ethnic origin which constitute a denial of fundamental human rights is a flagrant violation of the purposes and principles of the Charter.[51]

When both covenants were being drafted, it was accepted that prohibiting discrimination or distinction does not preclude positive measures taken in favour of disadvantaged groups. When Article 26 of the Covenant on Civil and Political Rights was being written, it was recognized that "the word, 'discrimination' … was used … in a negative sense only, to mean a distinction of an unfavorable kind."[52] Similarly, it was said that the word "discrimination" "conveyed the idea of a distinction made without any objective basis."[53] The representatives of Chile, the Netherlands, and Uruguay pointed out that equality did not mean identity of treatment.

During discussions on the International Covenant on Economic, Social and Cultural Rights in 1962, the Indian representative pointed out that implementing non-discrimination raised certain problems, such as in the case of certain groups in under-developed countries. Thus, it was suggested that the committee add an article reading: "Special measures for the advancement of any socially and educationally backward sections of society shall not be construed as distinctions under this article."[12] The committee endorsed the point made by the Indian representative,[13] and the position adopted by the Third Committee followed that also made by the World Court in a case regarding minority schools in Albania.[14]

With regard to the rights of women, an authoritative General Comment 16 of the Committee on ESCRs has stated that the equal right of men and women to the enjoyment of all human rights "is one of the fundamental principles recognized under international law and enshrined in the main international human rights instruments." The Comment continues: "The travaux préparatoires state that article 3 was included in the Covenant, as well as in ICCPR, to indicate that beyond a prohibition of discrimination, "the same rights should be expressly recognized for men and women on an equal footing and suitable measures should be taken to ensure that women had the opportunity to exercise their rights…."[54] The essence of Article 3 of ICESCR is that the rights set forth in the Covenant are to be enjoyed by men and women on a basis of equality, a concept that carries substantive meaning. While expressions of formal equality may be found in constitutional provisions, legislation, and policies of governments, Article 3 also mandates the equal enjoyment of the rights in the Covenant for men and women in practice.[55] The principle of non-discrimination is the corollary of the principle of equality. Subject to what is stated in paragraph 15 below on temporary special measures, it prohibits differential treatment of a person or group of persons based on his/her or their particular status or situation, such as race, colour, sex, language, religion, political and other opinion, national or social origin, property, birth, or other status, such as age, ethnicity, disability, marital, refugee, or migrant status.[56] Gender-based and any other form of discrimination in relation to the rights to work and to housing, essential elements of a life of dignity, are also prohibited under international law.[57]

Ensuring a Life of Dignity

The pursuit of a life dignity across has yielded some good progress as evidenced by the economic growth and development of China, Japan, Malaysia, Singapore, South Korea, and Thailand. India has also made important strides. In nearly all, however, democracy and the rule of law remain aspirations. How did Asian countries seek to give effect to the principles of human dignity and equitable life chances?

In declaring a new humanism, after the "myopia" of the previous 150 years,[58] P.C. Chang indirectly called attention to the magnitude of the task of ensuring a life of dignity. He pointed out that human rights were too large a concept for one [42] commission and that all other organs of the United Nations were concerned with the carrying out of this concept. This foreshadowed the concerted multilateral effort envisioned under the Millennium Development Goals (MDGs) of 2000 and the successor Sustainable Development Goals (SDGS) of 2015.

In successive policy documents, the United Nations has sought to set development goals and pursue development strategies for tackling the massive economic and social problems, particularly extreme poverty, facing two thirds of the world's population. In the Millennium Declaration adopted on 8 September 2000, United Nations Heads of State and Government reaffirmed their commitment to the purposes and principles of the United Nations Charter and expressed their determination to establish a just and lasting peace all over the world. In order to ensure that globalization became a positive force for all the world's peoples, they agreed, inter alia, as follows:

- That certain fundamental values to be essential to international relations in the twenty-first century including freedom, equality, solidarity, tolerance, respect for nature, and shared responsibility.
- To spare no effort "to free our fellow men, women and children from the abject and dehumanizing conditions of extreme poverty."
- To halve by the year 2015 the proportions of the world's people whose income was less than one dollar a day as well as the same proportion of people from hunger.
- To halve the proportion of people unable to reach or to afford safe drinking water.
- To ensure that children everywhere, boys and girls alike, would be able to complete a full course of primary schooling.
- To similar goals were in relation to the reduction of maternal mortality, tackling HIV/AIDS and malaria, and to improving the lives of slum dwellers.
- To protect the vulnerable and to protect and assist children and civilian populations that suffer disproportionately the consequences of natural disasters, genocide and armed conflicts, and other humanitarian emergencies.
- To strengthen the capacity of all their countries to implement the principles of democracy and respect for human rights, including minority rights.

- To strengthen cooperation between the United Nations and national parliaments and to give greater opportunities to the private sector, NGOs, and civil society to contribute to the realization of United Nations goals and programmes.
- To request the General Assembly to review the progress made in implementing the provisions of their declaration and asked the Secretary-General "to issue periodic reports" for consideration by the General Assembly and "as a basis for further action."[59]

The Millennium Development Goals (MDGs) were derived from the Millennium Declaration. Most of the goals and targets were set to be achieved by the year 2015 on the basis of the global situation during the 1990s. During that decade a number of global conferences had taken place, and the main objectives of the development agenda had been defined. The MDGs laid down eight goals to be achieved by the year 2015. Goal 8 called for a global partnership for development with the following targets: addressing the special needs of the least developed countries, landlocked countries, and small island developing states; developing further an open, rule-based, predictable, non-discriminatory trading and financial system; dealing comprehensively with developing countries' debt; in cooperation with developing countries, developing and implementing strategies for decent and productive work for youth; in cooperation with pharmaceutical companies, providing access to affordable essential drugs in developing countries; in cooperation with the private sector, making available the benefits of new technologies, especially information and communications to developing countries.

The MDGs were based more on partnership and cooperation rather than on right but they have been invoked by the developing countries in support of the implementation of the right to development, particularly the alleviation of extreme poverty. The concept of preventable poverty requires that in and for all countries there be monitoring of situations of extreme poverty and national strategies to tackle them. Regional and international assistance should be targeted to such situations as a matter of priority. There are national, regional, and international bodies that can help identify such situations and call for action to redress them. The Committee on Economic, Social and Cultural Rights can take the lead on this. The Human Rights Council's Special Rapporteur on Extreme Poverty can do likewise. UNDP, the World Bank, and regional development banks or institutions can also play a part. It surely must be fair to expect priority attention to be devoted to the alleviation of extreme poverty as issues of prevention, protection, and justice. Regional prevention mechanisms can also play their part.

The Millennium Development Goals were renewed and reinvigorated in the Sustainable Development Goals in 2015 for the period up to 2030.

The foregoing has shown the emphasis given since the establishment of the United Nations to the pursuit of development and to the implementation of economic, social, and cultural rights alongside civil and political rights. It is acknowledged that development is needed for the full flowering of human rights—as much as human rights are necessary for the full flowering of development.

The importance of development for human rights, and the need to integrate human rights in the development process have been emphasized ever since and there is nowadays much discussion of rights-based approaches to development as well as the role of human rights in poverty reduction strategies. But while related to, these are not the same as the right to development and we need to examine the pith and substance of the idea in view of the emphasis, but differing interpretations, given to it by developing and developed countries.

Asian countries belonging to the Non-Aligned Movement (NAM) have emphasized the importance and centrality of the right to development in the mandate of the UN Human Rights Council and have complained that, since the adoption of the Declaration on the Right to Development a quarter century ago, very little had been shown in terms of implementation of this right by the international community. In the current globalization context, the NAM underscored the lack of autonomy of developing countries as regards decision-making to formulate development policies suitable to their realities: unfair trade rules and practices that restricted market access and allowed for export subsidies; a decrease in and failure to comply with commitments to official development assistance; and transfer of technology and heavy debt burdens, as factors of permanent "decapitalization" of developing countries. Elaborating on the right to development, the NAM reaffirmed the duty of states to cooperate for the creation of conditions conducive to realizing the right to development. It called for cooperation that was not subject to conditionality and was not treated as charity.[60]

The European Union and associated countries, for their part, reaffirmed their "firm commitment to the realization of the right to development and underscored the primary responsibility of states for the promotion and protection of all human rights, including the right to development; their responsibility to create internal conditions favourable to their development, and to cooperate at an international level in eliminating obstacles to development."[61]

As could be seen from the foregoing, the developing countries emphasized the international dimensions of the right to development and have been firmly opposed to discussing the national dimensions. The developed countries, on the other hand, emphasized the internal dimensions and saw international cooperation as related to it. This difference could be seen in the outcome of the deliberations of the Working Group that year, whose report called for the elaboration and implementation of a comprehensive and coherent set of standards. The developing countries have been advocating the drafting and adoption of a convention on the right to development. The report of the Working Group explained that these standards "could take various forms, including guidelines on the implementation of the right to development, and evolve into a basis for consideration of an international legal standard of a binding nature, through a collaborative process of engagement." This was diplomatic language for a convention.

The Non-Aligned Movement made this clear in an explanation recorded in Annex III to the report: "The Non-Aligned Movement interprets the phrase 'international legal standard of a binding nature' contained in paragraph 52 of the conclusions and recommendations to mean 'internationally legally binding convention.'"[62] Canada recorded its opposition to this: Canada "does not believe it is appropriate for the Working Group or high-level task force to consider the development of a legally binding instrument."[63] The European Union and Australia made similar reservations.[64]

Conclusion

This chapter outlined Asian propositions on human dignity, equality, and non-discrimination in the drafting of the UDHR, as well as subsequent challenges in ensuring life of dignity. It remains to be seen whether Asian, and generally, developing countries that form the majority at the United Nations will press for the drafting and adoption of an international convention on the right to development. Questions that arise include: what will be included in such an instrument, to what extent it will be broadly supported, and how it will interpret the right to development. In the meantime, we are left to examine what could be considered the elements of the right to development as already spelled out in consensual international practice, namely, practice that has a wide degree of international support. The International Covenant on Economic, Social and Cultural Rights, which has been accepted as binding well over 150 states, the 1986 Declaration on the Right to Development, and the ambitious Sustainable Development Goals are documents that suggest themselves for examination.

Notes

1. E/HR/6 29 April 1946 Summary Record of Meetings [of the "Nuclear" Commission on Human Rights] First meeting held on Monday, 29 April 1946, at 3 p.m.
2. E/CN.4/AC.1/3 4 June 1947 in Schabas, p. 282. The Preamble shall refer to the four freedoms and to the provisions of the Charter relating to human rights and shall enunciate the following principles:

    1. that there can be no peace unless human rights and freedoms are respected;
    2. that man does not have rights only; he owes duties to the society of which he forms part;
    3. that man is a citizen both of his State and of the world;
    4. that there can be no human freedom or dignity unless war and the threat of war is abolished.

3. "Essentials of Peace", GA Res. 290(IV), OP 6.
4. E/CN.4/SR.7, 31 January 1947 Summary Record of the Seventh Meeting [of the Commission on Human Rights] Held at Lake Success, New York, on Friday, 31 January 1947, at 11:00 a.m.
5. E/CN.4/SR.7 31 January 1947, Summary Record of the Seventh Meeting [of the Commission on Human Rights] Held at Lake Success, New York, on Friday, 31 January 1947.
6. E/CN.4/11 31 January 1947, Draft of a Resolution for the General Assembly Submitted by the Representative of India.
7. E/SR.69, p. 5.
8. E/CN.4/SR.14 4 February 1947 Original Text: French Summary Record of the Fourteenth Meeting [of the Commission on Human Rights] Held at Lake Success, New York, on Tuesday, 4 February 1947 at 2:00 p.m.

9. E/CN.4/AC.1/SR.2 11 June 1947 160 Summary Record of the Second Meeting [of the Drafting Committee of the Commission on Human Rights] Held at Lake Success, New York, on Wednesday, 11 June 1947 at 11:00 a.m.
10. E/CN.4/132 14 June 1948 Lebanon: Suggested Preamble for the Draft International Declaration on Human Rights, Schabas p. 1870.
11. E/CN.4/AC.2/SR.2 5 December 1947 Original Text: French Summary Record of the Second Meeting [of the Working Group on the Declaration of Human Rights] Held at the Palais des Nations, Geneva, on Friday 5 December 1947, at 3 p.m.
12. E/SR.69, p. 5.
13. E/CN.4/SR.15, 5 February, 1947. (Schabas, 205).
14. E/CN.4/AC.1/SR.21 4 May 1948 Summary Record of the Twenty-First Meeting [of the Drafting Committee, Second Session] Held at Lake Success, 4 May 1948 at 10.30 a.m.
15. A/PV.139 23 September 1948 Verbatim Record of the One Hundred and Thirty-Ninth Meeting [of the General Assembly] Held at the Palais de Chaillot, Paris, on Thursday, 23 September 1948, at 10.30 a.m.
16. A/C.3/243 7 October 1948 Recapitulation of Amendments to Article 1 of the Draft Declaration (E/800)
17. A/C.3/SR.9624 7 October 1948 Summary Record of the Ninety-Sixth Meeting [of the Third Committee] Held at the Palais de Chaillot, Paris, on Thursday, 7 October 1948, at 10:30 a.m.
18. A/C.3/314/Rev.1* 20 November 1948 Recapitulation of Amendments to the Preamble of the Draft Declaration (E/800) (In the chronological order of their submission to the Committee)
19. See, for example, the American Federation of Labor's Draft International Bill of Human Rights proposed to the Commission.
20. E/CT.2/2 20 August 1946 Committee on Arrangements for Consultation with Non-Governmental Organizations, in Schabas, p. 71–77.
21. E/CN.4/W.4 13 January 1947, Working Paper on an International Bill of Rights, Schabas p. 109.
22. E/CN.4/AC.1/3/Add.2 9 June 1947 Plan of the Draft Outline of an International Bill of Rights (Prepared by the Secretariat), Schabas pp. 305–306.
23. E/CN.4/SR.14 4 February 1947 Original Text: French Summary Record of the Fourteenth Meeting [of the Commission on Human Rights] Held at Lake Success, New York, on Tuesday, 4 February 1947 at 2:00 p.m.
24. E/CN.0.4/SR 14, 4 February, 1947, (Schabas, 200).
25. E/CN.4/11 31 January 1947.
26. E/CN.4/AC.2/SR.7 9 December 1947 Summary Record of the Seventh Meeting [of the Working Group on the Declaration of Human Rights]

Held at the Palais des Nations, Geneva, at 3 p.m. on Tuesday, 9 December, 1947

27. CESCR General Comment No. 14: The Right to the Highest Attainable Standard of Health (Art. 12), E/C.12/2000/4, 11 August 2000. Available at https://www.ohchr.org/en/hrbodies/cescr/pages/cescrindex.aspx
28. CESCR, General Comment No.3, The nature of States parties' obligations, 1990. Available at https://www.ohchr.org/en/hrbodies/cescr/pages/cescrindex.aspx
29. HRI/GEN/1Rev.9, pp. 90–91. See similarly, p. 105 ff on violations of the right to water; pp. 116–117 and 121–122 violations of article 3 on equal rights between men and women; pp. 133–134 on violations of article 15; pp. 147–148, violations of the right to work.
30. A/RES/41/128, 4 December 1986.
31. See, generally, S.R. Chowdhury, M.G. Denters and P. J. de Waart Eds., *The Right to Development in International Law* (Dordrecht: Martinus Nijhoff Publishers, 1992); and P. De Waart, P. Peters and E Denters, eds., *International Law and Development* (Dordrecht, Martinus Nijhoff, 1988).
32. Oscar Schachter, "Implementing the right to development: programme of action," in S.R. Chowdhury, M.G. Denters and P. J. de Waart Eds., *The Right to Development in International Law* (Dordrecht: Martinus Nijhoff Publishers, 1992), pp. 27–30.
33. Yash Ghai, Redesigning the State for 'Right to Development', in Nobel Foundation, *The Right to Development.* Edited by B. Andreassen (Oslo....) 2006, pp. 140–141 (pp. 140–166).
34. See, generally, M. Salomon, "The Nature of a Rights: The Right to a Process in the Right to Development" in *Franciscans International, Geneva, The Right to Development. Reflections on the First Four Reports of the Independent Expert on the Right to Development* (2003), pp. 82–104.
35. E/CN.4/1999/WG.18/2, 27 July 1999, para. 37.
36. Ibid., para. 47.
37. A/55/306, para. 15.
38. Ibid. para. 16–17.
39. Ibid., para. 20.
40. Ibid., para. 21.
41. Ibid., para. 22. In this same paragraph the Independent Expert stated that "the process must be distinguished from the outcomes of the process." In the preceding footnote, he had written that "the human rights approach to development is not the same thing as realizing the right to development." In paragraph 24 of his report, he stated that "the right to development at as whole will also have to be realized in a rights-based manner that is transparent accountable, participatory and non-discriminatory as well as equitable and just."

42. E/CN.4/2002/WG.18/4, para. 18.
43. Ghai, op. cit., p. 141.
44. Ibid.
45. IPU, *Democracy: Its Principles and Achievement* (Geneva: IPU, 1998), iv–vii).
46. Second meeting of the Commission on Human Rights, 27 January, 1947; E/CN.4/SR.2, 27 January, 1947, p. 1. (Schabas pp. 161–162).
47. Second meeting of the Commission on Human Rights, 27 January, 1947; E/CN.4/SR.2, 27 January, 1947, p. 1. (Schabas pp. 161–162).
48. E/CN.4/SR.1, 27 January, 1947. (Schabas, 159).
49. Carlos P. Romulo with Beth Day Romulo, Forty Years. A Third World Soldier at the UN. New York, Greenwood Press, 1986, pp. 71–72.
50. Hersch Lauterpacht, An International Bill of the Rights of Man (Oxford: Oxford University Press, 2013), p. 115. (First published in 1945).
51. Bertrand Ramcharan, *Contemporary Human Rights Ideas: Rethinking theory and Practice* (London, New York: Routledge, 2015), p. 70. See also Steve Farrior, Equality and Non-Discrimination under International Law, Volume 2, (New York: Routledge, 2015).
52. Ibid., p. 75.
53. Ibid.
54. Committee on Economic, Social and Cultural Rights (CESCR), *General Comment No. 16: The Equal Right of Men and Women to the Enjoyment of All Economic, Social and Cultural Rights (Art. 3 of the Covenant)*, 11 August 2005, E/C.12/2005/4, para.2, Available at: http://www.refworld.org/docid/43f3067ae.html [accessed 20 May 2018].
55. Ibid., para.6.
56. Ibid., para 10.
57. See ICESCR, General Comments 4 and 18.
58. E/SR.69, pp. 7–9.
59. *Millennium Declaration*, adopted by Heads of State and Government at the United Nations General Assembly, 2000, para. 31.
60. Working Group on the Right to Development, A/HRC/4/47, 14 March 2007, para. 19.
61. Working Group on the Right to Development, A/HRC/4/47, 14 March 2007, para. 20.
62. Working Group on the Right to Development, A/HRC/4/47, 14 March 2007, para. 60.
63. Working Group on the Right to Development, A/HRC/4/47, 14 March 2007, paras. 61–62.
64. Working Group on the Right to Development, A/HRC/4/47, 14 March 2007, paras. 63–64.

References

Primary Documents: United Nations Documents from Drafting Process in William Schabas.

A/C.3/243 7 October 1948 Recapitulation of Amendments to Article 1 of the Draft Declaration (E/800).

A/C.3/314/Rev.1* 20 November 1948 Recapitulation of Amendments to the Preamble of the Draft Declaration (E/800) (In the chronological order of their submission to the Committee).

A/C.3/SR.9624 7 October 1948 Summary Record of the Ninety-Sixth Meeting [of the Third Committee] Held at the Palais de Chaillot, Paris, on Thursday, 7 October 1948, at 10:30 a.m.

A/PV.139 23 September 1948 Verbatim Record of the One Hundred and Thirty-Ninth Meeting [of the General Assembly] Held at the Palais de Chaillot, Paris, on Thursday, 23 September 1948, at 10.30 a.m.

E/CN.4/SR 14, 4 February, 1947, in Schabas, p. 200.

E/CN.4/11 31 January 1947a.

E/CN.4/11 31 January 1947b, Draft of a Resolution for the General Assembly Submitted by the Representative of India.

E/CN.4/132 14 June 1948 Lebanon: Suggested Preamble for the Draft International Declaration on Human Rights, Schabas p. 1870.

E/CN.4/AC.1/3 4 June 1947 in Schabas, p. 282.

E/CN.4/AC.1/3/Add.2 9 June 1947 Plan of the Draft Outline of an International Bill of Rights (Prepared by the Secretariat), Schabas pp. 305–306.

E/CN.4/AC.1/SR.2 11 June 1947 160 Summary Record of the Second Meeting [of the Drafting Committee of the Commission on Human Rights] Held at Lake Success, New York, on Wednesday, 11 June 1947 at 11:00 a.m.

E/CN.4/AC.1/SR.21 4 May 1948 Summary Record of the Twenty-First Meeting [of the Drafting Committee, Second Session] Held at Lake Success, 4 May 1948 at 10.30 a.m.

E/CN.4/AC.2/SR.2 5 December 1947 Original Text: French Summary Record of the Second Meeting [of the Working Group on the Declaration of Human Rights] Held at the Palais des Nations, Geneva, on Friday 5 December 1947, at 3 p.m.

E/CN.4/AC.2/SR.7 9 December 1947 Summary Record of the Seventh Meeting [of the Working Group on the Declaration of Human Rights] Held at the Palais des Nations, Geneva, at 3 p.m. on Tuesday, 9 December, 1947.

E/CN.4/SR.1, 27 January, 1947. in Schabas, p. 159.

E/CN.4/SR.14 4 February 1947a Original Text: French Summary Record of the Fourteenth Meeting [of the Commission on Human Rights] Held at Lake Success, New York, on Tuesday, 4 February 1947 at 2:00 p.m.

E/CN.4/SR.14 4 February 1947b Original Text: French Summary Record of the Fourteenth Meeting [of the Commission on Human Rights] Held at Lake Success, New York, on Tuesday, 4 February 1947 at 2:00 p.m.
E/CN.4/SR.15, 5 February, 1947. in Schabas, p. 205.
E/CN.4/SR.7 31 January 1947, Summary Record of the Seventh Meeting [of the Commission on Human Rights] Held at Lake Success, New York, on Friday, 31 January 1947.
E/CN.4/SR.7, 31 January 1947 Summary Record of the Seventh Meeting [of the Commission on Human Rights] Held at Lake Success, New York, on Friday, 31 January 1947, at 11:00 a.m.
E/CN.4/W.4 13 January 1947, Working Paper on an International Bill of Rights, Schabas p. 109.
E/CT.2/2 20 August 1946 Committee on Arrangements for Consultation with Non-Governmental Organizations, in Schabas, pp. 71–77.
E/HR/6 29 April 1946 Summary Record of Meetings [of the "Nuclear" Commission on Human Rights] First meeting held on Monday, 29 April 1946, at 3 p.m.
E/SR.69, p. 5.
E/SR.69, pp. 7–9.
E/CN.4/SR.2, Second meeting of the Commission on Human Rights, 27 January, 1947 in Schabas pp. 161–162.
Second meeting of the Commission on Human Rights, 27 January, 1947; E/CN.4/SR.2, 27 January, 1947, p. 1. in Schabas, pp. 161–162.
GA Res. 290(IV), "Essentials of Peace."

CESCR General Comment No. 14: The Right to the Highest Attainable Standard of Health (Art. 12), E/C.12/2000/4, 11 August 2000. Available at https://www.ohchr.org/en/hrbodies/cescr/pages/cescrindex.aspx

CESCR, General Comment No. 3, The nature of States parties' obligations, 1990. Available at https://www.ohchr.org/en/hrbodies/cescr/pages/cescrindex.aspx

Chowdhury, S.R, M.G. Denters and P. J. de Waart Eds., *The Right to Development in International Law* (Dordrecht: Martinus Nijhoff Publishers, 1992).

Committee on Economic, Social and Cultural Rights (CESCR), *General Comment No. 16: The Equal Right of Men and Women to the Enjoyment of All Economic, Social and Cultural Rights (Art. 3 of the Covenant)*, 11 August 2005, E/C.12/2005/4, para.2, Available at: http://www.refworld.org/docid/43f3067ae.html [accessed 20 May 2018].

Farrior, Steve, Equality and Non-Discrimination under International Law, Volume 2, (New York: Routledge, 2015).

Ghai, Yash, Redesigning the State for 'Right to Development', in Nobel Foundation, *The Right to Development*. Edited by B. Andreassen (Oslo....) 2006, pp. 140–141 (pp. 140–166).

IPU, *Democracy: Its Principles and Achievement* (Geneva: IPU, 1998), iv.–vii).
Lauterpacht, Hersch. *An International Bill of the Rights of Man* (Oxford: Oxford University Press, 2013), p. 115. (First published in 1945).
Millennium Declaration, adopted by Heads of State and Government at the United Nations General Assembly, 2000, para. 31.
Ramcharan, Bertrand G, *Contemporary Human Rights Ideas: Rethinking theory and Practice* (London, New York: Routledge, 2015), p. 70.
Romulo, Carlos P. and Beth Day Romulo, *Forty Years. A Third World Soldier at the UN.* (New York, Greenwood Press, 1986).
Salomon, M. "The Nature of a Rights: The Right to a Process in the Right to Development" in Franciscans International, Geneva, *The Right to Development. Reflections on the First Four Reports of the Independent Expert on the Right to. Development* (2003), pp. 82–104.
Schachter, Oscar "Implementing the right to development: programme of action", in S.R. Chowdhury, M.G. Denters and P. J. de Waart Eds., *The Right to Development in International Law* (Dordrecht: Martinus Nijhoff Publishers, 1992), pp. 27–30.
United Nations, A/55/306, para. 15.
United Nations, A/RES/41/128, 4 December 1986.
United Nations, E/CN.4/1999/WG.18/2, 27 July 1999, para.37.
United Nations, E/CN.4/2002/WG.18/4, para. 18.
United Nations, HRI/GEN/1Rev.9, pp 90–91.
de Waart, P Peters and E Denters, eds., *International Law and Development* (Dordrecht, Martinus Nijhoff, 1988).
Working Group on the Right to Development, A/HRC/4/47, 14 March 2007

CHAPTER 8

Implementation

Introduction

At the time of the drafting of the Universal Declaration, India, in particular, emphasized the importance of measures of implementation. The Declaration itself only contained the idea of human rights education, which we discuss in a later chapter. Implementation policies were left to be considered during the drafting of the International Covenant on Civil and Political Rights and the International Covenant on Economic, Social and Cultural Rights. The subject of implementation gave rise to contentious debates, and, in the end, the two covenants merely provided for reporting procedures and, in the case of the International Covenant on Civil and Political Rights, for optional individual complaints and optional state-to-state complaints. While the former has given rise to an impressive body of case law, the latter has never been used.

The Problem of Implementation

A Memorandum on Implementation Prepared by the Secretariat at the Request of the Committee [for the Drafting Committee of the International Bill of Human Rights of the Commission on Human Rights] drew the attention of the Committee to a resolution of the Economic and Social Council of 21 June 1946, which stated:

R. Ramcharan, B. Ramcharan, *Asia and the Drafting of the Universal Declaration of Human Rights*,
https://doi.org/10.1007/978-981-13-2104-7_8

> Considering that the purpose of the United Nations with regard to the promotion and observance of human rights, as defined in the Charter of the United Nations, can only be fulfilled if provisions are made for the implementation of human rights and of an international bill of rights, the Council requests the Commission on Human Rights to submit at an early date suggestions regarding the ways and means for the effective implementation of human rights and fundamental freedoms, with a view to assisting the Economic and Social Council in working out arrangements for such implementation with other appropriate organs of the United Nations.[1]

The Secretariat memorandum offered the following path forward for consideration. It suggested successive stages that are:

> (a) the establishment of the right of the General Assembly and other organs of the United Nations, including possibly the Commission on Human Rights, to discuss and make recommendations in regard to violations of the Bill;
> (b) the establishment of the right of individuals to petition the United Nations as means of initiating procedure for enforcement of human rights;
> (c) the establishment of a special organ of the United Nations with jurisdiction and the duty to supervise and enforce human rights *motu proprio*;
> (d) the establishment of jurisdiction in this organ to consider cases of suspension of the Bill of Rights, either in whole or in part;
> (e) the establishment of local agencies of the United Nations in the various countries with jurisdiction to supervise and enforce human [3] rights therein.

Asians would make substantial contributions to the discussion on implementation.

The Asian Quest for Implementation Machinery at the Time of the Drafting of the Universal Declaration

From the Secretariat outline of the Draft Declaration, it was clear to Malik at the second meeting of the Drafting Committee on 11 June 1947 that most countries already had provisions in their constitutions relating to fundamental human rights and the question was whether or not these rights and freedoms were implemented.[2]

On Thursday 5 December 1946, at the 42nd meeting of the Third Committee (Social and Humanitarian Committee), Mr. Sapru of India "considered that a simple declaration would not suffice. He stressed that it was necessary not only to make a declaration, but to ensure that the countries which had adopted it would put it into practice. The Charter of the United Nations affirmed this principle of human rights and freedom, but it seemed that certain countries did not yet conform to it."[3]

Later, speaking in the Commission on Human Rights, Mrs. Mehta (India) stressed that the delegation of India could not give its consent to a solution consisting merely in drafting a Declaration. It would like to see measures for its implementation included in the Declaration, such as those proposed by the Secretariat in Articles 47 and 48 of its Draft Declaration. The Delegation of India was in favour of a preliminary declaration followed by conventions, and would like the Commission before going further to take a formal decision regarding the form of the text it would draw up.[4]

At the first session of the Commission, Mrs. Mehta offered a draft of a General Act on implementation, which read as follows:

> The General Assembly,
>
> Recognizing the fact that the United Nations has been established for the specific purpose of enthroning the natural rights of man to freedom and equality before the law, and for upholding the worth and dignity of human personality;
>
> Having taken note of the Preamble and the relevant clauses of the United Nations Charter, the resolutions of the Economic and Social Council; the Human Rights Clauses of the Trusteeship Agreements as approved by the First Assembly of the United Nations; and the Human Rights Clauses of the European Treaties,
>
> Resolves that the following be incorporated into a General Act of the United Nations Assembly:
>
> 1. (a) Every human being is entitled to the right of liberty, including the right to personal freedom; freedom of worship; freedom of opinion; freedom of assembly and association; and the right to access to the United Nations, without risk of reprisal, wherever there is an actual or threatened infringement of human rights.
> (b) Every human being has the right of equality, without distinction of race, sex, language, religion, nationality or political belief.

(c) Every human being has the right of security, including the right to work, the right to education, the right to health, the right to participate in government, and the right to property, subject only to the over-riding consideration of public weal when the State or its appropriate organs acquire it after paying equitable compensation.

2. (a) This General Act is an obligation undertaken by Member States of the United Nations, and comes into force within twelve calendar months from the date on which it is passed by the United Nations Assembly.
(b) Non-self-governing areas and areas under the trusteeship of the United Nations automatically come under the regime of this Act.
Non-Member States are eligible to adhere to this Act. Nothing mentioned in this Act shall be construed as not obligating the individual to his corresponding duties to his own State and to the international community under the United Nations.
No state Member of the United Nations, non-self-governing territory, trusteeship area or non-member of the United Nations which has adhered to this Act, shall have the right to suspend it in whole or in part once it was adhered to in due form.
The Security Council of the United Nations shall be seized of all alleged violations of human rights, investigate them and enforce redress within the framework of the United Nations.[5]

Two meetings later, Mrs. Mehta (India) stressed that she desired to see the International Bill of Rights become part of both international and domestic law. Most of the fundamental human rights had been incorporated by her government in the constitution which had been formulated, and after ratification they would become part of the national law. She was of opinion that the Bill should be in the form of both a Declaration and a Convention. She agreed with Colonel Hodgson that the Declaration should contain nothing which would not be implemented and felt that an article or clause should be inserted, either in the Declaration or in the Preamble, to the effect that the rights therein set out were to be implemented by the member states of the United Nations. She felt that adequate machinery for implementation already existed in the International Court of Justice and was opposed to the idea of creating new machinery.[6]

Lebanon's proposal in June 1947, for a draft of the Preamble for the future Declaration called upon every individual and every organ of society, national and international, to strive by teaching and education to promote their respect and by progressive measures to secure their universal recognition and observance.

The Implementation Machinery

Implementation has been, and remains, problematic. Unfortunately, gross violations of human rights are still taking place in many parts of the world and many countries lack adequate and effective national protection systems. Notwithstanding their ratifications of international human rights treaties and their participation in supervisory systems under these treaties, many countries still have a long way to go to achieve faithful implementation of the provisions of the treaties. Francis Fukuyama has written that political development requires a strong state, the rule of law, and democratic accountability.[7] Many countries of the world are without all three of these.

Universal Mechanisms

During the period of the Cold War, the principal adversaries sought to protect their friends and to admonish their adversaries. The principled international protection of human rights suffered. When the former colonies and dependent territories came into the United Nations, they pushed, in the 1960s, for the UN to deal with gross violations of human rights in the non-independent countries and in *apartheid* South Africa. Thus began a process whereby the UN, particularly its Commission on Human Rights, would discuss gross violations of human rights publicly, establish fact-finding exercises into allegations of gross violations, adopt resolutions condemning gross violations, and send envoys to countries for contacts within the framework of confidential petitions procedures. The Commission on Human Rights also appointed a number of fact-finders into broad-based or country-based violations which are collectively known as the UN human rights special procedures.

When UN investigative and other protection procedures came to be used to examine the human rights records of developing countries themselves, they used their voting majorities in the UN to stifle the Commission on Human Rights and its fact-finders. Dissatisfaction with the operations of the Commission on Human Rights led to its replacement in 2006 by a UN Human Rights Council whose practice is to favour approaches of dialogue and consensus over straight-talking when dealing with situations of gross violations of human rights. The developing countries have a majority on the Human Rights Council and use that majority to block condemnations of governments for gross violations of human rights save in some instances. This is a problem in the operations of the UN Human Rights Council.

The Human Rights Council does have a new procedure whose long-term results are still to be seen. This is its Universal Periodic Review process under which every country, once every four and a half years, submits a report on its efforts to implement UN human rights norms and participates in a review process with its peers on the Council. For the time being the process is still very diplomatic, and its ground rules do not allow for scrutiny of gross violations of human rights inside the country being reviewed.

The UPR process is proceeding on the basis of the UN human rights norms and could thus contribute to the entrenchment of universality. The process could, in the long term, lead to the establishment or strengthening of national protection systems but while questions are sometimes asked about the role of national human rights institutions, this has not been systematic so far. The UPR process could, in the long term, make an important contribution in encouraging the development and strengthening of national protection systems.

In the meantime, gross violations of human rights continue to take place across Asia, and regional and national protection systems are deficient or non-existent in many countries, while the international protection of human rights remains in its adolescence notwithstanding the existence of human rights treaty procedures, the UN Human Rights Council, and the Office of UN High Commissioner for Human Rights.

International mechanisms, notably the UPR, have been hailed as critical in the absence of effective regional mechanisms in Asia and the purely promotional role of the recently established ASEAN Intergovernmental Commission on Human Rights (AICHR).[8]

Regional Mechanisms

AICHR is the only regional human rights body in Asia that was created in 2009, pursuant to the ASEAN Charter of 2007. The Charter and AICHR responded to calls for ASEAN to pay greater attention to human rights since the 1993 World Conference in Vienna. The Charter promulgated new norms of good governance, democracy, human rights, and the rule of law for the region.

The creation of AICHR and the subsequent ASEAN Declaration of Human Rights 2012 heralded high hopes for a new era of human rights protection in the region. Deliberation over the human rights mechanism proved to be the most divisive process in ASEAN's history, leading to a pro-human rights camp (Cambodia, Laos, Myanmar, Vietnam) against others that were in favour of a strong mechanism (Indonesia, Philippines, and Thailand).

While it was a welcome development, the mandate of AICHR was received with disappointment internationally and locally, especially among civil society.[9] A purely promotional mandate was given to AICHR, which still lacks key aspects of a protection mechanism: representatives who are independent from their member states, a petitions system and participation by civil society.[10] The Commission holds its meetings in private and one is left to guess what their deliberations are about. Nevertheless, AICHR is engaged in useful promotional work and sensitization of policy makers, civil society, and the private sector on human rights norms and law.

Unlike other regions of the world, there is no regional court of human rights, such as the Inter-American Court, the European Court, and the African Court. Beyond academic discussions, this remains aspirational.[11]

National Mechanisms

At the end of the day, human rights must be protected inside each country. This makes it critical that every government should have in place an adequate and effective national protection system. A national protection system, while anchored in national law, should be consistent with and reflective of international human rights law.

A national protection system functions best under democracy and the rule of law. The Legislature, the Executive, the Judiciary, the Legal Profession, dedicated institutions such as a national human rights commission, and NGOs all have roles to play in the efficient design and performance of the national protection system.

The national constitution should include provisions reflecting international human rights norms of public policy (*jus cogens*), such as the total prohibition of torture in any circumstances. National legislation should incorporate all international human rights obligations of the State under international customary law and international treaties, and under mandatory decisions of the UN Security Council.

The national protection system should provide for effective safeguards against violations of international human rights norms from which no derogation is permitted under international law. The Judiciary should be free to invoke international human rights norms as reflected in international customary law, international treaties binding on the State, or general principles of law. Human rights education should be provided in all schools and higher institutions of learning.

A national protection system should include institutions such as a national commission on human rights or an ombudsperson. A national protection system should include arrangements to detect potential conflicts or gross violations of human rights and to prevent them.

A national protection system should provide for adequate and effective remedies to prevent violations of human rights and to provide redress in cases of breach. The absence of a remedy available to test an arguable claim for breach amounts to a violation of human rights.[12]

The right to an effective remedy may, in certain circumstances, require governments to provide for and implement provisional or interim measures to avoid continuing violations and to endeavour to repair at the earliest possible opportunity any harm that may have been done.[13]

A national protection system should be particularly attentive to the risks of genocide, ethnic cleansing, crimes against humanity, and war crimes and should provide effective guarantees against them. Human Rights Committee, General Comment 6/16 of 27 July 1982, has noted that states have the supreme duty to prevent wars, acts of genocide, and other acts of mass violence causing arbitrary loss of life.

A national protection system should provide for a system of regular visits by national, regional or international bodies to all places of detention. In the event of a violation of human rights the national protection system must provide for measures, beyond a victim-specific remedy, to be taken to avoid recurrence of the type of violation in question. Such measures may require changes in the State's laws or practices.[14]

A national protection system should provide for investigations of gross violations of human rights and for justice to the victims. A national protection system should provide for safeguards against deportation or extradition to a state where the deportee/extraditee may face serious risks of torture or arbitrary execution. A national protection system should be particularly protective of human rights defenders.

There are severe problems with gross violations of human rights throughout Asia and national protection systems are poor in the majority of countries. The Global Alliance of National Human Rights Institutions (GANHRI) considers applications for accreditation from national human rights institutions, and it uses three categories in its listing of such institutions. "A" status institutions are those that are considered to have complied with the United Nations principles on the independence of such institutions (the Paris Principles). "B" status institutions do not fully comply with the Paris Principles. "C" status institutions do not comply with the Paris Principles.

National human rights institutions (NHRIs) from the following countries have been accredited with "A" status by GANHRI at the time of writing: Afghanistan, Australia, India, Indonesia, Jordan, Malaysia, Mongolia, Nepal, New Zealand, the Philippines, Qatar, Republic of Korea, Samoa, and Timor Leste. Institutions from the following countries have been accorded "B" status: Bahrain, Iraq, Kazakhstan, Kyrgyzstan, Sri Lanka, Tajikistan, Maldives, Myanmar, Oman, and Thailand. Institutions from Hong Kong and Iran have been accorded "C" status, while the institution from Fiji has been suspended.[15]

In a forthcoming edited book on national human rights institutions in Southeast Asia undertaken by Asia Centre, a think-tank in Bangkok, authors highlight key problems affecting regional NHRIs, which include the lack of independence of the commissioners, failure to properly exercise their investigative mandates, inadequate expertise in the area of human rights, lack of financial resources, ineffectiveness in securing remedies, and inability to secure consideration of their reports and findings by legislative authorities.[16] The Commissions of the Philippines and Thailand have come under direct attack from their respective governments. In the latter case, the current military government had considered dismantling the commission altogether, though it was eventually preserved but under very trying working considerations.

NHRIs have performed good work in the face of such adversity. They have strived to uphold their mandates in difficult political contexts by calling attention to violations of civil and political rights and economic, social and cultural rights. For example, one of the burning regional issues that they have tackled, notably in Indonesia and Malaysia, is the plight of indigenous peoples whose lands are being usurped by national and private interests.

Strategies for a Life of Dignity in Asia

Legal Innovation

In his book, *The Bottom Billion: Why the Poorest Countries Are Failing and What Can Be Done About it*,[17] Professor Paul Collier argues for new "laws and charters" to cover the following areas: a Charter for National Resource Revenues, a Charter for Democracy, a Charter for Budget Transparency, a Charter for Post-Conflict Situations, and a Charter for Investment.[18]

The need for these charters is to help make sure that the society is organized to act for the common good and also to rule out the temptations of corruption. Professor Collier sees these charters being developed internationally to begin with, but there is no reason why a society in good faith pursuit of the right to development should not go ahead with the elaboration of its own charters on these vital issues.

There are other areas where particular legal attention would be needed, and some of these are discussed hereafter.

Preventable Poverty

A Swiss panel that prepared an Agenda for Human Rights on the occasion of the 60th anniversary of the Universal Declaration of Human Rights advocated the concept of preventable poverty, namely, identifying those parts of the population whose plight could be alleviated using the resources already available to the state and acting to alleviate or head off their poverty.[19] This concept should find reflection in the national legal order and policy of every country.

The acclaimed Indian Nobel economics laureate, Amartya Sen, an economist, philosopher, and public thinker, who wrote the much-cited work, *Development as Freedom*, has just published another powerful book, *The Idea of Justice (2009)*, in which he argues that instead of approaching the issue of justice from the traditional perspective of a social contract and of being concerned with identifying what perfectly just social and institutional arrangements might be, one should concentrate instead on preventing and reducing injustices in society as a concrete way of rendering justice.

In Sen's approach, principles of justice are defined in terms of the lives and freedoms of the people involved. The focus on actual lives in the assessment of justice has implications for the nature and reach of the idea of justice. A realization-focused perspective emphasizes the importance of the *prevention* of manifest injustice in the world, rather than seeking the perfectly just.

Sen insists on the role of public reasoning and discussions in establishing what can make societies less unjust. He assesses democracy in terms of public reasoning and offers a view of democracy as "government by discussion." Democracy has to be judged, he writes, not just by the institutions that formally exist but by the extent to which different voices from diverse sections of the people can actually be heard.

The Committee on Economic, Social and Cultural Rights, a body established by the ECOSOC and operating under the International Covenant on Economic, Social and Cultural Rights, adopted a statement on poverty in 2001 in which it noted that sometimes poverty arises when people have no access to existing resources because of who they are, what they believe, or where they live. Discrimination may thus cause poverty, just as poverty may cause discrimination.[20]

The scheme of the United Nations Charter and of the International Covenant on Economic, Social and Cultural Rights is that governments should use their own resources to maximum effect in meeting the needs of their people that there should be no discrimination in the allocation of resources and that governments should cooperate for mutual benefit in the realization of the rights stated in the Charter, the UDHR, and the International Covenant. Nowadays there is understandable emphasis on the implementation of the right to development, on how globalization impacts on the ability to governments to fulfil their human rights obligations, and on the adverse effects of an inequitable international economic order. These are all deserving issues, but they do not gainsay the obligation of a government to meet the basic needs of the people, especially those in extreme poverty.

Goal 1 of the MDGs targeted the eradication of extreme poverty and hunger, specifically the halving by 2015 of people whose income was less than $1 a day and the halving by 2015 of people who suffered from hunger. The UN reported in 2006 that chronic hunger—measured by the proportion of people lacking the food needed to meet their daily needs—had declined in the developing countries, but progress overall was not fast enough and an estimated 824 million people in the developing world were affected by chronic hunger in 2003.[21]

Legal Empowerment of the Poor

The Commission on Legal Empowerment of the Poor (2008)[22] found that in too many countries the laws, institutions, and policies governing economic, social, and political affairs deny a large part of society the chance to participate on equal terms. The rules of the game are unfair. This is not only morally unacceptable it stunts economic development and can readily undermine stability and security. The outcomes of governance, the cumulative effect of policies and institutions on peoples' lives, will only change if the processes of governance are fundamentally changed.

The Commission's assessment was that poverty is man-made, by action and inaction, and a failure of public policies and of markets. Most poor people do not live under the shelter of the law but far from the law's protection and the opportunities it affords. Where the law works for everyone, it defines and enforces the rights and obligations of all. This allows people to interact with one another in an atmosphere that is certain and predictable. Thus the rule of law is a vital source of progress. It creates an environment in which the full spectrum of human creativity can flourish and prosperity can be built.

The Commission understood legal empowerment to be a process of systemic change through which the poor and excluded become able to use the law, the legal system, and legal services to protect and advance their rights and interests as citizens and economic actors. The Commission recognized that: "The elements of legal empowerment are grounded in the spirit and letter of international human rights law, and particularly in Article 1 of the Universal Declaration of Human Rights, which declares, 'All human beings are born free and equal in dignity and rights.'" [23]

The Commission emphasized that democracy was an indispensable means, a just end. It emphasized that legal empowerment of the poor can only be realized through systemic change aimed at unlocking the civic and economic potential of the poor. It put forward four pillars of legal empowerment of the poor: access to justice and the rule of law, property rights, labour rights, and business rights. In their convergence and through their synergy, legal empowerment of the poor can be achieved.

(a) First pillar: Access to Justice and the Rule of Law

In the presentation of the Commission, legal empowerment of the poor was impossible when, *de jure* or de facto, poor people are denied access to a well-functioning justice system. Legal empowerment measures in this domain must:

- Ensure that everyone has the fundamental right to legal identity and is registered at birth;
- Repeal or modify laws and regulations that are biased against the rights, interests, and livelihoods of poor people:

- Facilitate the creation of state and civil society organizations and coalitions, including paralegals who work in the interest of the excluded;
- Establish a legitimate state monopoly on the means of coercion, through, for example, effective and impartial policing;
- Make the formal judicial system, land administration systems, and relevant public institutions more accessible by recognizing and integrating customary and informal legal procedures with which the poor are already familiar.

The Commission, as will be seen from the above, paints with a broad brush, and one is still left with the challenge of concrete action to facilitate access to justice and the rule of law.

(b) Second pillar: Property Rights

As presented by the Commission, a fully functioning property system is composed of four building blocks: a system of rules that defines the bundle of rights and obligations between people and assets reflecting the multiplicity and diversity of property systems around the world; a system of governance; a functioning market for the exchange of assets; and an instrument of social policy. Legal empowerment measures in this domain must:

- Promote efficient governance of individual and collective property in order to integrate the extralegal economy into the formal economy and ensure it remains easily accessible to all citizens;
- Ensure that all property recognized in each nation is legally enforceable by law and that all owners have access to the same rights and standards:
- Create a functioning market for the exchange of assets that is accessible, transparent, and accountable;
- Broaden the availability of property rights, including tenure security, through social and other public policies, such as access to housing, low interest loans, and the distribution of state aid;
- Promote an inclusive property rights system that will automatically recognize real and immoveable property bought by men as the co-property of their wives or common law partners.

Again, the Commission paints with a broad brush.

(c) Third Pillar: Labour Rights

The Commission calls for fulfilment of the ILO's Fundamental Principles and Rights at Work and the Decent Work agenda. It recommended the following strategies to provide protection and opportunity to workers in the informal economy:

- Respect, promote, and realize freedom of association so that the identity, voice, and representation of the working poor can be strengthened in the social and political dialogue about reform and its design;
- Improve the quality of labour regulation and the functioning of labour market institutions, thereby creating synergy between the protection and productivity of the poor;
- Ensure effective enforcement of a minimum of a minimum package of labour rights for workers and enterprises in the informal economy that upholds and goes beyond the Declaration of Fundamental Principles and Rights at Work.
- Increase access to employment opportunities in the growing and more inclusive market economy;
- Expand social protection for poor workers in the event of economic shocks and structural changes;
- Promote measures and guarantee access to medical care, health insurance, and pensions;
- Ensure that legal empowerment drives gender equality, thus meeting the commitments under ILO standards that actively promote the elimination of discrimination and equality of opportunity for, and treatment of women, who have emerged as a major force in poverty reduction in poor communities.

Broad brush strokes thus continued in the Commission's recommendations.

(d) Fourth Pillar: Business Rights

The Commission held it to be self-evident that the poor are entitled to rights not only when working for others but also in developing their own businesses. Legal empowerment measures in this domain must:

- Guarantee basic business rights, including the right to vend, to have a work and a work space, and to have access to necessary infrastructure and services (shelter, electricity, water, sanitation);
- Strengthen effective economic governance that makes it easy and affordable to set up and operate a business, to access markets, and to exit a business if necessary;
- Expand the definition of "legal person" to include legal liability companies that allow owners to separate their business and personal assets, thus enabling prudent risk-taking;
- Promote inclusive financial services that offer entrepreneurs in the developing world what many of their counterparts elsewhere take for granted—savings, credit, insurance, pensions, and other tools for risk management;
- Expand access to new business opportunities through specialized programmes to familiarize entrepreneurs with new markets and help them comply with regulations and requirements and that support backward and forward linkages between larger and smaller firms.

Here also, the Commission maintained a broad brush approach.

(e) Assessment

The recommendations of the Commission are laudatory and help draw attention to the need to act to strengthen legal empowerment of the poor. However, it would be fair to say that they did not build on concrete earlier recommendations of the International Commission of Jurists on the provision oflegal services to the poor, ofthe International Labour Organization supervisory bodies, or of the human rights treaty bodies, especially the Human Rights Committee and the Committee on Economic, Social and Cultural Rights. After one has read the Commission's recommendations, one then still has to turn to the concrete norms and recommendations of the international human rights treaty regime in order to take forward the process of strengthening legal empowerment of the poor. The recommendations of the International Commission of Jurists provide a good point of departure.

Public Interest Litigation

This principle of fairness towards the poor and the needy is at the heart of the concept of public interest litigation, sometimes also referred to as social action litigation, whose traces may be found in the United States but which has seen pronounced expression in India. In this work we raise for consideration whether the courts of developing countries should embark on a course towards public interest litigation and thereby make a new contribution to the cause of justice of their needy people.

First, the courts can take this initiative on their own. Judges of the Indian Supreme Court first admitted the public interest litigation in the 1970s because they felt that the courts must be in a position to respond to the plight of the poorest and most disadvantaged sectors of the Indian population. The highest court of Guyana, the Guyana Court of Appeal, has, since its establishment, clearly laid down the principle that it would develop a jurisprudence tailored to the circumstances of Guyana, drawing upon the historic commonwealth jurisprudence as well as upon international and comparative jurisprudence. We documented this in our book on the Guyana Court of Appeal.[24] There is no doubt in our mind that our courts can develop public interest jurisprudence in favour of the poor and the disadvantaged in our midst.

The concept of public interest litigation was initiated by Krishna Iyer J. in 1976. Its full scope was elaborated by Bhagwati J in S.P. *Gupta* vs. *Union of India*, 1982. Public interest litigation is an exception to the traditional rule of locus standi, according to which only those directly affected could approach the court. Under the public interest jurisprudence, any member of the public having sufficient interest can maintain an action for judgement and seek redress for public injury.

The practice of the Indian Supreme Court, according to its guidelines, allows any member of the public having sufficient interest may maintain an action or petition by way of PIL if:

- There is a personal injury or injury to a disadvantaged section of the population for whom access to the legal justice system is difficult.
- The person bringing the action has sufficient interest to maintain an action of public injury.
- The injury must have arisen because of breach of public duty or violation of the constitution or of the law.
- It must seek enforcement of such public duty and observance of constitutional law or legal provisions.

Public interest litigation has become a process for the enforcement of public duties enjoined by law for amelioration of the downtrodden and helpless victims. The judiciary could take cognizance of a simple letter or newspaper article as a petition. It is invoked when access to reasonable life – to live with dignity – is threatened. Public interest litigation has proved to be an instrument of social justice.

It has been used to order minimum wages for poor workers; abolish bonded labour and child labour; ensure proper working conditions for labourers; uphold the right to education and to proper health and sanitary services; protect the rights of prisoners, pavement, and slum dwellers; order inspection of hospitals, mines, prisons, women, and children homes; stop harassments and exploitation; punish those found guilty of dowry deaths and police excesses; control environmental pollution and labour from hazardous occupation; and arrange for proper compensation.

Different sections of people such as the dalits, tribals, landless labourers and others, who have suffered from economic exploitation and different sorts of social indignities, have been the beneficiaries of PIL. The Supreme Court has hauled up certain states of the Union for their failure to prepare lists of families below the poverty line, who were to be given food at lower rates, and for their indifference to stop deaths due to hunger.

Where needed, the Court initiates fact-finding by its own instrumentalities. One method by which the Court gathers facts is by the appointment of commissioners. The Court has appointed district judges, journalists, lawyers, mental health professionals, civil servants, and expert bodies as commissioners.

Achieving a Life of Dignity: The Indian Example

Notwithstanding their championship of the right to development internationally, few, if any, countries follow up by seeking to implement it nationally. As we shall see below, there has been little follow-up action on the right to development as such in the national legal order, even if there are impressive efforts for development. There are parts of their development policies that would come within the frame of the right to development (RTD), and the judiciaries of countries such as India have provided some important statements on the implementation of economic, social, and cultural rights.

Championing RTD at the National Level

Justice A.S. Anand, Chairperson of the National Human Rights Commission of India and former Chief Justice of that country, addressed the UN Human Rights Council on the "Right to Development" during its first session, on 27 June 2006.[25] The Indian Commission, he explained, had taken the view that the right to development was inherent in the right to a life with dignity under Article 21 of the Indian Constitution, which is an enforceable right.

Elaborating on this, he explained that for a programme of poverty eradication one had to look at a number of indices together, and a right to development approach would imply considering improvement in each of the indices through schemes that had to be implemented following the rights approach, where the beneficiaries were empowered to participate in the decision-making and executing the different schemes, transparently and accountably, and sharing the benefits equitably.

Non-discrimination, he noted, was central to the implementation of the right to development. Another important factor having a bearing on the development debate was the issue of corruption, as a violator of human rights. Good governance was not possible unless it was free from corruption. He added:

> It would be in the fitness of things that we aim at ensuring distributive justice in the national as well as the global context. To achieve that, there has to be a paradigm shift from Human Development as seen merely in terms of economic growth, to Human Development as a basic human right.

The universality of human rights, he continued, with focus on human dignity and concern for accountability, made them uniquely appropriate for re-shaping development cooperation, fostering good governance, and combating discrimination, disease, and despair with the ultimate aim of reaching the goal of achieving "human rights for all."[26]

India's Planning Commission

The Indian Planning Commission has worked for economic and social justice in India, and in effect for the implementation of the right to development, for the past 60 years. In the spirit of advancing economic and social justice and human rights, the latest, the 11th five-year plan of India's Planning Commission, aims at:

- Rapid growth (at nine per cent per annum) that can reduce poverty and create employment opportunities;
- Access to essential services in health and education especially for the poor.

- Equality of opportunity;
- Empowerment through education and skill development;
- Employment opportunities underpinned by the National Rural Employment Guarantee;
- Environmental sustainability;
- Recognition of women's agency; and
- Good governance.

The goal of access to essential services in health and education, especially for the poor, is worthy of some elaboration. The thinking of the Indian Planning Commission is that access to basic facilities such as health, education, clean drinking water, and so on impacts directly on welfare in the short run, while in the longer run it determines economic opportunities for the future. Since access to these services for the mass of the population depends not only upon their income levels but upon the delivery of these services through publicly funded systems, the Eleventh Plan envisages a major expansion in the supply of these services. It hopes that the high growth being targeted over the plan period will help in providing ample resources to fund these programmes by way of higher tax revenues that would become available and a larger borrowing capability.

The Planning Commission, the supreme planning body in India, was set up in March 1950 by a Resolution of the Central Government. It is not a statutory or constitutional body. It was placed outside of the conventional ministries and departments with a view to preventing it from falling into a rut and to facilitate development of supra-departmental views. The Commission format was intended to provide flexibility in response to emerging needs and to build up a brains trust for development.

Its functions from the outset were fivefold:

- Formulation of five-year plans for the most effective and balanced utilization of the country's resources;
- Working out priorities in the plan;
- Assessment of national resources and devising ways and means of augmenting them;
- Determination of the best machinery to secure the successful implementation of the plan;
- Periodic evaluation of the progress of the plan with a view to suggesting adjustments if necessary.

The composition and structure of the Commission have evolved since its establishment some 60 years ago. More recently the Commission has consisted of a full-time deputy chairman and eight other full-time members. The day-to-day work of the Commission is in the hands of the deputy chairman, who has the rank of a cabinet minister, while the other full-time members have the rank of ministers of state (equivalent to a junior minister). The chair of the Commission is the prime minister who, however, only participates from time to time on matters of special importance. Different ministers have, from time to time, served as part-time ex officio members. There are those who have criticized the membership of the prime minister and the ministers. The deputy chairman, who is also minister of planning, is invited to attend all Cabinet meetings, and when necessary other members also attend the meetings of the Cabinet or its Committees.

The Planning Commission is an advisory body to the government. It may take the initiative in suggesting new policies and programmes and in coordinating those originating from other agencies of government. To support the Planning Commission there is also a small Ministry of Planning. We shall not go into details of its composition here. There is a Minister of State in this Ministry whose main task is to act as spokesman of the Commission and to be answerable to Parliament for the Commission's work.

The main work of the Planning Commission is organized through divisions which include a General Planning Division responsible for a comprehensive study of the country as a whole and whose work and conclusions are prerequisites for studies relating to individual sectors. Special Planning Divisions are concerned with the study of particular sectors of social and economic development. Other divisions include those on educational health and family welfare; labour, employment, and manpower; rural development; village and small industries; rural energy; development policy; and backward classes.[27]

Professor Arvind Panagariya in a recent book, *India: The Emerging Giant*, discusses the issues of poverty, inequality, and economic reforms. He traces India's efforts with varying degrees of success to help alleviate poverty and to reduce inequality. These are issues at the heart of implementation of the right to development. Professor Panagariya submits that poverty alleviation strategies are more important than strategies for the redistribution of wealth so as to tackle the phenomenon of inequality.[28]

Conclusion

The problem of implementation was broached as the UDHR was being drafted. It has remained a considerable challenge since then. This chapter has discussed a broad range of efforts in which Asian States have joined like-minded countries in other regions of the world to press for policies and strategies to promote human dignity and equitable life chances for humanity. There is still a long way to go on many of the issues discussed in this chapter, and it is to be hoped that Asia will in the future pursue the quest for human dignity and equitable life chances in a spirit of freedom, democracy, and the rule of law.

Notes

1. Journal of the Economic and Social Council, No. 29, p. 521.
2. E/CN.4/AC.1/SR.2 11 June 1947 160 Summary Record of the Second Meeting [of the Drafting Committee of the Commission on Human Rights] Held at Lake Success, New York, on Wednesday, 11 June 1947 at 11:00 a.m.
3. A/C.3/SR.42, 5 December, 1946, reproduced in Schabas, p. 87.
4. E/CN.4/SR.25, Schabas, p. 1111.
5. E/CN.4/11.
6. E/CN.4/SR 27, Schabas, p. 1121.
7. Francis Fukuyama, *Political Order And Political Decay: From the Industrial Revolution to the Globalization of Democracy* (New York: Farrar, Straus & Giroux, 2014).
8. James Gomez and Robin Ramcharan (2017), The Universal Periodic Review of Southeast Asia: Civil Society Perspectives. Palgrave Macmillan.
9. James Gomez and Robin Ramcharan, The Protection of Human Rights in Southeast Asia: Improving the Effectiveness of Civil Society," Asia-Pacific Journal on Human Rights and the Law, Volume 13, Issue 2, 2012, pp. 27–43.
10. See Robin Ramcharan, "ASEAN's Human Rights Commission: Policy Considerations for Enhancing its Capacity to Protect Human Rights, UCL Human Rights Review, December 2010.
11. See Hao Duy Phan, "A Blueprint For a Southeast Asian Court Of Human Rights," *Asian-Pacific Law & Policy Journal*, Vol. 10, No.2, pp. 384–433.
12. See Human Rights Committee, *Faure v. Australia*, 2001.
13. See Human Right Committee, General Comment 31.
14. See Human Rights Committee, General Comment 31.

15. GANHRI, Chart of the Status of National Institutions. Accreditation status as of 14 October 2016; consulted on the internet on 14 June 2017, no internet citation shown.
16. James Gomez and Robin Ramcharan (expected 2018), *National Human Rights Institutions in Southeast Asia: The Challenge of Protection*. Singapore: Palgrave Macmillan.
17. Paul Collier, *The Bottom Billion: Why the Poorest Countries Are Failing and What Can Be Done About it* (Oxford: Oxford University Press, 2007).
18. Ibid., Chapter 9, pp. 135–156.
19. *Protecting Dignity: An Agenda for Human Rights, 2008*. Swiss Initiative to Commemorate the 60th Anniversary of the UDHR. http://www.udhr60.ch/.
20. ECOSOC, E/C.12/2001/10 (10 May 200), para. 11.
21. UN, *The Millennium Development Goals Report* 2006 (New York: UN, 2006), 5.
22. See Making the Law Work for Everyone. Volume I, Report on Legal Empowerment of the Poor. UNDP, New York, 2008.
23. Ibid, p. 4.
24. B.G. Ramcharan, The Guyana Court of Appeal. London, Cavendish Press, 2000.
25. Intervention on Behalf of the National Human Rights Commission of India on "Right to Development" at First Session of the United Nations Human Rights Council by Dr. Justice A.S. Anand, Chairperson, National Human Rights Commission of India (former Chief Justice of India) on 27 June 2006 at Geneva. Original text on the internet.
26. Ibid.
27. See, generally, Indian Planning Commission, *Eleventh Plan* (2008); S.R. Maheshwari, Indian Administration: S.K. Misra and V.K. Puri, Indian Economy.
28. Arvind Panagariya, *India: the Emerging Giant*. (Oxford: Oxford University Press, 2009). See Chap. 7 "Declining Poverty: the Human Face of Reforms" and Chap. 8, "Inequality: A Lesser Problem."

References

Primary Documents: United Nations Documents from Drafting Process in William Schabas:

E/CN.4/AC.1/SR.2 11 June 1947 160 Summary Record of the Second Meeting [of the Drafting Committee of the Commission on Human Rights] Held at Lake Success, New York, on Wednesday, 11 June 1947 at 11:00 a. m.

E/CN.4/SR.25, Schabas, p. 1111.

E/CN.4/SR 27, Schabas, p. 1121.

A/C.3/SR.42, 5 December, 1946, reproduced in Schabas, p. 87.

E/CN.4/11.
Annand, A.S. Chairperson, Intervention on Behalf of the National Human Rights Commission of India on 'Right to Development' at First Session of the United Nations Human Rights Council by National Human Rights Commission of India (former Chief Justice of India) on 27 June, 2006 at Geneva. Original text on the Internet.
Collier, Paul. *The Bottom Billion. Why the Poorest Countries are Failing and What Can be Done About it* (Oxford: Oxford University Press, 2007).
ECOSOC, E/C.12/2001/10 (10 May 2001, para. 11).
ECOSOC, *Journal of the Economic and Social Council*, No. 29, p. 521.
Fukuyama, Francis. *Political Order And Political Decay: From the Industrial Revolution to the Globalization of Democracy* (New York: Farrar, Straus & Giroux, 2014).
GANHRI, Chart of the Status of National Institutions. Accreditation status as of 14 October, 2016; Consulted on the internet on 14 June, 2017, no internet citation shown.
Gomez, James and Robin Ramcharan, *The Universal Periodic Review of Southeast Asia: Civil Society Perspectives* (Singapore: Palgrave Macmillan, 2017).
Gomez, James and Robin Ramcharan, The Protection of Human Rights in Southeast Asia: Improving the Effectiveness of Civil Society," *Asia-Pacific Journal on Human Rights and the Law*, Volume 13, Issue 2, 2012, pp. 27–43.
Gomez, James and Robin Ramcharan, *National Human Rights Institutions in Southeast Asia: The Challenge of Protection.* (Singapore: Palgrave Macmillan, expected 2018).
Hao Duy Phan, "A Blueprint For a Southeast Asian Court Of Human Rights," *Asian-Pacific Law & Policy Journal*, Vol. 10, No. 2, pp. 384–433.
Human Right Committee, General Comment 31.
Human Rights Committee, *Faure v. Australia*, 2001.
Human Rights Committee, General Comment 31.
Indian Planning Commission, *Eleventh Plan* (2008).
Panagariya, Arvind, *India: the Emerging Giant.* (Oxford: Oxford University Press, 2009).
Protecting Dignity: An Agenda for Human Rights, 2008. Swiss Initiative to Commemorate the 60th Anniversary of the UDHR. http://www.udhr60.ch/
Ramcharan, Bertrand, *The Guyana Court of Appeal* (London, Cavendish Press, 2000).
Ramcharan, Robin. "ASEAN's Human Rights Commission: Policy Considerations for Enhancing its Capacity to Protect Human Rights," *UCL Human Rights Review*, December 2010.
UNDP, *Making the Law Work for Everyone. Volume I, Report on Legal Empowerment of the Poor.* UNDP, New York, 2008.
United Nations, *The Millennium Development Goals Report* 2006 (New York: UN, 2006), 5.

CHAPTER 9

The Future of the UDHR: Building on the Past and the Present

Introduction

The Universal Declaration is a political text that was debated and adopted by many states, including Asian States. As Waltz has noted, "It is the political recognition that accompanies such negotiation, rather than any supposed intellectual lineage, that gives the UDHR legitimacy as a standard for good behaviour by states and by peoples."[1] Dialogue on the UDHR has continued since 1948, with some setbacks for universalism but also with an increasing number of states from developing parts of the world participating in the dialogue and affirming their adherence to universal standards promulgated in the UDHR.

Since 1948, as this chapter will argue, the list of rights enumerated has gained in acceptance at key international human rights forums, has been incorporated into many domestic systems in Asia, and has provided a standard for civil society in Asia to hold their governments to account. A final component that must be added to the toolkit is the need for human rights education to deepen respect for the Universal Declaration.

Growing Adherence to the UDHR: Bandung, Tehran, and Vienna

The Syrian delegate, Abdul Rahman Kayali, stated during the UN General Assembly plenary session that approved the UDHR:

R. Ramcharan, B. Ramcharan, *Asia and the Drafting of the Universal Declaration of Human Rights*,
https://doi.org/10.1007/978-981-13-2104-7_9

> Civilization [has] progressed slowly through centuries of oppression and tyranny, until finally the present declaration [has] been drawn up. It was not the work of a few representatives in the Assembly or in the Economic and Social Council; it was the achievement of generations of human beings who [have] worked towards that end. Now at last the peoples of the world [will] hear it proclaimed that their aim has been reached by the United Nations.[2]

Bandung 1955

The UDHR would gain further traction at the Bandung Summit of Asian and African states from 18 to 24 April 1955, crucially from Communist China and newly formed African states that had not participated in the drafting process. While the Bandung Summit focused principally on the quest for self-determination and an end to colonial rule that was noted at the beginning of this work, human rights featured significantly in the discussions. As Roland Burke has demonstrated, African and Asian states came to a consensus statement that affirmed the UDHR.[3] Burke has called attention to the enthusiasm for human rights in the immediate post-colonial moment and that human rights featured very much in speeches to the conference. Immediate preoccupations of racism and colonialism featured more prominently. Nevertheless, of the 25 nations who gave addresses in the opening session on 18–19 April, at least 11 invoked human rights. The speeches came from a diverse collection of states and encompassed the full range of political systems in attendance. Speakers came from diverse political systems, including His Royal Highness, Foreign Minister Sardar Mohammed Naim of Afghanistan and Prime Minister Zhou Enlai of Communist China. It also included ideologically disparate states as Egypt, Iran, Japan, Jordan, Lebanon, Thailand, Turkey, South Vietnam, and Yemen.

In the closing session, Burke noted that human rights featured prominently and four delegations nominated its recognition as one of the achievements of the conference. The Afghan delegate, Naim, praised the conference for proving "that all of us, from different parts of Asia and Africa, have felt and acted as one, for the achievement of our common desire ... [the] protection of human rights." Nasser of Egypt endorsed it as "a tremendous success," not least because of the "deep concern and full support which all the Asiatic and African countries have shown with regard to questions of human rights." Prime Minister Mohammed Ali, Pakistan, extolled human rights as one of the core beliefs that defined the

Asian-African attitude towards world affairs and pronounced that, "the peoples of Asia and Africa ... stand for the fundamental principles of Human Rights and Self-determination."[4]

Most importantly, the universal character of human rights received strong affirmation at the Afro-Asian meeting. Support for universality was apparent early on as speakers invoking both the UDHR and the Draft Covenant on Human Rights in the opening session. For example, Prince Wan of Thailand offered a brief philosophical digression on the common nature of rights, and asserted that "Buddhism, Islam and Christianity all teach the same lesson – the dignity and worth of man, faith in fundamental human rights, and respect for fundamental freedom for all without distinction as to creed, colour or race."[5]

Enthusiasm by many Third World delegates for human rights was evident in discussions in the Political Committee, which echoed debates at the time of the drafting of the UDHR. Charles Malik, who was a delegate at the Conference, put forward a proposal for the Conference to recognize the UDHR. While this initiative won backing from Sri Lanka, Iran, Iraq, Japan, Pakistan, Thailand, Turkey, and South Vietnam, it was opposed by China, India, Indonesia, and North Vietnam.

At this stage in world affairs, Communist China, while agreeing in principle that the conference should endorse human rights in some form, was vocal in its opposition the acceptance of the UDHR on the basis that it was not a member of the UN at the time the UDHR was drafted. Indeed, at least one third of the states represented at Bandung were not involved in the adoption of the UDHR, as they were yet to be admitted to the organization and, in some cases, were still to win their independence. Burke noted that with every new state that appeared, there was the need to explain the UDHR and persuade them of its virtue. Thus, as the Chinese objections demonstrated, "the Universal Declaration was not self-evidently universal for those who had not participated in its creation. The battles of 1948 had to be re-fought, at least on some level, with every new state that entered the organization."[6]

The task of persuading the new states at Bandung fell on the shoulders of Malik and Romulo. For Malik, Bandung operated as "a small United Nations, a United Nations in miniature ... meeting together and deliberating in matters and by ways that were almost identical with the methods and ways of the United Nations."[7] The key source of division was not with regard to the content of the UDHR, but in Zhou's opposition to it as a text produced by a body at which his country was not represented. Romulo would confirm the nature of Zhou's objection to the UDHR noting that Zhou had originally signified objection to any conference statement predicated on a United Nations precept, principle, or position, declaring that:

> since the People's Republic of China was not a member of the United Nations, and therefore had no opportunity to participate in the formulation of such United Nations statement or policies, "his country" could not be expected to attach its name to any conference statement tied to the United Nations.[8]

In subsequent deliberations about the UDHR, however, a consensus position evolved. The consensus human rights paragraph revealed a modest but significant success for the proponents of human rights. The Communique at Bandung, concluded with a clear acknowledgement of the UDHR as a universal standard in section "C. Human Rights and Self-determination":

1. The Asian-African Conference declared its full support of the fundamental principles of Human Rights as set forth in the Charter of the United Nations and took note of the Universal Declaration of Human Rights as a common standard of achievement for all peoples and all nations.[9]

Malik, as per Burke, has noted that the Chinese considered the human rights question a serious one, and their lack of familiarity with the Declaration made them cautious about offering a full affirmation of a document they themselves acknowledged as highly significant: "[H]ere we had an important text-which was illustrated in their announcements-that they could not possibly fairly be expected to endorse it and the utmost they could say was that 'we took note of it.'"[10]

Tehran 1968

Such endorsement was not present in the speeches delivered by some delegates at the Tehran International Conference on Human Rights from 22 April to 13 May 1968 but featured in the final proclamation.

At this meeting, new and dictatorial regimes, including the despotic Shah in Iran, made statements lambasting human rights at a time when the United States was cautious in negotiating the conventions on human rights, was undergoing the turmoil of the civil rights movement, and was mourning the recent assassination of Martin Luther King. Burke has also provided a riveting account of the Tehran conference. The Shah and others, echoing Communist Soviet policy, proposed greater emphasis on economic development and a consequent diminution in civil and political rights. Burke has noted that:

> The first International Conference on Human Rights was a serious setback for the evolution of the UN rights project. It inaugurated two decades in which collective rights were exalted as the most sacred precept of the human rights program, invariably at the expense of individual rights. Concentrated state power was lauded as the path to freedom, as opposed to a serious threat to it.[11]

The universal values of the UDHR were nevertheless upheld in the Proclamation of Tehran, which proclaimed inter alia:

> 2. The Universal Declaration of Human Rights states a common understanding of the peoples of the world concerning the inalienable and inviolable rights of all members of the human family and constitutes an obligation for the members of the international community;
>
> ....
>
> The International Conference on Human Rights,
>
> 3. Affirming its faith in the principles of the Universal Declaration of Human Rights and other international instruments in this field,
> 4. Urges all peoples and governments to dedicate themselves to the principles enshrined in the Universal Declaration of Human Rights and to redouble their efforts to provide for all human beings a life consonant with freedom and dignity and conducive to physical, mental, social and spiritual welfare.[12]

Vienna 1993

The end of Cold War ideological divisions led to global endorsement of the universality of human rights at Vienna in 1993 by all UN member states at the time. The Vienna Declaration and Programme of Action stipulated that

5. All human rights are universal, indivisible and interdependent and interrelated. The international community must treat human rights globally in a fair and equal manner, on the same footing, and with the same emphasis. While the significance of national and regional particularities and various historical, cultural and religious backgrounds must be borne in mind, it is the duty of States, regardless of their political, economic and cultural systems, to promote and protect all human rights and fundamental freedoms.[13]

It is worth mentioning that the declaration continued to state that,

> As stated in the Declaration on the Right to Development, the human person is the central subject of development.
>
> While development facilitates the enjoyment of all human rights, the lack of development may not be invoked to justify the abridgement of internationally recognized human rights.

The status of the UDHR was reviewed by international jurist Hurst Hannum. He noted in 1995 that it remained "the primary source of global human rights standards, and its recognition as a source of rights and law by states throughout the world distinguishes it from conventional obligations."[14] He continued, "Virtually every international instrument concerned with human rights contains at least a preambular reference to the Universal Declaration, as do many declarations adopted unanimously or by consensus by the U.N. General Assembly."[15]

Some 20 years after the Vienna Declaration, Vitit Muntarbhorn of Thailand would call attention to its impact at the conceptual level for "the document acknowledged that while the world can bear in mind regional and national "particularities," it is the duty of states to promote and protect human rights and freedoms." In other words, "if there is a conflict between those particularities and the universality of human rights, it is the latter which must prevail. Vienna also interlinked between human rights, democracy and development." He went on to note a major lesson of Vienna: "the crunch is the implementation of human rights comprehensively at the national level." He noted that, given the nexus between power and human rights, "it is imperative to build checks and balances to prevent abuse of power and promote accountability, as well as broad public participation in the realization of human rights. Worldwide, eternal vigilance is thus the key."[16]

One positive step in this direction is the incorporation of the UDHR into many Asian national legal systems. While the UPR process provides a comprehensive record of national constitutional, legal, and policy developments across Asia, the following section looks briefly at the UDHR in Asia.

Increasing "Constitutionalisation" of International Human Rights Standards in Asia

Although Asia does not have a regional convention nor a court of human rights, Jiunn-rong Yeh has argued that Asia "has been developing transnational human rights discourses, frameworks and institutions for quite some time…driven by globalization and its related complexities."[17] Asian States have increasingly incorporated international human rights standards in their national political systems through various ways: (1) national incorporation of core human rights conventions, (2) international human rights references by domestic courts, and (3) establishment of national human rights institutions. A sub-regional system, AICHR, has also emerged.

National Incorporation

While Asian States continue to advance their adherence to universal values, as noted in the introduction, many if not all[18] have incorporated the UDHR's provisions and subsequent Conventions in into their national systems. In the UPR process states continue to call attention to the constitutional provisions related to upholding universal standards. While it is beyond the scope of this work to provide an exhaustive survey, a few examples will suffice.

Part II of India's Constitution adopted in 1949 by the National Assembly 1951, "Fundamental Rights," which was drafted in tandem with the participation of Indian drafters of the UDHR,[19] provides inter alia for:

> Right to Equality 14. The State shall not deny to any person equality before the law or the equal protection of the laws within the territory of India.
>
> [Non-discrimination] 15. (1) The State shall not discriminate against any citizen on grounds only of religion, race, caste, sex, place of birth or any of them.

Right to Freedom 19. (1) All citizens shall have the right—(a) to freedom of speech and expression; (b) to assemble peaceably and without arms; (c) to form associations or unions; (d) to move freely throughout the territory of India; (e) to reside and settle in any part of the territory of India; 1 [and]

Right against Exploitation 23. (1) Traffic in human beings and other similar forms of forced labour are prohibited and any contravention of this provision shall be an offence punishable in accordance with law.

Right to Freedom of Religion 25. (1) Subject to public order, morality and health and to the other provisions of this Part, all persons are equally entitled to freedom of conscience and the right freely to profess, practise and propagate religion.

Right to Constitutional Remedies 32. (1) The right to move the Supreme Court by appropriate proceedings for the enforcement of the rights conferred by this Part is guaranteed.

(2) The Supreme Court shall have power to issue directions or orders or writs, including writs in the nature of habeas corpus, mandamus, prohibition, quo warranto and certiorari, whichever may be appropriate, for the enforcement of any of the rights conferred by this Part.[20]

The Constitution of Japan, which came into effect in 1947, echoes closely the UDHR by stipulating in its preamble that "…laws of political morality are universal; and that obedience to such laws is incumbent upon all nations who would sustain their own sovereignty and justify their sovereign relationship with other nations."[21] Chapter III, "Rights and Duties of the People," stipulates inter alia that:

Article 11. The people shall not be prevented from enjoying any of the fundamental human rights. These fundamental human rights guaranteed to the people by this Constitution shall be conferred upon the people of this and future generations as eternal and inviolate rights.

Article 12. The freedoms and rights guaranteed to the people by this Constitution shall be maintained by the constant endeavor of the people, who shall refrain from any abuse of these freedoms and rights and shall always be responsible for utilizing them for the public welfare.

Article 13. All of the people shall be respected as individuals. Their right to life, liberty, and the pursuit of happiness shall, to the extent that it does not interfere with the public welfare, be the supreme consideration in legislation and in other governmental affairs.

Article 14. All of the people are equal under the law and there shall be no discrimination in political, economic or social relations because of race, creed, sex, social status or family origin.

...

Article 18. No person shall be held in bondage of any kind. Involuntary servitude, except as punishment for crime, is prohibited. Article 19. Freedom of thought and conscience shall not be violated. Article 20. Freedom of religion is guaranteed to all.

Article 21. Freedom of assembly and association as well as speech, press and all other forms of expression are guaranteed.

...

Article 25. All people shall have the right to maintain the minimum standards of wholesome and cultured living.

...

Article 31. No person shall be deprived of life or liberty,....

Other countries, if not all,[22] have incorporated the standards of the UDHR and core Conventions. In the case of Timor Leste, Article 23 of its Constitution states that fundamental rights enshrined in the Constitution shall be interpreted in accordance with the Universal Declaration of Human Rights. Article 9 provides that East Timor's legal system adopts the general or customary principles of international law and that "rules provided for in international conventions, treaties and agreements shall apply" in its legal system, and all rules that are contrary to the provisions of international conventions, treaties, and agreements applied in the internal legal system shall be invalid. Cambodia's constitution, in Article 31, expressly recognizes respect for human rights under the United Nations Charter, the Universal Declaration of Human Rights, and the covenants and conventions relating to human rights, and women's and children's rights.

By 1995, Hannum noted a plethora of constitutions worldwide that referred to the status of international law including references to the UDHR. He cited Asian countries as follows:

Afghanistan (1990)

Art. 134: "Afghanistan respects and observes the U.N. Charter and Universal Declaration of Human Rights and other accepted principles of international law."

Bangladesh (1991)

Art. 25: "The State shall base its international relations on… respect for international law and the principles enunciated in the U.N. Charter."

Cambodia (1993)

Art. 31: "The Kingdom of Cambodia shall recognize and respect human rights as stipulated in the United Nations Charter, the Universal Declaration of Human Rights, the covenants and conventions related to human rights, women's and children's rights."

Japan (1947)

Art. 98: "The treaties concluded by Japan and established laws of nations shall be faithfully observed."

Kazakhstan (1993)

Preamble: "The constitution shall possess supreme legal force, and its norms shall be directly applied. Laws and other acts which contradict the provisions of the Constitution shall not have legal force."

Art. 3: "International legal acts concerning rights and freedoms of men and citizens recognized by the Republic of Kazakhstan shall have priority before [domestic] laws in the territory of the Republic."

Kyrgyzstan (1993)

Art. 12(1): "The Constitution shall have supreme legal force and direct effect in the Kyrghyz Republic."

Art. 12(3): "International treaties and other norms of international law which have been ratified by the Kyrghyz Republic shall be a component and directly applicable part of legislation of the Kyrghyz Republic."

Art. 16(1): "In the Kyrghyz Republic basic human rights and freedoms shall be recognized and guaranteed in accordance with universally accepted norms and principles of international law, international treaties and agreements on the issues of human rights which have been ratified by the Kyrghyz Republic."

Art. 16(2): "Every person in the Kyrghyz Republic shall enjoy the right… [there follows a list of fifteen specific rights]."

"The enumeration of rights and freedoms in the Constitution shall not be interpreted as negating or infringing upon other universally recognized human rights and freedoms."

Mongolia (1992)

Art. 10(1): "Mongolia shall adhere to the universally recognized norms and principles of international law and pursue a peaceful foreign policy."

Art. 10(2): "Mongolia shall fulfill in good faith its obligations under international treaties to which it is a Party."

Art. 10(3): "The international treaties to which Mongolia is a Party, shall become effective as domestic legislation upon the entry into force of the laws on their ratification or accession."

Art. 10(4): "Mongolia shall not abide by any international treaty or other instruments incompatible with its Constitution."

Republic of Korea (1987)

Art. 6(1): "Treaties duly concluded and promulgated in accordance with the Constitution and the generally recognized rules of international law shall have the same effect as the domestic laws of the Republic of Korea."

Turkmenistan (1992)

Art. 5: "The Constitution of Turkmenistan shall be the supreme Law of the State; its rules and provisions shall be applied directly. Laws and other legal acts which contradict the Constitution shall have no legal force."

Art. 6: "Turkmenistan shall acknowledge the priority of generally recognized norms of international law. Turkmenistan shall be an authorized member of the world community, observing in its foreign policy the principles of peaceful co-existence, non-use of force, and non-interference in the internal affairs of other states."

Uzbekistan (1992)

Preamble: "The people of Uzbekistan, solemnly declaring their adherence to human rights and principles of state sovereignty.... recognizing priority of the generally accepted norms of the international law...."

Art. 13: "Democracy in the Republic of Uzbekistan shall rest on the principles common to all mankind, according to which the ultimate value is the human being, his life, freedom, honour, dignity and other inalienable rights."

Art. 15: "The constitution and the laws of the Republic of Uzbekistan shall have absolute supremacy in the Republic of Uzbekistan."[23]

In recent years, post-Suharto Indonesia has come to be a standard bearer of democratic transition and human rights in Southeast Asia as it has amended its 1945 Constitution to incorporate universal human rights standards, which continues to adhere to the Pancasila principles.[24] Article

28, A–J, of the Constitution, amended between 1999 and 2002, provides as follows:

Chapter XA Human Rights

Article 28 The freedom to associate and to assemble, to express written and oral opinions, etc., shall be regulated by law.

Article 28A Every person shall have the right to live and to defend his/her life and existence.

Article 28B (1) Every person shall have the right to establish a family and to procreate based upon lawful marriage. (2) Every child shall have the right to live, to grow and to develop, and shall have the right to protection from violence and discrimination.

Article 28C (1) Every person shall have the right to develop him/herself through the fulfilment of his/her basic needs, the right to get education and to benefit from science and technology, arts and culture, for the purpose of improving the quality of his/her life and for the welfare of the human race. (2) Every person shall have the right to improve him/herself through collective struggle for his/her rights to develop his/her society, nation and state.

Article 28D (1) Every person shall have the right of recognition, guarantees, protection and certainty before a just law, and of equal treatment before the law. (2) Every person shall have the right to work and to receive fair and proper remuneration and treatment in employment. (3) Every citizen shall have the right to obtain equal opportunities in government. (4) Every person shall have the right to citizenship status.

Article 28E (1) Every person shall be free to choose and to practice the religion of his/her choice, to choose one's education, to choose one's employment, to choose one's citizenship, and to choose one's place of residence within the state territory, to leave it and to subsequently return to it. (2) Every person shall have the right to the freedom to believe his/her faith (kepercayaan), and to express his/her views and thoughts, in accordance with his/her conscience. (3) Every person shall have the right to the freedom to associate, to assemble and to express opinions.

Article 28F Every person shall have the right to communicate and to obtain information for the purpose of the development of his/her self and social environment, and shall have the right to seek, obtain, possess, store, process and convey information by employing all available types of channels.

Article 28G (1) Every person shall have the right to protection of his/herself, family, honour, dignity, and property, and shall have the right to feel secure against and receive protection from the threat of fear to do or not do something that is a human right. (2) Every person shall have the right to be free from torture or inhumane and degrading treatment, and shall have the right to obtain political asylum from another country.

Article 28H (1) Every person shall have the right to live in physical and spiritual prosperity, to have a home and to enjoy a good and healthy environment, and shall have the right to obtain medical care. (2) Every person shall have the right to receive facilitation and special treatment to have the same opportunity and benefit in order to achieve equality and fairness. (3) Every person shall have the right to social security in order to develop oneself fully as a dignified human being. (4) Every person shall have the right to own personal property, and such property may not be unjustly held possession of by any party.

Article 28I (1) The rights to life, freedom from torture, freedom of thought and conscience, freedom of religion, freedom from enslavement, recognition as a person before the law, and the right not to be tried under a law with retrospective effect are all human rights that cannot be limited under any circumstances. (2) Every person shall have the right to be free from discriminative treatment based upon any grounds whatsoever and shall have the right to protection from such discriminative treatment. (3) The cultural identities and rights of traditional communities shall be respected in accordance with the development of times and civilisations. (4) The protection, advancement, upholding and fulfilment of human rights are the responsibility of the state, especially the government. (5) For the purpose of upholding and protecting human rights in accordance with the principle of a democratic and law-based state, the implementation of human rights shall be guaranteed, regulated and set forth in laws and regulations.

Article 28J (1) Every person shall have the duty to respect the human rights of others in the orderly life of the community, nation and state. (2) In exercising his/her rights and freedoms, every person shall have the duty to accept the restrictions established by law for the sole purposes of guaranteeing the recognition and respect of the rights and freedoms of others and of satisfying just demands based upon considerations of morality, religious values, security and public order in a democratic society.[25]

Incorporation by the Courts

Incorporation of international human rights law into domestic legal systems has also been carried out by judicial interpretation. A prime example of this is India's court system, which has increasingly referred to international human rights standards and conventions in its jurisprudence.

Decisions or interpretations by international courts regarding those rights and documents have also been incorporated. This has been the case, notes Yeh, in the new constitutions of newer "third-wave democracies," where "there has often been a demand for judicial reference to international law or at least international human rights law, and some even directly pronounce that international laws are part of their domestic laws." Yeh calls this a domestic "constitutionalisation" process of international norms which has facilitated not only judicial conversations regarding external norms but also constitutional functions of international norms. For example, Yeh calls attention to the fact that Indonesia, South Korea, and Taiwan have ensured that international human rights laws are directly applicable in domestic law through a monistic view on the relationship between domestic and international laws.[26] India's judicial system in particular has championed international human rights standards, especially through its public interest litigation. The courts would also progressively integrate international human rights law into its domestic rulings.[27] The "creeping influence" of the international human rights law and the UDHR on Singapore public law has been noted by Li-Ann Thio, who examines the impact of the UDHR in national courts and its significance in terms of developing a human rights culture in the thinking and operation of legal actors, such as the bench and bar.[28] Thio noted a "A consciousness about international instruments like the Universal Declaration of Human Rights ('UDHR'), a UN General Assembly resolution, was present in the early constitutional discourse of the newly independent Republic of Singapore."[29] The UDHR, continues Thio, "has been invoked before Singapore courts in adjudicating rights, in recognising the persuasive value of international law norms as a valuable aid to constitutional interpretation."[30] She notes a slow erosion of the resistance to international law: "although a monist sensibility is evident, insofar as clearly established CIL norms automatically form part of the Singapore domestic legal order, without need for a further act of incorporation."[31]

National Human Rights Institutions

Many countries in Asia have converged with international practice by establishing NHRIs. They include Bangladesh (2009), India (1993), Indonesia (1993), Malaysia (2000), Mongolia (2001), Myanmar (2011), Nepal (2000), the Philippines (1987), Thailand (2001), Sri Lanka (1996), and South Korea (2011). All of them apply the Paris Principles which provide a shared ground for national human rights institutions in Asia to guide the development of human rights within the region. An Asia Pacific Forum of NHRCs serves as a dialogue forum to exchange information with regard how to spread and implement international human rights norms in this region.

Regional Constitutionalisation

While no Asia-wide regional convention and institution exist, the ASEAN Intergovernmental Commission on Human Rights, despite the well-known challenges facing its protection capacity, provides a framework for the regional constitutionalisation of international human rights standards. The ASEAN Charter, which was adopted in 2007 and gave the organization legal personality, announced in its Preamble, ASEAN's adherence to "…respect for and protection of human rights and fundamental freedoms" which is also a key purpose stipulated in Article 1. The Terms of Reference of AICHR, created pursuant to Article 14 of the Charter, stipulates a key purpose:

> To uphold international human rights standards as prescribed by the Universal Declaration of Human Rights, the Vienna Declaration and Programme of Action, and international human rights instruments to which ASEAN Member States are parties.[32]

Members committed themselves to the principle of "upholding the Charter of the United Nations and international law, including international humanitarian law, subscribed to by ASEAN Member States."[33]

Article 2.2 committed members to upholding "[r]espect for international human rights principles, including universality, indivisibility, interdependence and interrelatedness of all human rights and fundamental freedoms" and also to "impartiality, objectivity, non-selectivity, non-discrimination, and avoidance of double standards and politicisation…."

AICHR would draft the ASEAN Declaration of Human Rights, which reaffirmed further their commitment to the UDHR, the Charter of the UN, the Vienna Declaration and Programme of Action, and other international human rights instruments to which ASEAN members are party. Article 10 stipulates member states affirmation of civil and political rights, and Article 26 stipulates affirmation of economic, social, and cultural rights in the UDHR.[34]

AICHR's approach a decade on has been to engage in promotion of human rights through thematic studies and educational activities. On the educational front it has conducted research, trainings, and workshops on key issues.

Rights education across Asia is a key tool in the advancement of the UDHR in Asia in education.

Human Rights Education in Asia

At the time of the drafting of the Universal Declaration of Human Rights, Asian States such as China attached importance to the promotion of education about human rights. On 16 June 1948, China and the United States made the following proposal concerning education for the forthcoming Declaration of Human Rights:

> It is recommended that the Economic and Social Council pass a resolution containing the following proposal: Immediately after action is taken by the General Assembly on the Declaration of Human Rights, the Secretary-General of the United Nations shall be requested, acting with the advice of the Commission on Human Rights and interested specialized agencies and in cooperation with Member States, to institute a comprehensive programme of education designed to bring before the people of the world the principles set forth in the Declaration in such a manner that they and their Governments may be encouraged to take steps within their own borders to bring about the conditions which the Declaration envisages as being essential to the full realization of human rights and fundamental freedoms.[35]

This initiative culminated in a resolution adopted by the UN General Assembly just after the Assembly had adopted the Universal Declaration, in which the General Assembly underlined that the adoption of the Universal Declaration was an historic act, destined to consolidate world peace through the contribution of the United Nations towards the liberation of individuals from the unjustified oppression and constraint to which they had too often been subjected. The General Assembly therefore called for the text of the Declaration to be disseminated among all peoples throughout the world. In particular, the Assembly recommended to the governments of member states that they show their adherence to Article 56 of the United Nations Charter by using every means within their power solemnly to publicize the text of the Declaration and to cause it to be disseminated, displayed, read, and expounded principally in schools and other educational institutions, without distinction based on the political status of the countries or territories. In addition, the Assembly requested the Secretary-General of the UN to have the Declaration widely disseminated and, to that end, to publish and distribute texts not only in the official languages of the UN but also by using every means at the disposal of the UN, in all languages possible, and invited the specialized agencies and non-governmental organizations of the world to do their utmost to bring the Declaration to the attention of their members.[36]

Unfortunately, on account of under-development, poverty, conflicts, and poor governance, human rights education in Asia has not kept faith with the vision of the founders. This section outlines briefly look at the state of human rights education in Asia.

On 19 December 2011, the UN General Assembly adopted the United Nations Declaration on Human Rights Education and Training.[37] The Declaration provided that everyone has the right to know, seek, and receive information about all human rights and fundamental freedoms and should have access to human rights education and training. Human rights education and training is essential for the promotion of universal respect for and observance of all human rights and fundamental freedoms for all (Article 1).

States, and where applicable relevant governmental authorities, the Declaration continued, had the primary responsibility to promote and ensure human rights education and training, developed and implemented in a spirit of participation, inclusion, and responsibility. States should take steps, individually and through international assistance and cooperation, to ensure to the maximum of their available resources, the progressive implementation of human rights education and training by appropriate means, including the adoption of legislative and administrative measures and policies (Article 7). States should develop, or promote the development of, at the appropriate level, strategies and policies and, where appropriate, action plans and programmes to implement human rights education and training (Article 8).

Various actors within society, the Declaration continued, including, inter alia, educational institutions, the media, families, local communities, civil society institutions, including NGOs, human rights defenders and the private sector have an important role to play in promoting and providing human rights education and training. (Article 10). Voluntary funding for projects and initiatives in the field of human rights education and training should be encouraged. States should take appropriate measures to ensure the effective implementation of and follow-up to the present Declaration and make the necessary resources available in this regard. (Article 14).

On 14 September 2016, the UN Human Rights Council organized a panel discussion on the implementation of the Declaration. Its deliberations were summarized by the Office of High Commissioner for Human Rights in a report presented to the 35th session of the Council. Several delegates emphasized that human rights education was a prerequisite for realizing all human rights. Human rights embody a set of values that guarantee respect for dignity and equality for all, and can only be exercised and protected if all people know them. In that regard, delegates highlighted the value of the United Nations Declaration for Human Rights Education and Training. They noted that the Declaration had played a very important role in highlighting the right to human rights education.

Human rights education, they continued, is a lifelong process that concerns all ages and all parts of society at all levels. It develops the knowledge and skills of learners to promote, defend, and apply human rights in their daily. Several delegates stressed the need for a sound methodology that was participatory, learner-centred, and action-oriented and took into account different cultural contexts.

Some Asian States participated in the discussion. Indonesia informed the meeting that its Fourth National Action Plan on Human Rights (2015–2019) enabled the inclusion of human rights in the professional training of police and military officers. Thailand and Vietnam highlighted the importance of not only providing training on human rights but also engaging media professionals and journalists in the implementation of human rights education programmes, particularly public awareness campaigns.

Delegates concluded that the adoption of the 2030 Agenda for Sustainable Development, which specifically included human rights education under target 4.7, provided a momentum for furthering human rights education.[38]

The State of Human Rights Education in Asia

Against this background, one might ask what the situation of human rights education is in Asia. The answer is, "in the early stages in some countries and not yet begun in others." The website of the Office of High Commissioner for Human Rights has a summary of national initiatives undertaken within the UN Decade for Human Rights Education (1995–2004). The information was last updated as of October 2003. A further Decade is underway but the OHCHR has not yet updated the information on its website.[39] Basing oneself on the website of the OHCHR, the following picture emerges of the state of human rights education.

Australia reported that in December 1998, the Attorney-General had announced the establishment of a National Committee on Human Rights Education, which brought together the expertise of business, community organizations, and the government in an endeavour to enhance human rights education in Australia.

China reported that human rights education was being provided through legal education programmes for all citizens, focusing on the study of the law and on how to apply it. Successive five-year plans had been implemented, reaching millions of people. As a result of these programmes, citizens were more familiar with the law and were increasingly using it for suing public officials, while the latter were more careful to act in accordance with the law.

Fiji reported that the Constitution of July 1998 had provided for the establishment of a human rights commission, whose tasks included the promotion of human rights education.

India reported that it had constituted a Coordination Committee, under the Chairmanship of the Secretary (sic), comprising of secretaries of other ministries and departments. The Committee had requested the National Human Rights Commission to draft a national plan of action for human rights education. That task had been accomplished in 2001, when the National Action Plan for Human Rights Education had been finalized. The plan focused on strategies for human rights awareness-raising and for sensitizing specific target groups (students, officers in the administration of justice, etc.). Civil society was involved in the implementation of human rights education programmes, as well as the National Human Rights Commission. The Government also reported on specific activities undertaken in the secondary and higher education sector, including the establishment of a curriculum revision committee to revise textbooks; the development of a number of training modules for teachers in English, Hindi, and local languages by the National Council for Teacher Education; the provision of financial assistance by the University Grants Commission, to universities and colleges for the development of specific courses in human rights. The Government further reported on a project to establish a national resource centre at the Indira Gandhi National Open University, which would include human rights materials, with a focus on educational tools.

Jordan reported that a series of laws had been passed over the period 1999–2001 focusing on the importance of creating a democratic and human rights climate in schools. Information on international and national human rights law had been incorporated into school curricula and textbooks; teaching materials, including on the issue of teaching methodologies, had been developed. Human rights awareness-raising programmes had been designed to promote the role of women leaders, the rights of the child, and conflict resolution methodologies. In cooperation with the Royal Human Rights Committee, the Ministry of Education had contributed to the training of administration of justice officials. In cooperation with the Mizan Institute, human rights and children's rights clubs had been set up in a number of Jordanian schools. Jordan was further planning to develop human rights training for educational managers, in cooperation with the UNESCO, and to establish a human rights education and training centre.

The Islamic Republic of Iran reported that, in cooperation with the UNDP and OHCHR, the Faculty of Law and Political Science of the University of Tehran was implementing a project for strengthening national capacities for human rights research and training, which would bring together faculty members, students, and university graduates. It was expected that as a result of the project, a volume of literature on different crucial human rights subjects would be published.

Japan reported that the Headquarters for the Promotion of Human Rights Education had been established in December 1995. In July 1997, a broad national plan of action for human rights education had been released, which included the promotion of human rights education and training at all levels (school, general public, corporations and civil society movements, professionals), specific programmes for special groups (women, children, the aged, people with disabilities, people with HIV infection), and the promotion of international cooperation and other public information activities, such as symposia and conferences.

New Zealand reported that since 1993, the New Zealand Human Rights Commission, as mandated in its statute, had been developing human rights education and awareness programmes. In 1999, an agreement had been signed with the New Zealand Association of Citizen's Advice Bureau, which maintained more than 90 offices on the national territory, providing each office with a human rights education presence. In addition, the Human Rights Unit of the Ministry of Foreign Affairs had been engaged in raising awareness of human rights issues in the country.

Pakistan reported that plans were underway to set up a national committee. The Human Rights Wing of the Ministry of Law, Justice and Human Rights had been entrusted with the responsibility of human rights education at the national level. The Human Rights Wing had been working on a national plan for human rights education. The national action plan would introduce the subject of human rights through curriculum development at school, college, and university levels, and through extra-curricular activities such as debates, essays, paintings, puppet shows, songs, stage plays, community service, and linkages with under-privileged schoolchildren. The UNESCO was providing printed material to approximately 300 schools involved in the project on human rights education.

The Philippines reported that a National Plan of Action for Human Rights Education had been prepared by the Philippine Commission on Human Rights. The Plan included clear objectives, target audiences, strategies, and programmes, including the creation of a human rights training, documentation, and research centre. In the implementation of the Plan, the Commission had entered into a number of formal agreements with other national partners for human rights education, to define in detail specific areas of responsibility.

The Republic of Korea reported that a variety of measures had been undertaken to promote human rights awareness, including the dissemination of human rights treaties through their publication and translation into Korean, the intensified provision of human rights education to public officials, the organization of a national programme of public lectures and symposia on human rights, and the provision of legal aid services, through which fundamental human rights were publicized in medium- and small-sized cities coupled with farming and fishing communities.

Sri Lanka reported that a Management Committee responsible for the formulation of a national plan of action for human rights education had been established. The Committee was composed of ten members, five representing the governmental sector and five the non-governmental and civil society sector. The Committee had been established with the technical assistance of the OHCHR and UNDP.

Syria, prior to the ongoing civil war, reported on work undertaken towards the integration of international humanitarian law into academic curricula, as well as on plans for the future integration in school curricula, in cooperation with the International Committee of the Red Cross. Education activities were also being undertaken to foster religious tolerance in the formal education system.

Thailand reported that a sub-committee on the rights of the child had been established following Thailand's ratification of the Convention on the Rights of the Child. It promoted child rights education and other issues. The Office of the National Commission on Women's Affairs (ONCWA) had implemented legal literacy programmes for local women and published materials on the topic of women and the law.

In 1998, a National Committee had been established to draft the National Policy and Plan of Action on Human Rights, which had been completed and approved by parliament in October 2000. One of the 11 sections of the document concerned human rights education. The National Policy and Plan of Action on Human Rights was implemented through inter-ministry coordination, and the Ministry of Education was the focal point for the specific section on human rights education.

In addition to the foregoing countries, the OHCHR website carried information on two Central Asian states, Azerbaijan and Kazakhstan. In June 1998, a State Programme for Human Rights Protection had been approved and provided for the Government of Azerbaijan to take measures for the development of specialized training in human rights. Kazakhstan had sought to integrate human rights into school curricula at all levels of education. Such integration involved the study and the use of relevant international human rights treaties. Moreover, some universities had developed programmes on human rights teaching and research.

While awaiting updated studies by the UN, a recent study (2017) by Asia-Pacific Human Rights Information Center, *Human Rights Education in Asia-Pacific*, offers a general picture of the situation. A key point of the study is that while human rights education is important, it does not always appear as a singular programme, rather as a component of educational programmes and projects. Educational programmes address specific issues and limit their human rights content to those relevant to their focuses. In this context, the study asks: has human rights education lost its place as a specific area of education since it has been subsumed under different "educations"?[40] While the human rights component of all educational sectors is welcome," without sufficient presentation of human rights, these "educations" may sideline human rights content and stress other components."[41] Jefferson Plantilla, in his "Introduction" to the study, notes that:

> The challenge lies in ensuring proper learning and teaching of human rights. There should be adherence to the international principles that define human rights. There cannot be "localized" versions of human rights perpetuated by selective understanding of human rights or in support of the perspective that human rights should understood in relation to specific "contexts" (cultural, social, economic and political particularities).[42]

In this vein, one may note the human rights programme of Asia Centre in Bangkok, which undertakes evidence-based research on regional human rights issues. Also noteworthy are Mahidol University's Master of Arts Program in Human Rights and Master of Human Rights and Democratization. A Center for Human Rights Studies and Social Development (CHRSD) was created by Mahidol University in 1996, to provide education and research opportunities in the area of human rights. CHRSD together with the Raoul Wallenberg Institute of Human Rights and Humanitarian Law created the Southeast Asian Human Rights Studies Network (SEAHRN).[43] Under the Strengthening Human Rights and Peace Research and Education in Southeast Asia/ASEAN (SHAPE SEA) Program run by a network of academic institutions, members of the ASEAN University Network–Human Rights Education (AUN–HRE) and the Southeast Asian Human Rights Studies Network (SEAHRN) produce an annual *Human Rights Outlook in Southeast Asia*. It is the first human rights assessment report ever produced by scholars within the region. Its second volume offered a bleak picture of the situation in the region. Amidst positive economic progress,

> …[T]he region is also facing a drastic regression of human rights. As such, significant decline in democratic processes has been recorded in a majority of countries around the region, from Cambodia to the Philippines and Thailand where leaders now wield absolute power to curtail human rights especially pertaining to freedom of expression and assembly. Moreover, a number of countries have begun to use criminal charges and special legislation, including security and sedition laws, to restrict and silence academics and activists, as well as political opponents. Indeed, academic freedom has come under attack not only by political leaders but also by university administrations.

In addition, much like other parts of the world, populism has become the norm leaving accountability, transparency, and participation, the basic principles of human rights, hardly able to find a voice in governance. In the meantime, conflicts in the southern Philippines and Thailand have continued alongside ethno-religious conflicts in Myanmar's Rakhine State, resulting in a massive exodus of Rohingya refugees into neighbouring countries including some in Southeast Asia.[44]

Conclusion

In the preceding chapter on implementation, we saw that Asia is experiencing severe problems of gross violations of human rights. So, on a region-wide basis, it might provoke ridicule to speak of the provision of human rights education. Halting gross violations of human rights is the highest priority.

Yet, one should acknowledge at least the recognition, in some states, of the potential role of human rights education and efforts being made in some of these states to develop human rights education. One has seen National Plans of Action, National Committees, the dissemination of information, the development of curricula, and the mobilization of civil society.

One could say that Asia is professing a commitment to the human rights values of the Universal Declaration of Human Rights even as it experiences severe problems of poverty, inequality, conflicts, and social injustice.

Notes

1. Susan Waltz, "Reclaiming and rebuilding the history of the Universal Declaration of Human Rights" Third World Quarterly, Volume 23, Number 3, 1 June 2002, pp. 437–448(12), p. 10.
2. Susan Waltz (2002), p. 44.
3. Roland Burke, "The Compelling Dialogue of Freedom: Human Rights at the Bandung Conference," *Human Rights Quarterly*, V.8, 2006, p. 947.
4. All citations in Burke (2006), pp. 947–9.
5. Burke, p. 948.
6. Burke (2006), p. 949.
7. Ibid.
8. Ibid.
9. Final Communiqué of the Asian-African conference of Bandung (24 April 1955),

10. Burke (2006), p. 950.
11. Roland Burke, "From individual rights to national development: the first UN International Conference on Human Rights, Tehran, 1968," *Journal of World History*. Vol. 19, No. 3 Sept. 2008, p275.
12. Proclamation of Teheran, Final Act of the International Conference on Human Rights, Teheran, 22 April to 13 May 1968, U.N. Doc. A/CONF. 32/41 at 3 (1968).
13. Vienna Declaration and Programme of Action Adopted by the World Conference on Human Rights in Vienna on 25 June 1993. https://www.ohchr.org/EN/ProfessionalInterest/Pages/Vienna.aspx
14. Hurst Hannum, "The Status Of The Universal Declaration Of Human Rights In National And International Law," *GA Journal of International & Comparative. Law*, 1995–1996, Vol 25, p. 4 (pp. 287 to 397).
15. Hurst Hannum, "The Status Of The Universal Declaration Of Human Rights In National And International Law," *GA Journal of International & Comparative. Law*, 1995–1996, Vol 25, p. 4 (pp. 287 to 397).
16. International Service for Human Rights (2013), "Vienna Declaration and Programme of Action + 20," p. 13 https://www.ishr.ch/sites/default/files/article/files/vdpa.pdf
17. Jiunn-rong Yeh, "The Development of Regional Human Rights Institutions in Asia – Dialectical and functional perspectives," in *Global Constitutionalism and Multi-layered Protection of Human Rights*, edited by SNU Asia-Pacific Law Institute. (Seoul: Constitutional Court of Korea, 2016).
18. Yeh notes that new democracies such as Mongolia, South Korea and Taiwan have not provided a privileged status for international human rights law within the domestic legal regime. Ibid.
19. See Manu Bhagavan (2010) "A New Hope: India, the United Nations and the Making of the Universal Declaration of Human Rights," *Modern Asian Studies* 44, 2 (2010) pp. 311–347.
20. The Constitution of India, 6 November 1949, https://www.india.gov.in/sites/upload_files/npi/files/coi_part_full.pdf
21. https://japan.kantei.go.jp/constitution_and_government_of_japan/constitution_e.html
22. Yeh notes that some new democracies such as Mongolia, South Korea and Taiwan have not provided a privileged status for international human rights law within the domestic legal regime....
23. Hurst Hannum, "The Status of the Universal Declaration of Human Rights in National and International Law," *Georgia Journal International and Comparative Law*, 1995–1996, Vol. 25, pp. 355–366 (289–388).
24. Zezen Zaenel Mutaqin, "The Strong State and Pancasila: Reflecting Human Rights in the Indonesian Democracy," Constitutional Review, December 2016, Volume 2, Number 2, pp. 159–188.

25. The Constitution of the Republic of Indonesia 1945, available at http://www.ilo.org/wcmsp5/groups/public/%2D%2D-ed_protect/%2D%2D-protrav/%2D%2D-ilo_aids/documents/legaldocument/wcms_174556.pdf
26. Yeh, p. 642.
27. See Hannum, p. 381 for a list of cases.
28. Li-Ann Thoio (2008) "Reading Rights Rightly: The UDHR and its Creeping Influence on the Development of Singapore Public Law," *Singapore Journal of Legal Studies*, pp. 264–291, December 2008.
29. Ibid., p. 265.
30. Ibid.
31. Ibid., p. 290.
32. ASEAN (2009), Terms of Reference, of AICHR, ASEAN Secretariat.
33. ASEAN (2009), Terms of Reference, of AICHR, ASEAN Secretariat.
34. ASEAN (2012), ASEAN Human Rights Declaration. ASEAN Secretariat. For a critical assessment of the relationship between the AHRD and the UDHR, See Catherine Renshaw (2013), "The ASEAN Human Rights. Declaration 2012," 13 *Human Rights Law Review,* 557 (2013), pp. 557–579.
35. E/CN.4/144, 16 June 1948.
36. General Assembly resolution 217D (III) of 10 December 1948.
37. United Nations General Assembly Resolution 66/137.
38. Human Rights Council, A/HRC/35/6, paras. 26, 27, 37, 38, and 49.
39. OHCHR website, Summary of national initiatives undertaken within the Decade for Human Rights (1995–2004), consulted on 14 June, 2017.
40. Asia Pacific Human Rights Information Centre (2017). Human Rights Education in Asia-Pacific (Volume Seven), p. 9.
41. Ibid., p. 10.
42. Ibid., p. 11.
43. See Alexa Johns, "Graduate Programs on Human Rights: Mahidol University," https://www.hurights.or.jp/archives/asia-pacific/section1/15AlexaJohns.pdf
44. SHAPE-SEA, *Human Rights Outlook in Southeast Asia: 2016* (Bangkok: Institute of Human Rights and Peace Studies (IHRP), 2017), p. vii.

References

Primary Documents: United Nations Documents from Drafting Process in William Schabas:

E/CN.4/144, 16 June 1948.

Association of Southeast Asian Nations (ASEAN), Terms of Reference, of AICHR, ASEAN Secretariat, 2009.

Association of Southeast Asian Nations (ASEAN), ASEAN Human Rights Declaration. ASEAN Secretariat, 2012.

Asia Pacific Human Rights Information Centre, Human Rights Education in Asia-Pacific (Volume Seven), (Osaka: Asian Human Rights Information Center, 2017).

Bhagavan, Manu, "A New Hope: India, the United Nations and the Making of the Universal Declaration of Human Rights," *Modern Asian Studies* 44, 2 (2010) pp. 311–347.

Burke, Roland, "From individual rights to national development: the first UN International Conference on Human Rights, Tehran, 1968," *Journal of World History*. Vol. 19, No.3 Sept. 2008, p. 275.

Burke, Roland. "The Compelling Dialogue of Freedom: Human Rights at the Bandung Conference," *Human Rights Quarterly*, V.8, 2006, p. 947.

Constitution of India, 6 November 1949, https://www.india.gov.in/sites/upload_files/npi/files/coi_part_full.pdf

Constitution of Japan.1947 https://japan.kantei.go.jp/constitution_and_government_of_japan/constitution_e.html

Constitution of the Republic of Indonesia 1945, available at http://www.ilo.org/wcmsp5/groups/public/%2D%2D-ed_protect/%2D%2D-protrav/%2D%2D-ilo_aids/documents/legaldocument/wcms_174556.pdf

Final Communiqué of the Asian-African conference of Bandung (24 April 1955).

Hannum, Hurst, "The Status Of The Universal Declaration Of Human Rights In National And International Law," *GA Journal of International & Comparative. Law*, 1995–1996, Vol 25, p. 4 (pp. 287 to 397).

Human Rights Council, A/HRC/35/6, paras. 26, 27, 37, 38 and 49.

International Service for Human Rights (2013), "Vienna Declaration and Programme of Action + 20," 2013, p. 13 https://www.ishr.ch/sites/default/files/article/files/vdpa.pdf

Johns, Alexa, "Graduate Programs on Human Rights: Mahidol University," Human Rights Education in Asia-Pacific (Volume One), (Osaka: Asia Pacific Human Rights Information Center, 2010), pp. 213–223 https://www.hurights.or.jp/archives/asia-pacific/section1/15AlexaJohns.pdf

Mutaqin, Zezen Zaenel. "The Strong State and Pancasila: Reflecting Human Rights in the Indonesian Democracy," Constitutional Review, December 2016, Volume 2, Number 2, pp. 159–188.

OHCHR website, Summary of national initiatives undertaken within the Decade for Human Rights (1995–2004), consulted on 14 June 2017.

Proclamation of Teheran, Final Act of the International Conference on Human Rights, Teheran, 22 April to 13 May 1968, U.N. Doc. A/CONF. 32/41 at 3 (1968).

Renshaw, Chatherine, "The ASEAN Human Rights Declaration 2012," 13 *Human Rights Law Review*, 557 (2013), pp. 557–579.

SHAPE-SEA, *Human Rights Outlook in Southeast Asia: 2016* (Bangkok: Institute of Human Rights and Peace Studies (IHRP), 2017).

Thio, Li-Ann (2008) "Reading Rights Rightly: The UDHR and its Creeping Influence on the Development of Singapore Public Law," *Singapore Journal of Legal Studies*, pp. 264–291, December 2008.

United Nations, General Assembly Resolution 66/137.

United Nations, General Assembly resolution 217D (III) of 10 December 1948.

Vienna Declaration and Programme of Action Adopted by the World Conference on Human Rights in Vienna on 25 June 1993. https://www.ohchr.org/EN/ProfessionalInterest/Pages/Vienna.aspx

Waltz, Susan, Reclaiming and rebuilding the history of the Universal Declaration of Human Rights," Third *World Quarterly*, Vol 23, No 3, 1 June 2002, p. 438 (pp 437–448).

Yeh, Jiunn-rong, "The Development of Regional Human Rights Institutions in Asia – Dialectical and functional perspectives," in *Global Constitutionalism and Multi-layered Protection of Human Rights*, edited by SNU Asia-Pacific Law Institute. (Seoul: Constitutional Court of Korea, 2016).

CHAPTER 10

Conclusion

The UDHR, writes Morsink, has become the "moral lingua franca of our age" and has performed a canonical function for our age, since 1948.[1] Referring to Lynn Hunt's examination of the French and American revolutions,[2] he writes that the UDHR provided an "abstract universalism" akin to that of the French declaration, a metaphysical grounding that, once let out of the bottle, would hold arbitrary rule to account.[3] In this vein, Glenn Hughes has argued that the key framers, though fully aware of Christian anthropology that informed Western concepts of dignity of the person, also grasped that a ratifiable Declaration, needed to be free of religious reference and that the notion of "inherency" sufficed "to suggest heuristically not only a universal human nature but also, crucially, a transcendent reality in which all persons participate."[4]

Waltz has noted that it is one thing to recognize human rights in Western philosophy; it is quite another thing to equate the two as being synonymous.[5] Rene Cassin, representative of France, is often given credit for representing the Western philosophy and having a powerful impact on the draft. While he was active in all phases of the drafting, it has been noted that "he did not enter the room until the baby was born."[6] John Humphrey was perhaps more instrumental in framing the first draft, which drew on many Asian constitutions, as we have seen.

Joe Hoover has captured the essence of current critical scholarship about the UDHR by pointing out that:

R. Ramcharan, B. Ramcharan, *Asia and the Drafting of the Universal Declaration of Human Rights*,
https://doi.org/10.1007/978-981-13-2104-7_10

> Our understanding of the significance of the UDHR tends to oscillate between two poles: On one side it can be seen as a moment of founding for the human rights regime, based on the documents unique status as a symbol of moral consensus ...while, on the other hand, it can be seen as a political imposition by the postwar liberal powers intent upon remaking the international order in their image.[7]

Morsink has refuted critics like human rights scholar Michael Ignatieff who advised human rights advocates to see human rights not as a language or proclamation of eternal verities but as a discourse for adjudication of conflict.[8] Indeed, one need not subscribe to the proponents of the "end-times for human rights," however well-intentioned as they may be to advance the cause of justice around the world.[9] Independent researcher Fengyu Duan has argued that even if Western influences were strong, the UDHR is not imperialistic because it offers criticism against colonialism, it is not the anti-thesis of diversity because it encourages heterogeneity as a way of life as long as human rights and fundamental freedoms are satisfied. "Thus we may argue that the declaration, which has transcended different cultures, is a universal document endorsed by different peoples all over the world. Hence its universality should not be disregarded."[10]

The study of the UDHR as a political project and global dialogue over rights with multiple cultural and philosophical influences continues to today.[11] Indeed, while some parts of the world were not present in the drafting process, many parts were, including Asia, which influenced and participated in the drafting of the UDHR. Some 250 delegates and advisors from 56 countries were accredited to participate in the construction of the Universal Declaration, but most scholarly attention has been directed to the role of a few delegations.[12] In light of new evidence by 2001, Waltz, for example, posited a role for small states, not only big powers. Charles Malik, a Lebanese, advised the United States that many states wanted to scrutinize the document line by line, whereas the United States wanted to move to a speedy adoption.[13]

This work has shown convincingly that Asia played an integral and even seminal role in the drafting of the Universal Declaration of Human Rights. We have seen how the constitutional provisions of ten Asian countries were central material sources in its drafting.

At the time of the drafting of the Universal Declaration, large parts of Asia were under foreign domination. Yet, the desire for freedom could be seen in the visions of a future Declaration advanced by China, India, Lebanon, Vietnam, and Indonesia.

Asia provided key inspirational drafters of the Declaration, notably Charles Malik, P.C. Chang, Mrs. Hansa Mehta, Carlos Romulo, and Mohammad Zafrullah Khan. Malik and Chang were the inspired philosophers. Mehta and Romulo joined them in pleading for dignity and equitable life chances for the world's peoples. Zafrullah Khan was a consensus-builder. Asia's quest for a new humanism and for an equitable international order shone throughout the process.

Glendon, in response to an interview question about what the UDHR would have looked like if Charles Malik were not present, noted that:

> What would have been absent would have been the spirit of the preamble, the spirit with which the document opens, the affirmation of the unity of the human family and the sections at the end which don't contain rights at all, but rather emphasize the conditions that are necessary if rights are to become a reality.
>
> So, for example, one of the very last articles was one that was drafted by Malik himself. It says, 'Everyone is entitled to a social and international order in which the rights and freedoms set forth in this declaration can be fully realized.' In the context of the declaration, that's a reminder of the importance of democracy and the rule of law in assuring that rights exist not only on paper, but in reality.[14]

The role of P.C. Chang of China is noted by many scholars and is being increasingly claimed by Chinese scholars.[15] Chang, who received a Ph.D. at Columbia Teacher College and was conversant with Western philosophy, constantly brought to bear Confucian culture.[16] Chang has been credited with determining the structure of the International Bill: Declaration, Covenant, and measures of implementation. Lydia Liu has demonstrated that P.C. Chang was one of the principal architects of the UDHR in 1946–1948, a passionate critic of cultural relativism and colonialism and resolved to refashion human rights into a universal moral idea. Debates in the drafting of the UDHR, she notes,

> show how Chang attempted a translingual reworking of the plural human within the framework of rights talk. The ground of universalism he fought to reclaim in his capacity as vice chair of the UN Commission on Human Rights was the presumed meeting ground between Confucian moral philosophy and European Enlightenment thought. That precarious ground, however, did not come from nowhere since the idea of the plural human had already been deeply embedded in the development of modern theories of political pluralism and in the human rights activism

> of prewar China (1927–37). I suggest that this earlier history of global engagement with human rights must also be brought into our rethinking of universalism.[17]

Sun Pinghua, while noting that P.C. Chang's contribution is not well known in China, has argued that "his great contribution to the development of the world human rights cause was not accidental."[18] Zhang Pengchun's had a rich life experience that "coined his sigh with deep emotions for human hardship, his deep thinking on human nature and the problems of human rights protection, which laid a solid foundation for the formation of his pluralist view of human rights."[19] In highlighting P.C. Chang's humanism, Sun writes that:

> During working in the UN, especially in the drafting process of the International Bill of Rights, Zhang Pengchun repeatedly expounded the justice of humanism from a humanism standpoint. He attacked the evil in human nature by reflecting human behavior viewed from Nazi Germany and Japanese imperialism inhuman atrocities. He advocated the training and development of "goodness" in human nature and actively promoted the spirit of humanism. When discussing the implementation measures of the human rights, he emphasized with his generous feelings and tolerant attitudes that the purpose of the implementation was not to punish crime, but to promote self-reform through education. This tolerant attitude also reflected Zhang Pengchun's humanism.[20]

For Sun, P.C. Chang "incorporated traditional Chinese culture into the UDHR, which made the Confucianism have a profound impact on the West, the world and the whole human society."[21] In a commentary in a Chinese magazine, *Human Rights*, Sun would boldly claim:

> It is Zhang Pengchun who proposed the master plan for drafting the Declaration… He was in fact the mastermind of the Declaration, contributing to the drafting of every item in the Declaration by using his wisdom and knowledge. The most remarkable thing was that Zhang Pengchun called for inclusion of the quintessence of both Eastern and Western cultures in the Declaration.[22]

Claiming P.C. Chang in this way takes place in the context of increasing rights discourse in China, especially after the 1989 Tiananmen incident. The older post-1949 emphasis on collective rights of anti-discrimination, anti-colonialism, self-determination, right to development, and economic and social rights have given way to a new emphasis after 1991. Since its White Paper on human rights in November 1991, China began to place emphasis on "Chinese" values and on "subsistence" rights, not merely on economic, social, and cultural rights. Ann Kent notes that it has not argued against universality of human rights but that civil and political rights are second-tier rights.[23]

Similar to Chinese exceptionalism is the "Asian values" arguments. Whereas "Asian values" was championed powerfully in Singapore's exceptionalism,[24] which also emphasized "rice over rights," Naruemon Thabchumpon has shown that in Thailand "Asian values" were never caught on. Instead "Thai style human rights notions" served a rhetorical purpose by local authorities and politicians for personal political gain and that new rights and rights institutions under the 1997 Constitution that have not served fully to protect rights and liberties of people.[25] Leena Avonious has shown that "the process of grounding of international human rights standards in Indonesia already started during the heyday of 'Asian values' debate."[26] Appeals to universal human rights principles served to shed the yolk of authoritarianism under General Suharto, who was ousted in 1997.[27] Indeed, over the past three decades, despite lagging practice, international human rights standards have become firmly grounded in Indonesia. In addressing exceptionalist claims and "Asian values" claims emanating from post-colonial states across the region, Damien Kingsbury has pointed out that "the right to meet, to discuss, to express views, and to disseminate views amongst one's community is basic not just to political freedom, but to the full and fair manifestation of the human condition."[28] From a very practical perspective, "People are different but...not in ways that are terribly important...not radically so."[29]

Asian States, as we have seen through the Bandung Conference, at Tehran, at the Vienna Conference, and in the recent national reports on human rights submitted to the Universal Periodic Review process of the Human Rights Council, have continued to profess their faith in universal human rights. At the same time, they point to severe challenges stemming from poverty, inequality, and historical injustices.

Asia also has massive problems of gross violations of human rights in numerous countries, and the challenge for the future will be to bring these gross violations to an end swiftly. Asia's challenge in the future will be to faithfully respect, protect, and ensure the rights enshrined in the Universal

Declaration, and to be faithful to the visions of the Universal Declaration that Asia advanced at the time of its drafting.

The obligation of each government to protect human rights is regulated by international law. This is the idea of international obligation. In respect of economic, social, and cultural rights, the key international instrument is the International Covenant on this topic (ICESCR). The elements of protection found in the ICESCR are realization through all appropriate means, including the adoption of legislation, non-discrimination, progressive realization, full realization of the efforts of individual countries to the maximum of its available resources, international assistance, and cooperation especially economic and technical.

"Each State Party to the present Covenant undertakes to take steps, individually and through international cooperation and assistance and cooperation, especially economic and technical, to the maximum of its available resources, with a view to achieving progressively the full realization including particularly the adoption of legislative measures."

Articles 55 and 56 of the UN Charter are relevant to the concept of international cooperation. The primary duty to protect economic, social, and cultural rights lies with each government. Judicial protection of economic, social, and cultural rights may be provided for in national law, but this is a rarity. The concept of a situation where there is a consistent pattern of gross violations of human rights is known in international and regional human rights jurisprudence but has so far been applied mainly in respect of civil and political rights.

The "social action litigation" jurisprudence of the Indian Supreme Court recognizes the concept of a situation where there is a consistent pattern of gross violations of economic, social, and cultural rights. Some national human rights commissions do endeavour to protect economic, social, and cultural rights. The Optional Protocol to the ICESCR has, at the time of writing, only yielded two decisions. So far only six Asian States have become parties to the Protocol or have signed it.[30]

The Independent Commission, which launched the concept of the Responsibility to Protect, did not discuss its coverage to ESCRts. The Summit Outcome Document of the General Assembly of 2005, which endorsed the concept of the Responsibility to Protect, did not extend it to ESCRts. However the document had elaborate development goals which have now been updated in the Sustainable Development Goals.

The following questions arise for reflection: should governments activate, nationally, regionally, and internationally, the concept of a consistent pattern of gross violations of economic, social, and cultural rights? Should they introduce and operationalize a new concept, that of the prevention of gross violations of economic, social, and cultural rights, placing the emphasis on the duty of governments, using their available resources, to prevent gross violations of ESCRts? Should they entrust the judiciary more with the protection of economic, social, and cultural rights? Is the idea of an international petitions procedure in respect of ESCRts a helpful one? How should the Human Rights Council, the Economic and Social Council, and the Security Council react to situations where it is established that a government is failing in its duty to protect economic, social, and cultural rights? What more could the Committee on Economic, Social and Cultural Rights do to protect ESCRts? What protection roles have the special rapporteurs on ESCRts played and what more could they do in the future? What roles have regional human rights bodies played in the protection of ESCRts? How can NGOs contribute more to the protection of ESCRts.

Implementation, prevention, protection, equality, and equity are the challenges of the present and the future in Asia. Ideas such as the following could be considered:

- Each National Parliament should consider establishing a Parliamentary Committee on the Responsibility to Protect.
- National Parliaments could hold periodic deliberations on the implementation of the Responsibility to Protect in their country.
- Every country could consider arranging for a National Assessment regarding the implementation of the Responsibility to Protect in that country.
- National Human Rights Institutions and NGOs can play an invaluable role when it comes to national implementation of the Responsibility to Protect generally and the preparation of national assessments as suggested above.
- Women's organizations in each country could play a leading role in highlighting the importance of the Responsibility to Protect and in monitoring its implementation in their respective country.
- National Military Establishments could keep under ongoing consideration the role they might play in implementing the Responsibility to Protect in their own country.
- National Police Forces could regularly review their role in implementing the Responsibility to Protect inside their respective country, particularly as regards protests, civil disturbances, and similar events.

- Education and training as regards the Responsibility to Protect should be given priority attention in every country.
- Universities and other institutions of higher learning in each country should highlight implementation of the Responsibility to Protect in their teaching and research activities.

Notes

1. J. Morsink, *Inherent human rights: philosophical roots of the universal declaration* (Philadelphia: University of Pennsylvania Press, 2009), p. 2.
2. Lynne Hunt, *Inventing Human Rights: A History* (New York: WW Norton, 2007). In this work, Hung shows that human rights require interlocking qualities: they must be natural (inherent in human beings), equal (the same for everyone), and universal (applicable everywhere).
3. Morsink (2009), p. 4.
4. Glenn Hughes. "The Concept Of Dignity In The Universal Declaration Of Human Rights," *The Journal of Religious Ethics*, Vol. 39, No. 1 (March 2011), p. 1 (pp. 1–24).
5. Susan Waltz, p. 56.
6. Ibid.
7. Joe Hoover, "Rereading the Universal Declaration of Human Rights: Plurality and Contestation, Not Consensus," *Journal of Human Rights*, Vol. 12, 2013, pp. 217–241., p. 219.
8. Morsink (2009), p. 6.
9. See Patrick Kelly, "What is Hope For?" in *Los Angeles Review of Books*, 7 June 2018. Kelly writes that it is incumbent on scholars to take a more critical approach and to move away from "uplifting and triumphalist story of the rise of human rights." Available at https://lareviewofbooks.org/article/what-is-hope-for/#!
10. Duan, Fengyu, The Universal Declaration of Human Rights and the Modern History of Human Rights (November 7, 2017), p. 38 Available at SSRN: https://ssrn.com/abstract=3066882 or https://doi.org/10.2139/ssrn.3066882
11. See, for example, Susan Waltz (2001), "Universalising Human Rights: The Role of Small States in the Construction of the Universal Declaration of Human Rights, *Human Rights Quarterly*," Volume 23, Number 1, February 2001, pp. 44–72.
12. Waltz (2001), pp. 55–56.
13. Waltz (2001?), p. 56. See also Rowland Brucken (2014). *A most uncertain crusade: the United States, the United Nations, and human rights, 1941–1953*/DeKalb, IL: Northern Illinois University Press. Brucken produces

evidence indicating that the United States participated reluctantly in the elaboration of rights and implementation mechanisms as states negotiated the international covenants.
14. Interview: Professor Mary Ann Glendon discusses the role of Charles Malik in drafting the Universal Declaration of Human Rights, on PBS program *Weekend All Things Considered, Public Broadcasting Station*, 26 March 2001.
15. See Lydia H. Liu, "Shadows of Universalism: The Untold Story of Human Rights around 1948," Critical Inquiry 40, no. 4 (Summer 2014): 385–417; "Zhang Pengchun's Contributions to the Drafting of the UDHR," *China Legal Science*, Vol. 4, Issue 5 (September 2016), pp. 114–132.
16. Waltz, 2001, p. 57.
17. Lydia H. Liu, "Shadows of Universalism: The Untold Story of Human Rights around 1948," Critical Inquiry 40, no. 4 (Summer 2014): 385–417.
18. Sun Pinghua, "Zhang Pengchun's Human Rights Philosophy of Pluralism," China Legal Science. Vol. 5, 109 (2017), p. 109.
19. Sun Pinghua, "Zhang Pengchun's Human Rights Philosophy of Pluralism," China Legal Science. Vol. 5, 109 (2017), p. 109.
20. Sun Pinghua (107), "Zhang Pengchun's Human Rights Philosophy of Pluralism," *China Legal Sci.*, 5109 (2017).
21. Sun Pinghua (2017), Zhang Pengchun's Human Rights Philosophy of Pluralism, *China Legal Sci.*, 5, 109 (2017), p. 132.
22. Zhang Pengchun (2011), "A Globally Famed Chinese Human Rights Activist," Human Rights, No. 6, p. 29 (29–30).
23. Ann Kent (2008), "Chinese Values and Human Rights," in *Human Rights in Asia: A Reassessment of the Asian Values Debate,* Edited by Leena Avonius and Damien Kingsbury (Palgrave Macmillan), See also Ann Kent (1991) Waiting for Rights: China's Human Rights and China's Constitutions, 1949–1989. Human Rights Quarterly. May 1991, Vol. 13 Issue 2, pp. 170–201.
24. Laurence Wai-Teng Leong, "From 'Asian Values' to Singapore Exceptionalism," in *Human Rights in Asia: A Reassessment of the Asian Values Debate,* Edited by Leena Avonius and Damien Kingsbury (Palgrave Macmillan, 2008), pp. 121–140.
25. Naruemon Thabchumpon (2008), "Human Rights in Thailand: Rhetoric or Substance," in pp. 141–158.
26. Leena Avonious (2008), "From Marsinah to Munir: Grounding Human Rights in Indonesia," *Human Rights in Asia: A Reassessment of the Asian Values Debate,* Edited by Leena Avonius and Damien Kingsbury (Palgrave Macmillan), p. 115 (pp. 99–120).

27. Leena Avonious (2008), "From Marsinah to Munir: Grounding Human Rights in Indonesia," *Human Rights in Asia: A Reassessment of the Asian Values Debate,* Edited by Leena Avonius and Damien Kingsbury (Palgrave Macmillan), pp. 99–120.
28. Damien Kingsbury (2008), "Universalism and Exceptionalism in Asia," in *Human Rights in Asia: A Reassessment of the Asian Values Debate,* Edited by Leena Avonius and Damien Kingsbury (Palgrave Macmillan) p. 36 (pp. 19–39).
29. Kingsbury cites anthropologist E.E. Evans-Pritchard and philosopher Paul Ricoeur, cited in Kingsbury, p. 25.
30. The OHCHR database is available at http://indicators.ohchr.org/.

References

Avonious, Leena (2008), "From Marsinah to Munir: Grounding Human Rights in Indonesia," in *Human Rights in Asia: A Reassessment of the Asian Values Debate,* Edited by Leena Avonius and Damien Kingsbury (Palgrave Macmillan), p. 115 (pp. 99–120).

Brucken, Rowland, *A most uncertain crusade: the United States, the United Nations, and human rights, 1941–1953* (DeKalb, IL: Northern Illinois University Press, 2014).

Duan, Fengyu, The Universal Declaration of Human Rights and the Modern History of Human Rights (7 November 2017). Available at SSRN: https://ssrn.com/abstract=3066882 or https://doi.org/10.2139/ssrn.3066882.

Glendon, Mary Ann, Interview on the role of Charles Malik in drafting the Universal Declaration of Human Rights, on PBS program *Weekend All Things Considered, Public Broadcasting Station*, 26 March 2001.

Hughes.v Glenn, "The Concept Of Dignity In The Universal Declaration Of Human Rights," *The Journal of Religious Ethics*, Vol. 39, No. 1 (March 2011), (pp. 1–24).

Hunt, Lynne, *Inventing Human Rights: A History* (New York: WW Norton, 2007).

Joe Hoover, "Rereading the Universal Declaration of Human Rights: Plurality and Contestation, Not Consensus," *Journal of Human Rights*, Vol. 12, 2013, pp. 217–241.

Kelly, Patrick, "What is Hope For?" in *Los Angeles Review of Books*, 7 June 2018. Available at https://lareviewofbooks.org/article/what-is-hope-for/#!

Kent, Ann. "Chinese Values and Human Rights," in *Human Rights in Asia: A Reassessment of the Asian Values Debate,* Edited by Leena Avonius and Damien Kingsbury (Palgrave Macmillan, 2008).

Kent, Ann, "Waiting for Rights: China's Human Rights and China's Constitutions, 1949–1989," *Human Rights Quarterly.* May 1991, Vol. 13 Issue 2, (pp 170–201).

Kingsbury, Damien, "Universalism and Exceptionalism in Asia," in *Human Rights in Asia: A Reassessment of the Asian Values Debate,* Edited by Leena Avonius and Damien Kingsbury (Palgrave Macmillan, 2008) p. 36 (pp. 19–39).

Leong, Laurence Wai-Teng, "From "Asian Values" to Singapore Exceptionalism," in *Human Rights in Asia: A Reassessment of the Asian Values Debate,* Edited by Leena Avonius and Damien Kingsbury (Palgrave Macmillan, 2008), pp. 121–140.

Liu, Lydia H, "Zhang Pengchun's Contributions to the Drafting of the UDHR," *China Legal Science*, Vol. 4, Issue 5 (September 2016), pp. 114–132.

Liu, Lydia H. "Shadows of Universalism: The Untold Story of Human Rights around 1948," Critical Inquiry 40, no. 4 (Summer 2014): 385–417.

Morsink, Johannes. *Inherent human rights: philosophical roots of the universal declaration* (Philadelphia: University of Pennsylvania Press, 2009).

Sun Pinghua (107), "Zhang Pengchun's Human Rights Philosophy of Pluralism", *China Legal Sci.*, 5 109 (2017).

Thabchumpon, Naruemon, "Human Rights in Thailand: Rhetoric or Substance," in *Human Rights in Asia: A Reassessment of the Asian Values Debate,* Edited by Leena Avonius and Damien Kingsbury (Palgrave Macmillan, 2008) pp. 141–158.

Waltz, Susan, "Universalising Human Rights: The Role of Small States in the Construction of the Universal Declaration of Human Rights, *Human Rights Quarterly*," Volume 23, Number 1, February 2001, pp. 44–72.

Zhang Pengchun, (2011), "A Globally Famed Chinese Human Rights Activist," Human Rights, No. 6, p. 29 (29–30).

References

Primary Documents: United Nations Documents from Drafting Process in William Schabas:

A/C.3/SR 98, reproduced in Schabas, p. 2173:

A/C.3/237 7 October 1948, in Schabas, p. 2144.

A/C.3/243 7 October 1948a Recapitulation of Amendments to Article 1 of the Draft Declaration (E/800).

A/C.3/243 7 October 1948b, in Schabas, p. 2147.

A/C.3/247.

A/C.3/264 12 October 1948, in Schabas, pp. 2206.

A/C.3/314/Rev.1* 20 November 1948 Recapitulation of Amendments to the Preamble of the Draft Declaration (E/800) (In the chronological order of their submission to the Committee).

A/C.3/SR 100, reproduced in Schabas, p. 2190.

A/C.3/SR 100, reproduced in Schabas, p. 2196.

A/C.3/SR 96, reproduced in Schabas, p. 2152

A/C.3/SR 98, reproduced in Schabas, p. 2173.

A/C.3/SR 98, reproduced in Schabas, p. 2169.

A/C.3/SR 98, reproduced in Schabas, p. 2171:

A/C.3/SR 99, reproduced in Schabas, p. 2184.

A/C.3/SR. 127 (Schabas, pp. 2491–2492).

A/C.3/SR. 147, reproduced in Schabas, p. 2685.

A/C.3/SR. 98, reproduced in Schabas, op.cit., p. 2169.

A/C.3/SR.10032 12 October 1948, in Schabas, p. 2191.

R. Ramcharan, B. Ramcharan, *Asia and the Drafting of the Universal Declaration of Human Rights*,
https://doi.org/10.1007/978-981-13-2104-7

A/C.3/SR.139, reproduced in Schabas, p. 2603.
A/C.3/SR.146, reproduced in Schabas, p. 2673.
A/C.3/SR.42, 5 December, 1946, reproduced in Schabas, p. 87.
A/C.3/SR.9624 7 October 1948 Summary Record of the Ninety-Sixth Meeting [of the Third Committee] Held at the Palais de Chaillot, Paris, on Thursday, 7 October 1948, at 10:30 a.m.
A/C.3/SR.9930 11 October 1948, in Schabas, p. 2181.
A/PV. 182, reproduced in Schabas, op. cit. P. 3056.
A/PV. 182, reproduced in Schabas, op. cit. p. 3058.
A/PV. 182, reproduced in Schabas, op. cit. p. 3058. (PV means proces verbale).
A/PV. 182, reproduced in Schabas, op. cit. pp. 3054–3055.
A/PV.139 23 September 1948 Verbatim Record of the One Hundred and Thirty-Ninth Meeting [of the General Assembly] Held at the Palais de Chaillot, Paris, on Thursday, 23 September 1948, at 10.30 a.m.
A/PV.180, reproduced in Schabas, op. cit, p. 3028.
A/PV.180, reproduced in Schabas, op. cit. P. 3034.
A/PV.180, reproduced in Schabas, pp. 3027–3029.
A/PV.183, reproduced in Schabas, op. cit. P. 3073.
A/PV.183, reproduced in Schabas, pp. 3080–3081.
E.CN.4/SR 8, 31 January, 1947.(Schabas, 173).
E/422 (Schabas, 245).
E/439, 14 March, 1947; Summary record of the Six to eight meeting of the Economic and Social Council. (Schabas, 241).
E/CN.4/SR 14, 4 February, 1947a, (Schabas, 200).
E/CN.4/SR 14, 4 February, 1947b, (Schabas, 200).
E/CN.4/SR 14, 4 February, 1947c, (Schabas, 200).
E/CN.4/11.
E/CN.4/11 31 January 1947a.
E/CN.4/11 31 January 1947b, Draft of a Resolution for the General Assembly Submitted by the Representative of India.
E/CN.4/11 31 January, 1947c, reproduced in Schabas, pp. 175–176.
E/CN.4/132 14 June 1948a Lebanon: Suggested Preamble for the Draft International Declaration on Human Rights, Schabas p. 1870.
E/CN.4/144, 16 June, 1948b.
E/CN.4/2002/WG.18/4, para. 18.
E/CN.4/AC.1/18, 3 May, 1948. reproduced in Schabas, op. cit. pp. 1475–76.
E/CN.4/AC.1/3 4 June 1947a in Schabas, p. 282.
E/CN.4/AC.1/3/Add.2 9 June 1947b Plan of the Draft Outline of an International Bill of Rights (Prepared by the Secretariat), Schabas pp. 305–306.

E/CN.4/AC.1/ASR 3, reproduced in Schabas, p. 734.
E/CN.4/AC.1/SR.12, reproduced in Schabas, p. 847.
E/CN.4/AC.1/SR.12, reproduced in Schabas, p. 848.
E/CN.4/AC.1/SR.13, reproduced in Schabas, p. 863.
E/CN.4/AC.1/SR.2 11 June 1947d160 Summary Record of the Second Meeting [of the Drafting Committee of the Commission on Human Rights] Held at Lake Success, New York, on Wednesday, 11 June 1947 at 11:00 a.m.
E/CN.4/AC.1/SR.2 11 June 1947e160 Summary Record of the Second Meeting [of the Drafting Committee of the Commission on Human Rights] Held at Lake Success, New York, on Wednesday, 11 June 1947 at 11:00 a.m.
E/CN.4/AC.1/SR.21 4 May 1948 Summary Record of the Twenty-First Meeting [of the Drafting Committee, Second Session] Held at Lake Success, 4 May 1948 at 10.30 a.m.
E/CN.4/AC.1/SR.21, reproduced in Schabas op cit., pp. 1489–1490.
E/CN.4/AC.1/SR.8, reproduced in Schabas, p. 807.
E/CN.4/AC.2/SR.2 5 December 1947 Original Text: French Summary Record of the Second Meeting [of the Working Group on the Declaration of Human Rights] Held at the Palais des Nations, Geneva, on Friday 5 December 1947, at 3 p.m.
E/CN.4/AC.2/SR.7 9 December 1947 Summary Record of the Seventh Meeting [of the Working Group on the Declaration of Human Rights] Held at the Palais des Nations, Geneva, at 3 p.m. on Tuesday, 9 December, 1947f.
E/CN.4/SR 27, Schabas, p. 1121.
E/CN.4/SR 7, 31 January, 1947. (Schabas 169).
E/CN.4/SR 8, 31 January, 1947g, (Schabas 171).
E/CN.4/SR. 14, reproduced in Schabas, p. 391.
E/CN.4/SR.1, 27 January, 1947h. (Schabas, 159).
E/CN.4/SR.1, 27 January, 1947i. (Schabas, 159).
E/CN.4/SR.14 4 February 1947a Original Text: French Summary Record of the Fourteenth Meeting [of the Commission on Human Rights] Held at Lake Success, New York, on Tuesday, 4 February 1947 at 2:00 p.m.
E/CN.4/SR.14 4 February 1947b Original Text: French Summary Record of the Fourteenth Meeting [of the Commission on Human Rights] Held at Lake Success, New York, on Tuesday, 4 February 1947 at 2:00 p.m.
E/CN.4/SR.15, 5 February, 1947j. (Schabas, 205).
E/CN.4/SR.2, 27 January, 1947k, p. 1. (Schabas pp. 161–162).
E/CN.4/SR.25, Schabas, p. 1111.
E/CN.4/SR.41, reproduced in Schabas, p. 1305.
E/CN.4/SR.7 31 January 1947, Summary Record of the Seventh Meeting [of the Commission on Human Rights] Held at Lake Success, New York, on Friday, 31 January 1947.

E/CN.4/SR.7, 31 January 1947 Summary Record of the Seventh Meeting [of the Commission on Human Rights] Held at Lake Success, New York, on Friday, 31 January 1947, at 11:00 a.m.

E/CN.4/Sub.2/SR. 11, reproduced in Schabas, p. 1087.

E/CN.4/Sub.2/SR.23, reproduced in Schabas, p. 1098.

E/CN.4/W.4 13 January 1947l, Working Paper on an International Bill of Rights, Schabas p. 109.

E/CN.4?AC.1/SR. 14, reproduced in Schabas, op. cit. p. 871.

E/CT.2/2 20 August 1946 Committee on Arrangements for Consultation with Non-Governmental Organizations, in Schabas, p. 71–77.

E/HR/19, 15 May, 1946: *Draft Report of the Commission on Human Rights to the Second Session of the Economic and Social Council.* Rapporteur Mr K.C. Neogi (India), in Schabas p. 49.

E/HR/6 29 April 1946 Summary Record of Meetings [of the "Nuclear" Commission on Human Rights] First meeting held on Monday, 29 April 1946, at 3 p.m.

E/SR.19, 31 May, 1946a.

E/SR.20, 31 May, 1946b (Schabas, p. 65–66).

E/SR.20, 31 May, 1946c. (Schabas, 65–66).

E/SR.69, in Schabas, p. 5.

E/SR.69, p. 5

E/SR.69, p. 5.

E/SR.69, pp. 7–9.

AICHR (2009), Terms of Reference. Accessible at: http://www.asean.org/storage/images/archive/publications/TOR-of-AICHR.pdf

Alfredsson, Gudmundur and Asbjorn Eide (Eds.), *The Universal Declaration of Human Rights: A common Standard of Achievement* (the Hague: Martinus Nijhoff, 1999).

Amerante, Domenico, "Post-modern Constitutionalism In Asia: Perspectives From The Indian Experience," *NUJS Law Review*, April to June 2013, p. 215. pp. 213–228.

Angeles, Marford and Michael Yusingco, "ASEAN Charter: deepening constitutionalism in Southeast Asia," *Asian Currents.* (Association of Asian Studies of Australia. 1 September, 2017) http://asaa.asn.au/asean-charter-deepening-constitutionalism-southeast-asia/

An-na'im, Abdullahi Ahmed (Ed.), Human Rights in Cross-cultural Perspectives: A Quest for Consensus. (Philadelphia: University of Pennsylvania Press, 1992).

Annand, A.S. Chairperson, Intervention on Behalf of the National Human Rights Commission of India on 'Right to Development' at First Session of the United Nations Human Rights Council by National Human Rights Commission of India (former Chief Justice of India) on 27 June, 2006 at Geneva. Original text on the Internet.

Asia Pacific Human Rights Information Centre. Human Rights Education in Asia-Pacific (Volume Seven), (Osaka: Asian Human Rights Information Center, 2017).

Association of Southeast Asian Nations (ASEAN), ASEAN Human Rights Declaration. ASEAN Secretariat, 2012.

Association of Southeast Asian Nations (ASEAN), Terms of Reference, of AICHR, ASEAN Secretariat, 2009.

Avonious, Leena, "From Marsinah to Munir: Grounding Human Rights in Indonesia," *Human Rights in Asia: A Reassessment of the Asian Values Debate*, Edited by Leena Avonius and Damien Kingsbury (Palgrave Macmillan), p. 115 (pp. 99–120).

Ayer, A.J. (1984), *Philosophy in the Twentieth Century* (New York, Vintage books), p. 18.

Beasley, W.G. *Japanese Imperialism 1894–1945.* (Oxford: Oxford University Press, 2014).

Beer, Lawrence (Ed.), "Preface," *Constitutionalism in Asia: Asian Views of the American Influence.* in Occasional Papers/Reprint Series on Contemporary Asian Studies, NUMBER 6–1988 (89). Beer noted by 1988a that "Asian nation-states now share adoption of a government institution invented by the United States in the eighteenth century, the single-document constitution setting forth a country's public principles, its governmental structures, and the relationships between its leaders and governed." (p.iii).

Beer, Lawrence, "Introduction: Constitutionalism in Asia and the United States," *Constitutionalism in Asia: Asian Views of the American Influence.* in Occasional Papers/Reprint Series on Contemporary Asian Studies, NUMBER 6–1988b (89) p. 8.

Bell, Daniel, *The China Model* (Princeton and Oxford, Princeton University Press, 2015).

Best, Antony, et al, *International History of the Twentieth Century* (London: Routledge, 2004) p. 405.

Bhagavan, Manu, "A New Hope: India, the United Nations and the Making of the Universal Declaration of Human Rights," *Modern Asian Studies* 44, 2 (2010) pp. 311–347.

Blackburn, Roger, *Cultural Relativism in the Universal Periodic Review of the UN Human Rights Council.* Institut CAtala International, Working Paper No.3, 2011. Available at https://www.upr-info.org/sites/default/files/general-document/pdf/-blackburn_upr_cultural_relativism.09.2011.pdf

Blackburn, S. *What Do We Really Know. The Big Questions of Philosophy.* (London, Quercus, 2009).

Blackburn, S. *Oxford Dictionary of Philosophy* (Oxford: Oxford U. Press, Third Edition, 2016).

Blanshard, Brand, *Reason and Analysis.* London, 1962.

Brucken, Rowland, *A most uncertain crusade: the United States, the United Nations, and human rights, 1941–1953* (DeKalb, IL: Northern Illinois University Press,....).

Bruun, Ole and Michael Jacobsen, Human Rights and Asian Values: Contesting National Identities and Cultural Representations in Asia (London: Routledge, 2003).

Bünte, Marco and B. Dressel, *'Politics and Constitutions in Southeast Asia.'* (London, New York: Routledge 2017). See especially first chapter of Part 3.

Burke, Roland, "From individual rights to national development: the first UN International Conference on Human Rights, Tehran, 1968," *Journal of World History.* Vol. 19, No.3 Sept. 2008, p. 275.

Burke, Roland, "The Compelling Dialogue of Freedom: Human Rights at the Bandung Conference," *Human Rights Quarterly,* V.8, 2006, p. 947.

Candela, Kacie, China's Notions of UN Reform: Filling the Growing Vacuum Left by the US," *Pass Blue,* January 3, 2018, p. 11. Accessed at http://www.passblue.com/2018/01/03/chinas-notions-of-un-reform-filling-the-growing-vacuum-left-by-the-us/ 1/7.

Cassin, Rene, "Twenty Years After the Universal Declaration. Freedom and Equality", *Journal of the International Commission of Jurists,* December 1967, Special Issue 1968, *International Year for Human Rights,* pp. 1–16, at. P. 1. Italics added.

Cerna, Christina, "Universality of Human Rights and Cultural Diversity: Implementation of Human Rights in Different Socio-Cultural Contexts," *Human Rights Quarterly, Vol. 16, No.4,* (1994), *pp. 740–752.*

CESCR General Comment No. 14: The Right to the Highest Attainable Standard of Health (Art. 12), E/C.12/2000/4, 11 August 2000. Available at https://www.ohchr.org/en/hrbodies/cescr/pages/cescrindex.aspx

CESCR, General Comment No.3, The nature of States parties' obligations, 1990. Available at https://www.ohchr.org/en/hrbodies/cescr/pages/cescrindex.aspx

Chang, Wen-Chen, Li-ann Thio, Kevin YL Tan, Jiunn-rong Yeh, *Constitutionalism in Asia: Cases and Materials* (West Sussex, UK: Hart Publishing, 2014); Kevin YL Tan and Li-ann Thio (Eds.) (forthcoming). *Constitutionalism in Southeast Asia.* (West Sussex, UK: Hart Publishing, n.d.).

Chen, Albert H.Y (Ed.), "The achievement of constitutionalism in Asia: moving beyond 'constitutions without constitutionalism'." In *Constitutionalism in Asia in the Early Twenty-First Century,* (Cambridge: Cambridge University Press, 2014) p. 1–32.

Chen, Albert H.Y. *Constitutionalism in Asia in the Early Twenty-first century.* (Cambridge: Cambridge University Press, 2014).

Chen, Hongyi, *Constitutionalism in Asia in the Early Twenty-First Century* (Cambridge: Cambridge University Press, 2014) p. 7.

Chi Kwan, Mark, *China and the World Since 1945: An International History.* (Oxon, New York: Routledge, 2012).

Chowdhury, S.R, M.G. Denters and P. J. de Waart (Eds.), *The Right to Development in International Law* (Dordrecht: Martinus Nijhoff Publishers, 1992).

Collier, Paul, *The Bottom Billion. Why the Poorest Countries are Failing and What Can be Done About it* (Oxford: Oxford University Press, 2007).

Commission on Human Rights(1946a) 1st Meeting held on Monday, Document E/HR/6.

Commission on Human Rights (1946b), E/36/Eev. 1, p. 3.

Commission on Human Rights (1946c), Report Of The Commission On Human Rights To The Second Session Of The Economic And Social Council. Document E/38/Rev.1, p. 5.

Commission on Human Rights (1947a), Report of the Commission on Human Rights, E/383 27 March 197.

Commission on Human Rights, 27 January, 1947b; E/CN.4/SR.2, 27 January, 1947, p. 1. (Schabas pp. 161–162).

Commission on Human Rights, 27 January, 1947c; E/CN.4/SR.2, 27 January, 1947, p. 1. (Schabas pp. 161–162).

Committee on Economic, Social and Cultural Rights (CESCR), *General Comment No. 16: The Equal Right of Men and Women to the Enjoyment of All Economic, Social and Cultural Rights (Art. 3 of the Covenant)*, 11 August 2005, E/C.12/2005/4, para.2, Available at: http://www.refworld.org/docid/43f3067ae.html [accessed 20 May 2018].

Constitution of India, 6 November 1949, https://www.india.gov.in/sites/upload_files/npi/files/coi_part_full.pdf

Constitution of the Republic of Indonesia 1945, available at http://www.ilo.org/wcmsp5/groups/public/%2D%2D-ed_protect/%2D%2D-protrav/%2D%2D-ilo_aids/documents/legaldocument/wcms_174556.pdf

Constitution of Japan, 1947. Available at https://japan.kantei.go.jp/constitution_and_government_of_japan/constitution_e.html

Dalton, Dennis, *Course Guidebook on Power over People. Classical and Modern Political Theory.* (Virginia: The Teaching Company, 1998), pp. 132–134.

Dalton, Dennis, *The Indian Idea of Freedom* (Michigan: Academic Press, 1982).

Dimitrijevic, Vojin, *Customary Law As An Instrument For The Protection Of Human Rights*, Working Paper, Milano: Istituto per gli Studi di Politica Internazionale and D'Amato, Anthony, "Human Rights as Part of Customary International Law: A Plea for Change of Paradigms". Faculty Working Papers. Paper 88, 2010.

Donnelly, Jack, *Human Rights Quarterly*, Vol. 6, No. 4 (Nov., 1984), pp. 400–419.

Donnelly, Jack, *Universal Human Rights In Theory and Practice,* Ithaca: Cornell University Press, 2013. p. 53.

Douzinas, Coustas, *Human Rights and Empire. The Political Philosophy of Cosmopolitanism.* (London: Routledge-Cavendish, 2007.

Dyer, Geoff, (2014), *Contest of the Century*, New York: Vintage Books.

ECOSOC, E/C.12/2001/10 (10 May 200), para. 11.

Eldridge, Philip, *The Politics of Human Rights in Southeast Asia*, (Routledge, London and New York, 2002).

Elkins, Zachary, Tom Ginsburg and James Melton, "Imagining a world without the Universal Declaration of Human Rights," 6 September 2017, available online at http://www.law.nyu.edu/sites/default/files/upload_documents/Zachary%20Elkins%20Paper%20September%202017%20v.2.0%20%282%29.pdf

Fariss, C. "Respect for human rights has improved over time: Modeling the changing standard of accountability." *American Political Science Review*, Vol. 108, No. 2, May 2014, pp. 297–318.

Farrior, Steve, *Equality and Non-Discrimination under International Law*, Volume 2, (New York: Routledge, 2015).

Fengyu, Duan, "The Universal Declaration of Human Rights and the Modern History of Human Rights" (November 7, 2017), p. 38 Available at SSRN: https://ssrn.com/abstract=3066882 or https://doi.org/10.2139/ssrn.3066882.

Final Act of the International Conference on Human Rights, Tehran, 11 April to 13 May 1968. New York: United Nations. http://legal.un.org/avl/pdf/ha/fatchr/Final_Act_of_TehranConf.pdf

Final Communiqué of the Asian-African conference of Bandung (24 April 1955).

Finnemore, Martha and Kathryn Sikkink, (1998), "International Norm Dynamics and Political Change," International Organization, Vol. 52, No. 4, (Autumn, 1998), pp. 887–917.

Forsythe, David, "Hard times for human rights." *Journal of Human Rights,* Vol. 16, No. 2, 2017, pp. 242–253.

Foster, Ann, "Hansa Mehta, of UN Sub-Commission, Speaks for Women of India," *Christian Science Monitor*, 18 July 1946, p. 22.

Freeman, Michael, "Human Rights, Democracy and Asian Values," *The Pacific Review*, 9:3, 1997, 352–366.

Fukuyama, Francis, *Political Order and Political Decay* (London, Profile Books, 2014a), p. 360.

Fukuyama, Francis, *Political Order And Political Decay: From the Industrial Revolution to the Globalization of Democracy* (New York: Farrar, Straus & Giroux, 2014b).

GANHRI, Chart of the Status of National Institutions. Accreditation status as of 14 October, 2016; Consulted on the internet on 14 June, 2017, no internet citation shown.

Ghai, Yash, Redesigning the State for 'Right to Development', in Nobel Foundation, *The Right to Development.* Edited by B. Andreassen (Oslo….) 2006, pp. 140–141 (pp. 140–166).

Glendon, Mary, (1999a), "Foundations of Human Rights: The unfinished Business," *American Journal of Jurisprudence*, Vol. 44, No. 1, 1999, p. 7.

Glendon, Mary Ann, "Foundations of Human Rights: The Unfinished Business," *American Journal of Jurisprudence*, Vol. 44: No. 1, 1999b, p. 1 Available at: http://scholarship.law.nd.edu/ajj/vol44/iss1/1

Glendon, Mary A. *A World Made New: Eleanor Roosevelt and the Universal Declaration of Human Rights* (New York, Random House, 2001).

Glendon, Mary Ann, Interview on the role of Charles Malik in drafting the Universal Declaration of Human Rights, on PBS program *Weekend All Things Considered, Public Broadcasting Station, March 26,* 2001.

Gomez, James and Robin Ramcharan, (2017), *The Universal Periodic Review of Southeast Asia: Civil Society Perspectives* (Singapore: Palgrave Macmillan, 2017).

Gomez, James and Robin Ramcharan, The Protection of Human Rights in Southeast Asia: Improving the Effectiveness of Civil Society," *Asia-Pacific Journal on Human Rights and the Law*, Volume 13, Issue 2, 2012, pp. 27–43.

Gomez, James and Robin Ramcharan, *National Human Rights Institutions in Southeast Asia: The Challenge of Protection*. Singapore: Palgrave Macmillan, (expected 2018).

Guha, Ramachandra, *India After Gandhi: A History of the World's Largest Democracy* (PanMacmillan, 2017).

Hannum, Hurst, "The Status Of The Universal Declaration Of Human Rights In National And International Law," *GA Journal of International & Comparative. Law*, 1995–1996, Vol 25, p. 4 (pp. 287 to 397).

Hao, Duy Phan, "A Blueprint For a Southeast Asian Court Of Human Rights," *Asian-Pacific Law & Policy Journal*, Vol. 10, No.2, pp. 384–433.

Herlambang, "Understanding Pancasila Position as the Fundamental Norms (Grundnorm") of Indonesian Law," *Southeast Asian Journal of Contemporary Business, Economics and Law*, Vol. 13, No. 4, August 2017, p. 145 (pp. 145–155).

Hildebrand, Robert C. *Dumbarton Oaks. The Origins of the United Nations and the Search for Postwar Security* (Chapel Hill and London: The University of North Carolina Press, 1990), pp. 237–240.

Hill, Clauspeter and Joerg Menzel, *Constitutionalism in Southeast Asia*. Vol. 1. National Constitutions/ASEAN Charter. (Singapore: Konrad Adenauer Stiftung, 2009).

Ho, Ch Minh, *Selected Works*. (Hanoi, 1960–1962), Vol.3, pp. 17–21.

Hoover, Joe, "Rereading the Universal Declaration of Human Rights: Plurality and Contestation, Not Consensus," *Journal of Human Rights*, Vol 12, 2013, pp. 217–241, p. 219.

Hopgood, Stephen, *The Endtimes for Human Rights*. (Ithaca: Cornell University Press, 2014).

Hsia, Ching-Lin, *Studies in Chinese Diplomacy* (Harrisonburg, V.A.: The Commercial Press, 1925).

Hughes, Glenn, "The Concept Of Dignity In The Universal Declaration Of Human Rights," *The Journal of Religious Ethics*, Vol. 39, No. 1 (March 2011), p. 1 (pp. 1–24).

Human Right Committee, General Comment 31.

Human Rights Committee, *Faure v. Australia*, 2001.

Human Rights Committee, General Comment 31.

Human Rights Council, 34th session (HCR34) in March 2017: a resolution on the "Question of the realization in all countries of economic social and cultural rights" (A/HRC/34/L.4/Rev.1) and a resolution on "The right to food" (A/HRC/34/L.21).

Human Rights Council, A/HEC/WG.6/28/PAK/1, para. 2.

Human Rights Council, A/HRC/35/6, paras. 26, 27,37,38 and 49.

Human Rights Council, A/HRC/WG.6/17/CHN/1, para.4.

Human Rights Council, A/HRC/WG.6/17/MYS/1, para. 9.

Human Rights Council, A/HRC/WG.6/18/VNM/1, paras. 6–7.

Human Rights Council, A/HRC/WG.6/24/SGP/1, para. 4.

Human Rights Council, A/HRC/WG.6/25/THA/1, para. 14.

Human Rights Council, A/HRC/WG.6/27/IDN, para. 1.

Human Rights Council, A/HRC/WG.6/27/IND/1, para. 1.

Human Rights Council, A/HRC/WG.6/27/PHL/1, para. 3.

Humphrey, John, "International Protection of Human Rights. The Annals, Vol. 255 (January 1948), pp. 15–21.

Humphrey, John, "Memoirs of John P. Humphrey: The First Director of the United Nations Division of Human Rights," *Human Rights Quarterly*, 5:4 (November 1983), pp. 387–439.

Humphrey, John, *Human Rights. A Great Adventure*. Transnational Publishers, 1984.

Hunt, Lynne, *Inventing Human Rights: A History* (New York: WW Norton, 2007) In this work, Hung shows that human rights require interlocking qualities: they must be natural (inherent in human beings), equal (the same for everyone) and universal (applicable everywhere).

ICJ, North Sea Continental Shelf, Judgement of 20 February 1969, *International Court of Justice Reports*, 1969.

Indian Planning Commission, *Eleventh Plan* (2008).

Institute of International Law, *Report*, 1947.

Inter Parliamentary Union (IPU), *Democracy: Its Principles and Achievement* (Geneva: IPU, 1998), iv–vii).

International Court of Justice (ICJ), *Report* 1949.

International Service for Human Rights (2013), "Vienna Declaration and Programme of Action + 20," 2013, p. 13 https://www.ishr.ch/sites/default/files/article/files/vdpa.pdf

Jacobson, Thomas, *Ambassador Charles Malik and The Universal Declaration Of Human Rights, Focus on the Family*. Focus on the Family – August 28, 2008. International Government Affairs Department.

Johns, Alexa, "Graduate Programs on Human Rights: Mahidol University," Human Rights Education in Asia-Pacific (Volume One), (Osaka: Asia Pacific Human Rights Information Center, 2010), pp. 213–223 https://www.hurights.or.jp/archives/asia-pacific/section1/15AlexaJohns.pdf

Johnson, M. Glen and Janusz Symonides, *The Universal Declaration of Human Rights: A History of its Creation and Implementation*, 1948–1998, UNESCO Publications, 1998. http://unesdoc.unesco.org/images/0011/001144/114488E.pdf

Kelly, Patrick, "What is Hope For?" in *Los Angeles Review of Books*, 7 June 2018.

Kent, Ann, "Waiting for Rights: China's Human Rights and China's Constitutions, 1949–1989," *Human Rights Quarterly*. May 1991, Vol. 13 Issue 2, (pp. 170–201).

Kent, Ann, "Chinese Values and Human Rights," in *Human Rights in Asia: A Reassessment of the Asian Values Debate,* Edited by Leena Avonius and Damien Kingsbury (Palgrave Macmillan, 2008).

Khan, Muhammad Zafrulla Islam and Human Rights. London, The London Mosque, 1967, p. 10.

Killion, M. Ulric, "China's Amended Constitution: Quest for Liberty and Independent Judicial Review, *Washington. University Global Studies. Law Review*. Vol. 43, No.4, 2005, pp. 43–80, Available at http://openscholarship.wustl.edu/law_globalstudies/vol4/iss1/3

Kingsbury, Damien, "Universalism and Exceptionalism in Asia," in *Human Rights in Asia: A Reassessment of the Asian Values Debate,* Edited by Leena Avonius and Damien Kingsbury (Palgrave Macmillan, 2008) (pp. 19–39).

Kingsbury, D. and Leena Avonius (Eds.), *Human Rights in Asia: A Reassessment of the Asian Values Debate* (Springer, Palgrave Macmillan, 2008).

Kumarasingham, Harshan (Ed.), *Constitution-making in Asia: Decolonisation and State-Building in the Aftermath of the British Empire*. (London and New York: Routledge, 2016).

Lauren, Paul G. *The Evolution of International Human Rights: Visions Seen*. 2nd ed. (Philadelphia, University of Pennsylvania Press, 2003).

Lauterpacht, Hersch, *An International Bill of the Rights of Man* (Oxford: Oxford University Press, 2013), p. 115. (First published in 1945).

Leong, Laurence Wai-Teng, "From "Asian Values" to Singapore Exceptionalism," in *Human Rights in Asia: A Reassessment of the Asian Values Debate,* Edited by Leena Avonius and Damien Kingsbury (Palgrave Macmillan, 2008), pp. 121–140.

Lewis, William Draper and John R. Ellington, (Eds.), *Annals of the American Academy of Political and Social Science*, Issue 243(1).

Liu, Lydia H. "Shadows of Universalism: The Untold Story of Human Rights around 1948," Critical Inquiry 40, no. 4 (Summer 2014): 385–417.

Liu, Lydia H. "Zhang Pengchun's Contributions to the Drafting of the UDHR," *China Legal Science*, Vol. 4, Issue 5 (September 2016), pp. 114–132.

Macintyre, Alasdair, *A Study in Moral Theory* (Notre Dame Press, 2007).

Malik, Charles, Minister Plenipotentiary of Lebanon in the United States, Address on behalf of Mr Wadi Naim, Chairman of the Delegation of Lebanon, at the Third Plenary Session of the Conference at San Francisco on Saturday 28 April, 1945.

Malik, Habib C. (Ed.), *Charles Malik and the Universal Declaration.* Published by the Charles Malik Foundation in association with the Centre for Lebanese Studies, Oxford, 2000.

Malik, Habib C. *The Challenge of Human Rights. Charles Malik and the Universal Declaration.* (Charles Malik Foundation and Centre for Lebanese Studies, 59 Observatory Street).

Mauzy, Diane, "The human rights and 'Asian values' debate in Southeast Asia: Trying to clarify the key issues," *The Pacific Review*, Vol.10 No.2, 1997, p. 210 (pp. 210–236).

Mazower, Mark, "The Strange Triumph of Human Rights, 1933 – 1950, *The Historical Journal*, vol. 47, No. 2, 2004, pp. 379–398.

Mazower, Mak, "An international civilization? Empire, internationalism and the crisis of the mid-twentieth century," *International Affairs* Vol. 82, Issue 3 (2006) 553–566.

Millennium Declaration, adopted by Heads of State and Government at the United Nations General Assembly, 2000, para. 31.

Morsink, Johannes, *The Universal Declaration of Human Rights. Origins, Drafting and Intent.* (Philadelphia, University of Pennsylvania Press, 1999a).

Morsink, Johannes, *The Universal Declaration of Human Rights: Origins, Drafting, and Intent (Philadelphia:* University of Philadelphia 1999b/2010).

Morsink, Johannes, *Inherent human rights: philosophical roots of the universal declaration* (Philadelphia: University of Pennsylvania Press, 2009).

Moyn, S. *The Last Utopia: Human Rights in History* (Cambridge MA: Harvard University Press, 2012).

Mumford, s. *Metaphysics. A Very Short Introduction.* (Oxford, University Press, 2012).

Mutaqin, Zezen Zaenel, "The Strong State and Pancasila: Reflecting Human Rights in the Indonesian Democracy," Constitutional Review, December 2016, Volume 2, Number 2, pp. 159–188.

Nasu, Hitoshi and Ben Saul, *Human Rights in the Asia-Pacific Region: Towards Institution Building*, Routledge, 2011.

NGO Bangkok Declaration on Human Rights, World Conference on Human Rights, 19 April 19093, UN Doc. A Conf.157/PC/83.

NGO Bangkok Declaration on Human Rights, World Conference on Human Rights, 19 April 19093, UN Doc. A Conf.157/PC/83.

Normand, Roger and Sarah Zaidi, *Human Rights at the UN. The Political History of Universal Justice.* (Bloomington, Indiana University Press, 2008).

Nozick, Robert, "Justice Does Not Imply Equality," in Louis Pojman and Robert Westmoreland, *Equality: Selected Readings* (Oxford: Oxford University Press, 1997).

OHCHR website, Summary of national initiatives undertaken within the Decade for Human Rights (1995–2004), consulted on 14 June, 2017.

OHCHR, "The Core International Human Rights Instruments and their monitoring bodies," Available at https://www.ohchr.org/EN/ProfessionalInterest/Pages/CoreInstruments.aspx

Panagariya, Arvind, *India: the Emerging Giant.* (Oxford: Oxford University Press, 2009).

Paul Gordon Lauren's *The Evolution of International Human Rights,....*

Posner, E. *The Twilight of Human Rights Law* (Oxford: Oxford University Press, 2014).

Proclamation of Teheran, Final Act of the International Conference on Human Rights, Teheran, 22 April to 13 May 1968, U.N. Doc. A/CONF. 32/41 at 3 (1968).

Protecting Dignity: An Agenda for Human Rights, 2008. Swiss Initiative to Commemorate the 60th Anniversary of the UDHR. http://www.udhr60.ch/

Quing, Jiang, *A Confucian Constitutional Order.* (Princeton and Oxford: Princeton University Press, 2013).

Rachman, Gideon, *Easternization: War and Peace in the Asian Century.* (London: The Bodley Head, 2016).

Ramcharan, Bertrand G. *Contemporary Human Rights Ideas: Rethinking theory and Practice* (London, New York: Routledge, 2015), p. 70.

Ramcharan, Bertrand, *The Guyana Court of Appeal* (London, Cavendish Press, 2000).

Ramcharan, Robin, "ASEAN's Human Rights Commission: Policy Considerations for Enhancing its Capacity to Protect Human Rights," *UCL Human Rights Review*, December 2010.

Renshaw, Chatherine, "The ASEAN Human Rights Declaration 2012," 13 *Human Rights Law Review*, 557 (2013), pp. 557–579.

Rieff, David, "The End of Human Rights? Learning from the failure of the Responsibility to Protect and the International Criminal Court." *Foreign Policy. April 9 2018.* http://foreignpolicy.com/2018/04/09/the-end-of-human-rights-genocide-united-nations-r2p-terrorism/

Romulo, Carlos P. and Beth Day Romulo, *Forty Years. A Third World Soldier at the UN.* (New York, Greenwood Press, 1986).

Salomon, M. "The Nature of a Rights: The Right to a Process in the Right to Development" in *Franciscans International, Geneva, The Right to Development. Reflections on the First Four Reports of the Independent Expert on the Right to Development* (2003), pp. 82–104.

Samnoy, Ashild, *Human rights as international consensus: The Making of the Universal Declaration of Human Rights, 1945–1948*, Chr. Michelsen Institute Bergen, Norway, 1993, p. 1.

Sceats, Sonja and Shaun Breslin, *China and the International Human Rights System*. (London: Chatham House, 2012).

Schabas, William, T*he Universal Declaration of Human Rights, The travaux préparatoires*, Volumes 1 and 2. October 1946 to November 1947 (Cambridge: Cambridge University Press, 2013), p. 64.

Schachter, Oscar, "Implementing the right to development: programme of action", in S.R. Chowdhury, M.G. Denters and P. J. de Waart Eds., *The Right to Development in International Law* (Dordrecht: Martinus Nijhoff Publishers, 1992), pp. 27–30.

Sears, John, *Eleanor Roosevelt and the universal declaration Of human rights, Hyde Park:* Franklin and Eleanor Roosevelt Institute (FERI), https://drive.google.com/drive/folders/111xVhf6GvcjmhuAVJ7VIfYRhfygcxSAs

Seghal, Gita, "Who Wrote the Universal Declaration of Human Rights?" *Open Democracy*, 10 December 2014.

Sen, Amartya, "Human Rights and Asian Values," Sixteenth Annual Morgenthau Memorial Lecture on Ethics and Foreign Policy, May 25, 1997, https://www.carnegiecouncil.org/publications/archive/morgenthau/254

SHAPE-SEA, *Human Rights Outlook in Southeast Asia: 2016* (Bangkok: Institute of Human Rights and Peace Studies (IHRP), 2017), p. vii.

Sikkink, Kathryn, Evidence for Hope: Making Human Rights Work in the 21st Century. Princeton: Princeton University Press, 2017, p. 56.

Sohn, Louis B. "The Universal Declaration of Human Rights", in *Journal of the International Commission of Jurists*, loc. cit. I, pp. 17–26, at.pp. 25–26.

Stone, Julius, *The League of Nations and the Protection of Minorities*. (London: Stevens. 1932).

Pinghua, Sun, "Zhang Pengchun's Human Rights Philosophy of Pluralism," China Legal Science. Vol. 5, 109 (2017), p. 109.

Thabchumpon, Narumon, "Human Rights in Thailand: Rhetoric or Substance," in *Human Rights in Asia: A Reassessment of the Asian Values Debate*, Edited by Leena Avonius and Damien Kingsbury (Palgrave Macmillan, 2008) pp. 141–158.

Thio, Li-Ann, "Reading Rights Rightly: The UDHR and its Creeping Influence on the Development of Singapore Public Law," *Singapore Journal of Legal Studies*, pp. 264–291, December 2008.

UNDP. *Making the Law Work for Everyone*. Volume I, Report on Legal Empowerment of the Poor. UNDP, New York, 2008.

United Nations. "Essentials of Peace", GA Res. 290(IV), OP 6.

United Nations, General Assembly resolution 217D (III) of 10 December, 1948.

United Nations General Assembly Resolution 66/137.

United Nations General Assembly, A/RES/41/128, 4 December 1986.

UN, *The Millennium Development Goals Report* 2006 (New York: UN, 2006), 5.

Vienna Declaration and Programme of Action Adopted by the World Conference on Human Rights in Vienna on 25 June 1993. https://www.ohchr.org/EN/ProfessionalInterest/Pages/Vienna.aspx

Waart, ePeters D and E Denters (Eds.), *International Law and Development* (Dordrecht, Martinus Nijhoff, 1988).

Waltz, Susan, (2002), Reclaiming and rebuilding the history of the Universal Declaration of Human Rights," Third *World Quarterly*, Vol 23, No 3, 1 June 2002, p. 438 (pp. 437–448).

Waltz, Susan, "Universalising Human Rights: The Role of Small States in the Construction of the Universal Declaration of Human Rights, *Human Rights Quarterly*," Volume 23, Number 1, February 2001, pp. 44–72.

Warnock, G.J. "Reason", in *The Encyclopedia of Philosophy*. Paul Edwards, Editor in Chief, London, Macmillan, 1967, Vol. 7, pp. 83–85.

weaicolumbia, P.C. Chang. October 8 [2014] Event "Around 1948: Human Rights and Global Transformation. Video, Photos, and Audio. (no paging in text).

Williams, Bernard, "The idea of Equality," in Contemporary Political Philosophy: An Anthology, Robert Goodin and Philip Pettit, Eds. ((Malden, MA; Oxford; Victoria, Australia: Blackwell 2006), p. 451. Originally published in Peter Laslett and W.G. Runciman, Philosophy, Politics and Society (Oxford: Blackwell, 1962).

Woodcock, Andrew, "Jacques Maritain, Natural Law and the Universal Declaration of Human Rights," *Journal of the History of International Law*, Vol. 8, pp. 2006, pp. 245–266.

Worden, Andrea, "China Pushes 'Human Rights With Chinese Characteristics' at the UN," *China Change*, October 9, 2017. https://chinachange.org/2017/10/09/china-pushes-human-rights-with-chinese-characteristics-at-the-un/ 4/12.

Working Group on the Right to Development, A/HRC/4/47, 14 March 2007a, para. 19.

Working Group on the Right to Development, A/HRC/4/47, 14 March 2007b, para. 20.

Working Group on the Right to Development, A/HRC/4/47, 14 March 2007c, para. 60.

Working Group on the Right to Development, A/HRC/4/47, 14 March 2007d, paras. 61–62.

Working Group on the Right to Development, A/HRC/4/47, 14 March 2007e, paras. 63–64.

Yeh, Jiunn-rong, "The Development of Regional Human Rights Institutions in Asia – Dialectical and functional perspectives," in *Global Constitutionalism and Multi-layered Protection of Human Rights*, edited by SNU Asia-Pacific Law Institute. (Seoul: Constitutional Court of Korea, 2016).

Zakaria, Fareed, *The Future of Freedom: Illiberal Democracy at Home and Abroad*. London and NY: WW Norton and Co. 2007. First published in 2003; Zakaria, "The rise of illiberal democracy," *Foreign Affairs*, Nov/Dec, 1997, pp. 22–43.

Zhang Pengchun (2011), "A Globally Famed Chinese Human Rights Activist," Human Rights, No. 6, p. 29 (30, 31).

Zuber, Valentine, *Le Culte des Droits de l'Homme*. (Paris: Galimard, 2014). Zuber traces the passage from a religious based order to a new secular, humanist order at the time of the French Revolution.

Index[1]

[1] Note: Page numbers followed by 'n' refer to notes.

R. Ramcharan, B. Ramcharan, *Asia and the Drafting of the Universal Declaration of Human Rights*,
https://doi.org/10.1007/978-981-13-2104-7

FSC
www.fsc.org
MIX
Papier | Fördert
gute Waldnutzung
FSC® C083411

Kolibri 360 GmbH
Ferdinand-Jühlke-Straße 7
99095 Erfurt, Deutschland
produktsicherheit@kolibri360.de